Founding
the Republic

FOUNDING THE REPUBLIC

A Documentary History

Edited by JOHN J. PATRICK

Primary Documents in American History and Contemporary Issues

GREENWOOD PRESS
Westport, Connecticut • London

This work is dedicated with love to my mother,
Elizabeth Lazar Patrick, who dedicated her life
to her children.

Library of Congress Cataloging-in-Publication Data

Founding the Republic : a documentary history / edited by John J.
  Patrick
     p. cm. — (Primary documents in American history and
  contemporary issues series, ISSN 1069–5605)
   Includes bibliographical references and index.
   ISBN 0–313–29226–4 (alk. paper)
    1. United States—Politics and government—1775–1783—Sources.
  2. United States—Politics and government—1783–1809—Sources.
  I. Patrick, John J. II. Series.
  E210.F68 1995
  973.3—dc20   95–7537

British Library Cataloguing in Publication Data is available.

Library of Congress Catalog Card Number: 95–7537
ISBN: 0–313–29226–4
ISSN: 1069–5605

First published in 1995

Greenwood Press, 88 Post Road West, Westport, CT 06881
An imprint of Greenwood Publishing Group, Inc.

Printed in the United States of America

The paper used in this book complies with the
Permanent Paper Standard issued by the National
Information Standards Organization (Z39.48-1984).

10 9 8 7 6 5 4 3 2 1

Contents

Series Foreword   xi

Introduction   xiii

Chronology of Key Events in the Founding of the United
States of America   xix

**PART I: The Decision for Independence: Reasons For and
           Against Separation from Britain, 1775–1776**   1

Document 1: Declaration of the Causes and Necessity of
              Taking Up Arms (July 6, 1775)   7

Document 2: Proclamation by the King for Suppressing
              Rebellion and Sedition (August 23, 1775)   12

Document 3: *Common Sense* (Thomas Paine, January 10,
              1776)   14

Document 4: *The True Interest of America Impartially Stated*
              (Published Anonymously by The Reverend
              Charles Inglis, March 1776)   19

Document 5: Resolution for Independence (June 7, 1776)   24

Document 6: Notes on the Debate in Congress on
              Independence (Thomas Jefferson, June 7–
              July 4, 1776)   25

Document 7: The Declaration of Independence (July 4, 1776)   29

**Part II: Making Constitutions for the New American States:
            Debates on Models of Good Government,
            1776–1780**   35

Document 8:   *The People the Best Governors: Or a Plan of
               Government Founded on the Just Principles of
               Natural Freedom* (Published Anonymously in
               New Hampshire, 1776)   41

Document 9:   *Thoughts on Government: Applicable to the Present
               State of the American Colonies* (In a Letter from a
               Gentleman [John Adams] to His Friend,
               April 1776)   45

Document 10:   The Virginia Declaration of Rights
               (June 12, 1776)   52

Document 11:   Preamble to the Pennsylvania Constitution
               (August 1776)   56

Document 12:   Pennsylvania Declaration of Rights (August
               1776)   58

Document 13:   *The Essex Result* (Theophilus Parsons,
               Newburyport, Massachusetts, 1778)   61

Document 14:   Preamble to the Massachusetts Constitution
               (1780)   65

Document 15:   The Massachusetts Declaration of Rights (1780)   67

**PART III: Problems of Equality and Liberty in the New
             American States, 1776–1792**   73

Document 16:   Letter to John Adams (Abigail Adams,
               March 31, 1776)   79

Document 17:   Letter to James Sullivan (John Adams,
               May 26, 1776)   81

Document 18:   Petition Against Slavery to the General Court
               of Massachusetts (January 13, 1777)   85

Document 19:   Quock Walker's Case (1783)   87

Document 20:   Memorial and Remonstrance Against Religious
               Assessments (James Madison, June 20, 1785)   89

Document 21:   The Virginia Statute for Religious Freedom
               (Thomas Jefferson, January 16, 1786)   94

Document 22: Letter from Three Seneca Leaders to President
              George Washington (1790)   97

Document 23: A Sermon Against Slavery (The Reverend
              James Dana, September 9, 1791)   99

Document 24: Letter to Thomas Jefferson (Benjamin Banneker,
              August 19, 1791)   102

Document 25: Letters to Benjamin Banneker and to the
              Marquis de Condorcet (Thomas Jefferson,
              August 30, 1791)   106

**PART IV: The Crisis of Government Under the Articles of
            Confederation, 1781–1787**   109

Document 26: The Articles of Confederation (1781)   115

Document 27: Circular Letter to the State Governors (George
              Washington, June 8, 1783)   125

Document 28: Letter to Samuel Adams (Richard Henry Lee,
              March 14, 1785)   127

Document 29: Letter to George Washington (John Jay,
              June 27, 1786)   129

Document 30: Letter to John Jay (George Washington,
              August 1, 1786)   131

Document 31: Proceedings of the State Commissioners at
              Annapolis, Maryland (September 11–14, 1786)   133

Document 32: Letter to Edward Carrington (Thomas
              Jefferson, January 16, 1787)   136

Document 33: Letter to James Madison (Thomas Jefferson,
              January 30, 1787)   138

Document 34: Northwest Ordinance (July 13, 1787)   140

**PART V: The Federal Convention and the Constitution,
           1787**   147

Document 35: Letter to George Washington (James Madison,
              April 16, 1787)   155

Document 36: Virginia Plan (Reported by James Madison,
              May 29, 1787)   159

Document 37: Debate on the Virginia Plan (June 6, 1787)   163

Document 38:   Report of the Committee of the Whole
              (June 13, 1787)   167

Document 39:   New Jersey Plan (June 15, 1787)   170

Document 40:   Debate on the New Jersey and Virginia Plans
              (June 16, 1787)   173

Document 41:   Debate on Slavery (August 21–22, 1787)   177

Document 42:   Signing the Constitution and Concluding the
              Convention (September 17, 1787)   181

Document 43:   The Constitution of the United States of
              America, Signed by Thirty-Nine Delegates to
              the Federal Convention (September 17, 1787)   184

**Part VI: Debate on the Constitution: Federalists Versus
            Anti-Federalists, 1787–1788**   197

Document 44:   Essay I (Brutus, October 18, 1787)   203

Document 45:   *The Federalist* 1 (Publius [Alexander Hamilton],
              October 27, 1787)   207

Document 46:   Letter to the General Court of Massachusetts
              (Elbridge Gerry, November 3, 1787)   210

Document 47:   Objections to the Constitution (George Mason,
              November 22, 1787)   213

Document 48:   *The Federalist* 10 (Publius [James Madison],
              November 22, 1787)   216

Document 49:   Letter IV (Agrippa [James Winthrop],
              December 4, 1787)   222

Document 50:   *The Federalist* 39 (Publius [James Madison],
              January 16, 1788)   225

Document 51:   *The Federalist* 51 (Publius [James Madison],
              February 6, 1788)   229

Document 52:   Essay XV (Brutus, March 20, 1788)   233

Document 53:   *The Federalist* 78 (Publius [Alexander
              Hamilton], May 28, 1788)   237

Part VII: The First Federal Congress and the Bill of Rights, 1788–1792   243

Document 54: Letter to James Madison (Thomas Jefferson, December 20, 1787)   249

Document 55: Amendments to the U.S. Constitution Proposed by the Massachusetts Ratifying Convention (February 6, 1788)   251

Document 56: Amendments to the U.S. Constitution Proposed by the New York Ratifying Convention (July 26, 1788)   253

Document 57: Letter to Thomas Jefferson (James Madison, October 17, 1788)   255

Document 58: Speech in the U.S. House of Representatives (James Madison, June 8, 1789)   258

Document 59: Amendments Passed by the U.S. Congress (September 25, 1789)   262

Document 60: The Bill of Rights, Amendments I–X to the U.S. Constitution (Ratified December 15, 1791 and Certified by Thomas Jefferson, Secretary of State, in a Letter to the State Governors, March 1, 1792)   265

Index   269

Series Foreword

This series is designed to meet the research needs of high school and college students by making available in one volume the key primary documents on a given historical event or contemporary issue. Documents include speeches and letters, congressional testimony, Supreme Court and lower court decisions, government reports, biographical accounts, position papers, statutes, and news stories.

The purpose of the series is twofold: (1) to provide substantive and background material on an event or issue through the text of pivotal primary documents that shaped policy or law, raised controversy, or influenced the course of events; and (2) to trace the controversial aspects of the event or issue through documents that represent a variety of viewpoints. Documents for each volume have been selected by a recognized specialist in that subject with the advice of a board of other subject specialists, school librarians, and teachers.

To place the subject in historical perspective, the volume editor has prepared an introductory overview and a chronology of events. Documents are organized either chronologically or topically. The documents are full text or, if unusually long, have been excerpted by the volume editor. To facilitate understanding, each document is accompanied by an explanatory introduction. Suggestions for further reading follow the document or the chapter.

It is the hope of Greenwood Press that this series will enable students and other readers to use primary documents more easily in their research, to exercise critical thinking skills by examining the key documents in American history and public policy, and to critique the variety of viewpoints represented by this selection of documents.

Introduction

A GLOBAL PERSPECTIVE ON THE AMERICAN FOUNDING ERA

During the last quarter of the eighteenth century, Americans founded an extraordinary constitutional republic. They combined ancient and modern ideas to invent a fresh blend of the principles and practices of free government, which has influenced political thinkers and practitioners throughout the world from their times to our own. Political theorists of ancient Greece and Rome and of the eighteenth-century European Enlightenment had written brilliantly about such concepts as republican government, federations, and separation of powers, but these and other venerable ideas were given new vitality and practicality by the American founders, who innovatively defined and implemented them through several American state constitutions and the federal Constitution of 1787. Further, the idea of a written constitution and methods of making constitutions were given new meaning, so that modern theories and practices of constitutionalism throughout the world tend to be based on the American model.

Concepts of free government, taken for granted by Americans today, were daring and practically unique in the world of the 1780s, where monarchies and aristocracies, not republican governments, prevailed. Although Americans inherited English legal traditions, notably rights based on the rule of law, they moved beyond this heritage to novel political thoughts and practices. By today's standards, the free government of eighteenth-century America seems stunted and flawed. But by the world-class standards of their own times, the founders had broken new ground and planted new seeds for the growth and development of human rights and liberty during the next two centuries. Although participation in government was limited to a minority of the population in the United States of the founding era, the proportion of Americans with the right to vote or otherwise take part in their governance was unparalleled in the world of the 1780s. And from this rather small start, the rights to political and personal liberty were extended eventually to nearly all citizens of the republic.

Slavery, of course, was a cruel contradiction to the founders' ideas about individual rights and dignity. But slavery in the United States, if awful, was not unique in the world of the 1780s. It had existed variously in the world since ancient times. Pronouncements of the American founders about the universality of individual rights, however, were quite unusual, and they became irrepressible standards to which abolitionists appealed in their successful crusade against slavery.

THE FOUNDING-ERA CONSENSUS

The founders and their followers tended to agree that security for individual rights was an irrefutable purpose of good government. This idea has been shared by most Americans throughout their history, which explains why reformers in the United States have appealed effectively to this principle in their campaigns to extend political and personal freedoms to dispossessed groups. Other ideas on good government accepted pervasively by Americans of the 1770s and 1780s were republicanism, federalism, and constitutionalism.

A republican government was the only form of political order acceptable to Americans, who had rebelled against the aristocratic and monarchical British rule. Americans agreed generally that a republican government, comprised of the people's elected representatives, should be based on the people's consent and accountable to them.

Unitary national government was inconceivable to most Americans of the founding era, who generally agreed to the principle of federalism. They desired some sort of division and sharing of powers between the sovereign state governments and a government of the whole, the United States of America.

Americans also were committed to constitutionalism. They insisted upon a government of the people, limited by the supreme law of a written constitution, to secure the rights of individuals. They believed that the people should both empower and limit government through their constitution by granting it sufficient power to provide order and safety and limiting it sufficiently to prevent tyranny.

THE FOUNDING-ERA DEBATE

The founders' attempts to combine power and restraint, order and liberty, in their political system produced profound arguments on the meaning and practices of good government. However, this founding-era debate was a conflict within a broad consensus on the desirability of government that would be republican, federal, and constitutional, with the primary purpose of securing the fundamental rights of individuals. The sharp disputes were about the exact definitions and practical applications of the generally accepted concepts in the operations of government and the lives of citizens.

The arguments on the nature and practice of republicanism, federalism, constitutionalism, and individual rights began in earnest during the first quarter of 1776, and they intensified after the Declaration of Independence, July 4, 1776. For example, Thomas Paine's *Common Sense*, an argument for American independence, also included his recommendations on good government. John Adams agreed with Paine's argument for an independent United States of America, but disagreed vehemently with Paine's model of republican government. So, Adams offered his own model in *Thoughts on Government*, which circulated throughout the land. The different views of Paine and Adams represented clashing positions that framed the founding-era debate on good government. Paine's ideas, for example, influenced development of the Pennsylvania Constitution of 1776. By contrast, Adam's thoughts became foundations of the Massachusetts Constitution of 1780. The views of Adams were precursors of Federalist political thought, which produced and defended the federal Constitution of 1787. Paine's ideas were forerunners of Anti-Federalist political thought, which opposed the Constitution during the ratifying debates of 1787–1788.

The arguments on the Constitution between Federalist and Anti-Federalists represented the peak of the founding-era controversy. This debate was a profound extension of earlier arguments about constitution-making in the thirteen American states. Both Federalists and Anti-Federalists believed in republicanism, federalism, constitutionalism, and individual rights as essential elements of good government. They argued, however, about whether or not the Constitution of 1787 was an adequate instrument for the appropriate practice of the core political principles. Careful comparative analysis of selected *Federalist* papers and their Anti-Federalist counterpoints yields deep understanding of their conflicting views.

THE CONTINUING RELEVANCE OF THE FOUNDING-ERA DEBATE

The contending ideas of the Federalists and Anti-Federalists have generated alternative visions of constitutional government throughout U.S. history. For example, the nullification crisis of 1832, a debate on the nature of American federalism, was rooted in the founding-era arguments that pitted Anti-Federalist notions of states' rights and powers against Federalist ideas on national authority vis-à-vis the states. Further, there were prominent Anti-Federalist ideas in the Populist and Progressive campaigns to reform government from the 1890s until the 1920s. Current constitutional debates about term limits and the selection and tenure of federal judges are merely two of several examples of live controversies about good government in the United States, which can be traced to the 1770s and 1780s.

The great founding-era scholar, Herbert Storing, stated emphatically and eloquently the ongoing importance and relevance of the controversies on the Constitution of 1787: "If the foundation of the American polity was laid by the Federalists, the Anti-Federalist reservations echo through American history; and it is in the dialogue, not merely in the Federalist victory, that the country's principles are to be discovered."[1] So, the political ideas and issues of the 1770s and 1780s are forever relevant to Americans interested in the paradoxical problem of preserving the best characteristics of their constitutional tradition and improving upon the rest of it.

The core principles of American constitutional government, which have framed more than 200 years of political debate in the United States, have increasingly become interesting to people around the world, who have thrown off the shackles of totalitarian communism and are seeking keys to free government. Examination of the political problems, principles, and arguments of the American founding era, for example, are being used to inform the debates of contemporary constitution-makers in Central and Eastern Europe.

THE ORGANIZATION AND CONTENTS OF THIS VOLUME

The documents collected in this volume illustrate the American debate, from 1775 to 1792, on the principles and practices of good government. Documents were selected to exemplify contending views on the founding-era arguments about the meaning and practice of republican government, federalism, constitutionalism, and individual rights. They were also chosen because of their central place in the American political tradition, from the 1770s until the present. The focus is on core ideas and issues that have stimulated and challenged citizens throughout U.S. history to combine in a workable constitutional government such contrapuntal ideas as liberty with order, majority rule with minority rights, national authority with state powers, and the public good with private rights of individuals.

Alternative positions on issues are presented in various kinds of primary sources. There are, for example, official governmental documents of the Continental Congress, American state governments, and the first federal Congress. There are newspaper articles, pieces of personal correspondence, and entries from private journals. Finally, there are the greatest American founding documents, such as the Virginia Declaration of Rights, the Declaration of Independence, the Articles of Confederation, the Northwest Ordinance, the Constitution of the United States, selected *Federalist* papers, and the federal Bill of Rights. The full texts of several key documents have been presented. Many other documents have been abridged to enhance the readability and coherence of alternative arguments on the central political ideas and issues of the founding period.

The volume includes seven parts. An introductory essay presents the main theme, ideas, and issues of each part. It is followed by a set of documents that pertain to the theme, ideas, and issues. Each document is prefaced with an explanatory headnote, which includes questions to guide the reader's analysis of the primary source.

Part I treats the American decision to declare independence from Britain, 1775–1776. Part II covers constitution-making in the new American states, 1776–1780. Part III deals with issues of rights raised by women, African Americans, Native Americans, and members of religious minorities, 1776–1792. Part IV treats the problems of government under the Articles of Confederation, 1781–1787. Part V pertains to the issues, compromises, and achievements of the Constitutional Convention, 1787. Part VI covers the ratifying debate between Federalists and Anti-Federalists, 1787–1788. Finally, Part VII treats issues associated with enactment of the federal Bill of Rights, 1788–1792.

The text opens with a chronology of key events of the founding era debate on constitutional government. Documents are organized in chronological order within each part. At the end of each part, there is a select bibliography, containing suggestions for further reading on the themes, ideas, and issues raised by the preceding documents.

The contents of this volume emphasize political ideas, issues, and documents that undergird the civic tradition of Americans. Knowledge and appreciation of this tradition is a prerequisite to its preservation and improvement, a critical challenge of every generation of citizens in the United States of America.

NOTE

1. Herbert J. Storing, *What the Anti-Federalists Were For* (Chicago: The University of Chicago Press, 1981), p. 72.

Chronology of Key Events in the Founding of the United States of America

1775

April 19. Battles of Lexington and Concord mark the beginning of the American War of Independence.

July 6. Continental Congress sends petitions to King George III that declare "Causes and Necessity of Taking Up Arms" and seek reconciliation.

August 23. King George III rejects American petitions for reconciliation and proclaims the colonies in rebellion.

1776

January 10. Publication of *Common Sense* by Thomas Paine.

May 10. Congress approves motion by John Adams calling upon colonies to frame their own governments.

June 29. Virginia adopts a constitution for state government, which includes the Virginia Declaration of Rights, adopted on June 12.

July 2. The Continental Congress approves Richard Henry Lee's resolution for independence.

July 4. Congress approves the Declaration of Independence written principally by Thomas Jefferson.

1777

April 20. State of New York adopts a constitution for state government.

July 1. Vermont, which had seceded from New York in January, adopts a constitution for state government, the first one to abolish slavery.

1778

February 6. France offers treaty of alliance to the United States of America.

May 4. Continental Congress ratifies treaty of alliance with France.

1779

June 21. Spain declares war on Britain.

September 1. First popularly elected Constitutional Convention meets to draft a frame of government for the state of Massachusetts.

1780

March 1. Pennsylvania Act for Emancipation is the first law in America for gradual abolition of slavery.

March 20. Voters approve a constitution for Massachusetts in a state-wide referendum, the first time that people ratify their constitution by popular vote.

1781

March 1. Articles of Confederation officially become the law of the land following Maryland's ratification of the document, the last of the thirteen states to approve it.

October 18. British forces under General Cornwallis surrender to combined American and French forces at Yorktown, Virginia, which ends the British military offensive in America.

1782

September 27. Formal negotiations begin on a treaty of peace between Britain and the United States of America.

November 30. Provisional treaty of peace is signed by official representatives of the British and American governments.

1783

June 8. George Washington sends his "Circular Letter" to the governors of each state to draw attention to deficiencies of the Articles of Confederation.

September 3. The Treaty of Paris, a formal agreement of peace between the United States and Great Britain, is signed.

1784

January 14. Congress ratifies the Treaty of Paris.

March 1. Congress accepts the Virginia Act of Cession, which yields to the U.S. government the vast western land claims of the state of Virginia and opens this territory to national control and the eventual creation of new states.

1785

February 24. Congress appoints Thomas Jefferson to be U.S. Minister to France and John Adams to be U.S. Minister to Britain.

May 20. Congress passes the Land Ordinance of 1785, a plan for dividing and selling land in the western territories of the United States.

1786

January 16. Enactment by the Virginia state government of Thomas Jefferson's Statute for Religious Freedom.

September 14. State Commissioners at the Annapolis Convention issue a report calling for a convention in May 1787 to revise the Articles of Confederation.

1787

February 21. Congress approves a convention to revise the Articles of Confederation.

May 25. Federal Constitutional Convention convenes in Philadelphia and meets until mid-September to draft a new frame of government for the United States of America.

July 13. Congress enacts the Northwest Ordinance, a plan for governing the territory north and west of the Ohio River.

September 17. Constitutional Convention ends with signing of the new constitution by members of all twelve state delegations.

September 28. Congress votes to send the Constitution to the legislature of each state, which would convene state conventions to ratify or reject the proposed frame of government.

December 7. Delaware becomes the first state to ratify the Constitution.

1788

June 21. New Hampshire becomes the ninth state to ratify the Constitution, which satisfies the requirement in Article VII of the document for official approval by the states.

June 25. Virginia ratifies the Constitution.

July 26. New York ratifies the Constitution.

September 13. Congress sets dates for electing the president and first meetings of the new government under the Constitution.

October 10. Congress achieves its last quorum and holds its last official meeting under the Articles of Confederation.

1789

April 6. Both Houses of Congress, having achieved a quorum, conduct business, which includes official counting of ballots for the offices of President and Vice-President.

April 30. George Washington takes office as the first president under the new Constitution.

June 8. James Madison, a representative from Virginia, proposes addition of a bill of rights to the Constitution.

September 25. Both Houses of Congress approve by two-thirds vote twelve Amendments to the Constitution.

November 20. New Jersey is the first state to ratify eleven of the twelve proposed Amendments.

1790

May 29. Rhode Island is the last of the original thirteen states to ratify the Constitution.

June 7. Rhode Island ratifies all but the second of the twelve Amendments proposed by Congress.

1791

January 10. Vermont ratifies the Constitution.

March 4. Vermont is admitted by Congress to the Union as the fourteenth state.

November 3. Vermont ratifies the Bill of Rights.

December 15. Virginia ratifies all twelve Amendments proposed by Congress, which completes the ratification process for ten of these proposed Amendments, numbers 3–12, which become the Bill of Rights.

1792

March 1. Thomas Jefferson, secretary of state, notifies the state governors of ratification of ten amendments to the Constitution, the Bill of Rights.

Part I

The Decision for Independence: Reasons For and Against Separation from Britain, 1775–1776

British and American forces clashed at Lexington and Concord, Massachusetts during the morning of April 19, 1775. The fighting continued as the British soldiers marched back to their base at Charlestown, near Boston harbor. The British losses on this opening day of the American Revolutionary War were seventy-three killed, 174 wounded, and twenty-six missing. The Americans lost ninety-five militiamen.

Eight years passed before this Revolutionary War ended with British recognition of the independent United States of America. At first, however, most Americans were not sure that they wanted to sever long-standing ties to Britain, which had persisted for more than 160 years. So, for more than fourteen months, until July of 1776, they hotly debated among themselves the question of separation from Britain while they stubbornly resisted British troops trying to subdue them.

When the Second Continental Congress convened at Philadelphia on May 10, 1775, the primary topic was the war with Britain and the issue of independence. The central question was: Should the American colonies separate themselves from Britain and declare their independence?

John Dickinson of Pennsylvania was a leader of many delegates in Congress who ardently promoted reconciliation with the "mother country." John Adams of Massachusetts and his cousin Samuel fervently advocated separation. Most members of the Continental Congress, however, were undecided.

The reconciliationists argued that Americans had prospered during most of their long association with Britain. They pointed to the benefits of protection against foreign powers provided by the powerful armed forces of Britain. And they stressed the English language, legal institutions, and social traditions they shared with their "mother country."

By contrast, the separationists held that the British government had treated Americans as subordinates, whose political and economic rights could be abused with impunity. They believed Americans could adequately defend themselves without British help and would be more prosperous without British control of their economy.

American ambivalence about independence or reconciliation was revealed in two resolutions that the Continental Congress sent to the British King George III. On July 6, 1775, Congress adopted a Declaration of the Causes and Necessity of Taking Up Arms (see Document 1). Written primarily by John Dickinson of Pennsylvania and Thomas Jefferson of Virginia, this document presented numerous American grievances against the British government, many of which were included in the Declaration of Independence one year later. The authors simultaneously justified the armed resistance by Americans and expressed their desire for reconciliation with Britain and continuation of their fealty to the King. They promised that Americans would stop fighting whenever the British agreed to stop the abusive acts that had precipitated the conflict. But they warned that they would never submit to British tyranny. Two days later, on July 8, the Continental Congress approved the so-called "Olive Branch Petition," written solely by John Dickinson, which emphasized American loyalty to the king and urged him to halt the fighting and embrace reconciliation with the colonies.

King George and his ministers rejected the American petitions and responded with strong statements that seemed to be an unyielding declaration of war. On August 23, 1775, the King proclaimed the colonies in "open and avowed rebellion." He vowed to crush the rebellion "and to bring the traitors to justice" (see Document 2).

The hard-line actions of the British government pushed most previously undecided Americans, and some former proponents of reconciliation, toward support of independence. Thomas Paine's hard-hitting pamphlet, *Common Sense* (Document 3), both reflected and influenced the movement of public opinion from ambivalence to resistance against British rule. Paine wrote that his arguments for independence were "nothing more than simple facts, plain arguments, and common sense." Published in January 1776, Paine's *Common Sense* was an immediate best-seller. More than 120,000 copies were sold by the end of March 1776.

Americans loyal to Britain responded critically to Paine's pamphlet and argued the case for reconciliation (see Document 4). Despite the growth of public opinion in favor of independence, more than 20 percent of Americans were "loyalists."

The Continental Congress continued to vacillate. A majority of the thirteen state delegations appeared to favor separation from Britain. But opposition to independence prevailed in at least five delegations: Delaware, Maryland, New Jersey, New York, and Pennsylvania.

Congress finally faced a turning point on June 7, 1776, when Richard Henry Lee of Virginia presented a resolution that "these United Colonies are, and by right ought to be, free and independent States" (see Document 5). On June 11, the Continental Congress appointed a committee to draft a declaration of independence. The members were John Adams, Benjamin Franklin, Thomas Jefferson, Robert Livingstone, and Roger Sherman. This committee asked Jefferson, the best writer in the group, to compose a draft for the committee's consideration.

The arguments in Congress on independence, however, were far from over. A record of the debates was made by Thomas Jefferson (Document 6), who noted the opposition to an immediate decision for independence. As late as July 1, 1776, the delegations from Pennsylvania and South Carolina voted "no" in the Committee of the Whole, and Delaware abstained because its delegation was divided.

John Dickinson seized the moment to make a final, eloquent plea against independence. On July 1, he argued that Americans would be foolish to renounce the numerous advantages of union with Britain. He said the British government was the fairest and freest in the world. "Now, it is an established fact," said Dickinson, "that America can be well and happily governed by the English laws, under the same king and the same Parliament. Two hundred years of happiness are the proof of it; and we find it also in the present prosperity, which is the result of these venerable laws and of this ancient union."[1]

The delegates listened attentively to the well-respected Dickinson, but most had by this point decided for independence, and nothing he said could change their minds. On July 2, the delegations of Pennsylvania and South Carolina publicly reversed their previous day's resistance to independence. And with the sudden arrival of a new pro-independence delegate, Caesar Rodney, the formerly split Delaware delegation joined the nearly unanimous majority. Only the New York delegation abstained on July 2, 1776, when the Continental Congress voted for Richard Henry Lee's resolution of June 7 to declare independence from Britain.

On July 4, the Continental Congress discussed the formal Declaration of Independence written by Thomas Jefferson and approved, with minor changes, by the committee of five appointed the previous June by Congress. After intense discussion, the Congress approved Jefferson's draft with a few changes, the most notable being the deletion of a strong denunciation of the slave trade. John Hancock, president of the Continental Congress, was the only one to sign the document on July 4, which he did with a flourish.

On July 9, New York officially approved the Declaration, and Congress on July 15 added the word "unanimous" to the title of the document. The official signing ceremony was held on August 2 in Philadelphia, and fifty members of Congress wrote their names on the document on that day. Five more added their names to the Declaration during the autumn of 1776.

The Declaration of Independence (Document 7) was printed in newspapers and broadsides and was distributed and proclaimed throughout the thirteen United States of America. The document reflected public opinion, and the signers believed they had acted as genuine representatives of the popular will.

Many years later, on May 8, 1825, Thomas Jefferson wrote (in a letter to Henry Lee) that the Declaration of Independence "was intended to be an expression of the American mind" and not a highly original or innovative statement. The quick and general public acceptance of the Declaration in 1776 was proof that Jefferson masterfully had expressed the common American beliefs about the essence of good government and its relationship to individual rights. For example, the Declaration stated a compelling criterion by which to evaluate the worth of any government of any time or place: "That to secure these rights [to Life, Liberty, and the Pursuit of Happiness], Governments are instituted among Men, deriving their just powers from the consent of the governed." Any government that fails to "secure these rights," which all persons equally possess by virtue of their membership in the human species, is a bad government and "it is the Right of the People to alter or abolish it."

Shortly before his death, Jefferson fully recognized that the Declaration of Independence was destined to transcend for all time the period and place of its origin and to inspire people everywhere on Earth. On June 24, 1826, the eighty-three-year-old Jefferson, who would die ten days later on the fiftieth anniversary of American independence, wrote to Roger D. Weightman that the Declaration of Independence is "pregnant with our own and the fate of the world. . . . May it be to the world what I believe it will be, (to some parts sooner, to others later, but finally to all,) the Signal of arousing men . . . to assume the blessings and security of self government. . . . All eyes are opened, or opening to the rights of man."[2] And so the Declaration of Independence has been, as Jefferson predicted it would be, a global beacon for good government and individual rights.

Documents 1 through 7 illustrate various views and concerns of Americans facing the difficult decision of breaking their time-honored ties to Britain. And they reveal the strong American commitment to free government and natural rights that guided the founding of their new constitutional republic.

NOTES

1. Hezekiah Niles, ed., *Principles and Acts of the Revolution in America* (New York: A.S. Barnes and Co., 1876), p. 63.

2. Stephen L. Schechter, ed., *Roots of the Republic: American Founding Documents Interpreted* (Madison, Wis.: Madison House, 1990), p. 445.

DOCUMENT 1: Declaration of the Causes and Necessity of Taking Up Arms (July 6, 1775)

The Second Continental Congress convened in Philadelphia on May 10, 1775, about three weeks after the fighting at Lexington and Concord between men of the Massachusetts militia and regulars of the British army. The delegates, sixty-five men representing thirteen British colonies of North America, faced the daunting challenge of conducting a war against the world's greatest military power.

They quickly decided to raise a regular Continental Army and named George Washington of Virginia to command it. Then, the Congress named a five-man committee to explain to the British their reasons for armed resistance to the "mother country." Two members of the committee, John Dickinson of Pennsylvania (later Delaware) and Thomas Jefferson of Virginia were the authors of a document approved by Congress and sent to the British King, George III.

The document reveals the ambivalent feelings of the majority of the Congress. It is both a strong statement of grievances against Britain and a plea for peace and reconciliation. The Congress listed specific grievances against the British, such as violation of their traditional rights to trial by jury, interference with commerce and fishing rights, taxation without representation, and so forth. The Americans asserted that resistance against unjust acts was preferable to slavery. But, they also declared that they wanted to maintain their union with Britain and their loyalty to the King. What major reasons for fighting against Britain are strongly stated in the document? By contrast, what reasons for reconciliation are offered to the King? Which tendency of the document seems to be stronger—the statements of causes for conflict or of pleas for reconciliation?

IF IT WAS POSSIBLE for men who exercise their reason to believe that the Divine Author of our existence intended a part of the human race to hold an absolute property in and an unbounded power over others, marked out by His infinite goodness and wisdom, as the objects of a legal domination never rightfully resistible, however severe and oppressive, the inhabitants of these colonies might at least require from the Parliament of Great Britain some evidence that this dreadful authority over them has been granted to that body. But a reverence for our great Creator, principles of humanity, and the dictates of common sense must convince all those who reflect upon the subject that government was instituted to promote the welfare of mankind and ought to be administered for the attainment of that end.

The legislature of Great Britain, however, stimulated by an inordinate passion for a power not only unjustifiable but which they know to be peculiarly reprobated by the very constitution of that kingdom, and desperate of success in any mode of contest where regard should be had to truth, law, or right, have at length, deserting those, attempted to effect their cruel and impolitic purpose of enslaving these colonies by violence, and have thereby rendered it necessary for us to close with their last appeal from reason to arms. Yet, however blinded that assembly may be by their intemperate rage for unlimited domination so to slight justice and the opinion of mankind, we esteem ourselves bound, by obligations of respect to the rest of the world, to make known the justice of our cause.

Our forefathers, inhabitants of the island of Great Britain, left their native land to seek on these shores a residence for civil and religious freedom. At the expense of their blood, at the hazard of their fortunes, without the least charge to the country from which they removed, by unceasing labor and an unconquerable spirit, they effected settlements in the distant and inhospitable wilds of America, then filled with numerous and warlike nations of barbarians. Societies or governments, vested with perfect legislatures, were formed under charters from the Crown, and a harmonious intercourse was established between the colonies and the kingdom from which they derived their origin. The mutual benefits of this union became in a short time so extraordinary as to excite astonishment. It is universally confessed that the amazing increase of the wealth, strength, and navigation of the Realm arose from this source; and the minister, who so wisely and successfully directed the measures of Great Britain in the late war, publicly declared that these colonies enabled her to triumph over her enemies.

Toward the conclusion of that war, it pleased our sovereign to make a change in his counsels. From that fatal moment, the affairs of the British empire began to fall into confusion.... They have undertaken to give and grant our money without our consent, though we have ever exercised an exclusive right to dispose of our own property; statutes have been passed for extending the jurisdiction of Courts of Admiralty and Vice-Admiralty beyond their ancient limits; for depriving us of the accustomed and inestimable privilege of trial by jury, in cases affecting both life and property; for suspending the legislature of one of the colonies; for interdicting all commerce to the capital of another; and for altering fundamentally the form of government established by charter, and secured by acts of its own legislature solemnly confirmed by the Crown; for exempting the "murderers" of colonists from legal trial and, in effect, from punishment; for erecting in a neighboring province, acquired by the joint arms of Great Britain and America, a despotism dangerous to our very existence; and for quartering soldiers upon the colonists in time of profound peace. It has also been resolved in Parliament that colonists charged with committing certain offenses shall be transported to England to be tried.

But why should we enumerate our injuries in detail? By one statute it is declared that Parliament can "of right make laws to bind us in all cases whatsoever." What is to defend us against so enormous, so unlimited a power? Not a single man of those who assume it is chosen by us, or is subject to our control or influence; but, on the contrary, they are all of them exempt from the operation of such laws; and an American revenue, if not diverted from the ostensible purposes for which it is raised, would actually lighten their own burdens in proportion as they increase ours. We saw the misery to which such despotism would reduce us. We for ten years incessantly and ineffectually besieged the throne as supplicants; we reasoned, we remonstrated with Parliament, in the most mild and decent language.

Administration, sensible that we should regard these oppressive measures as freemen ought to do, sent over fleets and armies to enforce them. The indignation of the Americans was roused, it is true; but it was the indignation of a virtuous, loyal, and affectionate people. . . .

. . . General Gage, who in the course of the last year had taken possession of the town of Boston in the province of Massachusetts Bay, and still occupied it as a garrison, on the 19th day of April, sent out from that place a large detachment of his army, who made an unprovoked assault on the inhabitants of the said province, at the town of Lexington, as appears by the affidavits of a great number of persons, some of whom were officers and soldiers of that detachment, murdered eight of the inhabitants, and wounded many others. From thence the troops proceeded in warlike array to the town of Concord, where they set upon another party of the inhabitants of the same province, killing several and wounding more, until compelled to retreat by the country people suddenly assembled to repel this cruel aggression. Hostilities, thus commenced by the British troops, have been since prosecuted by them without regard to faith or reputation. . . .

The general, further emulating his ministerial masters by a proclamation bearing date on the 12th day of June, after venting the grossest falsehoods and calumnies against the good people of these colonies, proceeds to "declare them all, either by name or description, to be rebels and traitors, to supersede the course of the common law, and instead thereof to publish and order the use and exercise of the law martial." His troops have butchered our countrymen, have wantonly burned Charlestown, besides a considerable number of houses in other places; our ships and vessels are seized; the necessary supplies of provisions are intercepted; and he is exerting his utmost power to spread destruction and devastation around him.

We have received certain intelligence that General Carleton, the governor of Canada, is instigating the people of that province and the Indians to fall upon us; and we have but too much reason to apprehend that schemes have been formed to excite domestic enemies against us. In brief, a part of these colonies now feel, and all of them are sure of feeling, as far as the vengeance of administration can inflict them, the complicated calamities of fire, sword, and famine. We are reduced to the alternative of choosing an unconditional submission to the tyranny of irritated ministers, or resistance by force.

The latter is our choice. We have counted the cost of this contest and find nothing so dreadful as voluntary slavery. Honor, justice, and humanity forbid us tamely to surrender that freedom which we received from our gallant ancestors, and which our innocent posterity have a right to receive from us. We cannot endure the infamy and guilt of resigning succeeding generations to that wretchedness which inevitably awaits them, if we basely entail hereditary bondage upon them.

Our cause is just. Our union is perfect. Our internal resources are great; and, if necessary, foreign assistance is undoubtedly attainable. We gratefully acknowledge, as signal instances of the divine favor toward us, that His providence would not permit us to be called into this severe controversy until we were grown up to our present strength, had been previously exercised in warlike operation, and possessed of the means of defending ourselves. With hearts fortified with these animating reflections, we most solemnly, before God and the world, *declare* that, exerting the utmost energy of those powers which our beneficent Creator has graciously bestowed upon us, the arms we have been compelled by our enemies to assume, we will, in defiance of every hazard, with unabating firmness and perseverance, employ for the preservation of our liberties; being with one mind resolved to die free men rather than live slaves.

Lest this declaration should disquiet the minds of our friends and fellow subjects in any part of the empire, we assure them that we mean not to dissolve that union which has so long and so happily subsisted between us and which we sincerely wish to see restored. Necessity has not yet driven us into that desperate measure, or induced us to excite any other nation to war against them. We have not raised armies with ambitious designs of separating from Great Britain and establishing independent states. We fight not for glory or for conquest. We exhibit to mankind the remarkable spectacle of a people attacked by unprovoked enemies, without any imputation or even suspicion of offense. They boast of their privileges and civilization, and yet proffer no milder conditions than servitude or death.

In our own native land, in defense of the freedom that is our birthright and which we ever enjoyed till the late violation of it, for the protection of our property acquired solely by the honest industry of our forefathers and ourselves, against violence actually offered, we have taken up arms. We shall lay them down when hostilities shall cease on the part of the aggressors and all danger of their being renewed shall be removed, and not before.

With a humble confidence in the mercies of the supreme and impartial Judge and Ruler of the universe, we most devoutly implore His divine goodness to protect us happily through this great conflict, to dispose our adversaries to reconciliation on reasonable terms, and thereby to relieve the empire from the calamities of civil war.

Source: Worthington C. Ford, ed., *Journals of the Continental Congress,* Vol. 2 (Washington, D.C.: U.S. Government Printing Office, 1904), pp. 140ff.

DOCUMENT 2: Proclamation by the King for Suppressing Rebellion and Sedition (August 23, 1775)

King George III received two petitions sent to him in July by the Continental Congress: (1) the Declaration of the Causes and Necessity of Taking Up Arms, and (2) the so-called "Olive Branch Petition," which professed American loyalty to the king and hopes for peaceful settlement of all issues that divided Americans from the British. King George was the British sovereign, but his power, limited by law, was shared with the Parliament. The king and his ministers, however, tended to agree with the Parliament's policy of forcefully suppressing American resistance to British authority. So, the king refused to recognize the petitions for peace from America and declared the colonies in rebellion, which he vowed to crush.

News of the king's response to their petitions did not reach the colonies until the end of October 1776. It had a chilling effect on the American seekers of reconciliation with Britain and strengthened the forces for separation, who saw no recourse other than to settle the conflict by force of arms.

The king emphatically stated his position on the American challenges to British authority. He charged the leaders with treason and promised to capture and punish them. What are the main arguments of his Proclamation? What are his justifications for these arguments?

Whereas many of our subjects in divers parts of our Colonies and Plantations in *North America*, misled by dangerous and ill designing men, and forgetting the allegiance which they owe to the power that has protected and supported them; after various disorderly acts committed in disturbance of the publick peace, to the obstruction of lawful commerce, and to the oppression of our loyal subjects carrying on the same; have at length proceeded to open and avowed rebellion, by arraying themselves in a hostile manner, to withstand the execution of the law, and traitorously preparing, ordering and levying war against us: And whereas, there is reason to apprehend that such rebellion hath been much promoted and encouraged by the traitorous correspondence, counsels and comfort of divers wicked and desperate persons within this realm: To the end therefore, that none of our subjects may neglect or violate their duty through ignorance thereof, or through any doubt of the protection which the law will afford to their loyalty and zeal, we have thought fit, by and with the advice of our Privy Council, to issue our Royal Proclamation, hereby declaring, that not only all our Officers, civil and military, are obliged to exert their utmost endeavours to suppress such rebellion, and to bring the traitors to justice, but that all our subjects of this Realm, and the dominions thereunto belonging, are bound by law to be aiding and assisting in the suppression of such rebellion, and to disclose and make known all traitorous conspiracies and attempts against us, our crown and dignity; and we do accordingly strictly charge and command all our Officers, as well civil as military, and all others our obedient and loyal subjects, to use their utmost endeavours to withstand and suppress such rebellion, and to disclose and make known all treasons and traitorous conspiracies which they shall know to be against us, our crown and dignity; and for that purpose, that they transmit to one of our principal Secretaries of State, or other proper officer, due and full information of all persons who shall be found carrying on correspondence with, or in any manner or degree aiding or abetting the persons now in open arms and rebellion against our Government, within any of our Colonies and Plantations in *North America,* in order to bring to condign punishment the authors, prepetrators, and abetters of such traitorous designs.

Given at our Court at *St. James's* the twenty-third day of *August,* one thousand seven hundred and seventy-five, in the fifteenth year of our reign.

GOD save the KING.

Source: Peter Force, ed., *American Archives,* Fourth Series, Vol. 3 (Washington, D.C., 1837–), p. 240.

DOCUMENT 3: *Common Sense* (Thomas Paine, January 10, 1776)

The most influential public advocate of American independence was a recent immigrant from England, Thomas Paine. In November 1774, at the age of thirty-seven, he arrived in Philadelphia to begin a new life in a new country. In a short time, this newcomer became enthralled with the colonial cause against the British government.

Paine entered the fervent public debate about whether the American colonies should declare independence from Britain. In November 1775, he began to draft his case for immediate separation. This work, titled *Common Sense,* was published in January 1776. The byline of this pamphlet read, "written by an Englishman."

American readers responded enthusiastically to Paine's pamphlet. The first edition was quickly consumed, and the author proudly included his name on the title page of the second edition, published on February 14, which was extensively enlarged.

The following document is an abridgement of the shorter first edition of *Common Sense.* The excerpt presented here focuses on Paine's argument for American independence and on his recommendations about the kind of government Americans should establish for themselves. He claimed it made no sense that an island, Britain, should rule a continent, such as North America. Further, Paine claimed that Americans would enjoy greater prosperity as an independent country than they had known under British rule. Finally, he offered recommendations on how to establish a free and representative government, which would carry out the will of the people.

What was Thomas Paine's case for independence? Why did he believe that separation from Britain was the only reasonable choice for the American colonies? What did he recommend as the essential characteristics or institutions of an independent American government?

In the following pages I offer nothing more than simple facts, plain arguments, and common sense: and have no other preliminaries to settle with the reader, than that he will divest himself of prejudice and prepossession, and suffer his reason and his feelings to determine for themselves: that he will put on, or rather that he will not put off, the true character of a man, and generously enlarge his views beyond the present day.

Volumes have been written on the subject of the struggle between England and America. Men of all ranks have embarked in the controversy, from different motives, and with various designs; but all have been ineffectual, and the period of debate is closed. Arms as the last resource decide the contest; the appeal was the choice of the King, and the Continent has accepted the challenge.

It hath been reported of the late Mr. Pelham (who tho' an able minister was not without his faults) that on his being attacked in the House of Commons on the score that his measures were only of a temporary kind, replied, *"they will last my time."* Should a thought so fatal and unmanly possess the Colonies in the present contest, the name of ancestors will be remembered by future generations with detestation.

The Sun never shined on a cause of greater worth. 'Tis not the affair of a City, a County, a Province, or a Kingdom; but of a Continent—of at least one eighth part of the habitable Globe. 'Tis not the concern of a day, a year, or an age; posterity are virtually involved in the contest, and will be more or less affected even to the end of time, by the proceedings now. Now is the seed-time of Continental union, faith and honour. The least fracture now will be like a name engraved with the point of a pin on the tender rind of a young oak; the wound would enlarge with the tree, and posterity read it in full grown characters. . . .

I have heard it asserted by some, that as America has flourished under her former connection with Great-Britain, the same connection is necessary towards her future happiness, and will always have the same effect. Nothing can be more fallacious than this kind of argument. We may as well assert that because a child has thrived upon milk, that it is never to have meat, or that the first twenty years of our lives is to become a precedent for the next twenty. But even this is admitting more than is true; for I answer roundly, that America would have flourished as much, and probably much more, had no European power taken any notice of her. The commerce by which she hath enriched herself are the necessaries of life, and will always have a market while eating is the custom of Europe.

But she has protected us, say some. That she hath engrossed us is true, and defended the Continent at our expense as well as her own, is admitted; and she would have defended Turkey from the same motive, *viz.* for the sake of trade and dominion.

Alas! we have been long led away by ancient prejudices and made large sacrifices to superstition. We have boasted the protection of Great Britain; without considering, that her motive was *interest* not *attachment;* and that she did not protect us from *our enemies* on *our account;* but from *her enemies* on *her own account,* from those who had no quarrel with us on any *other account,* and who will always be our enemies on the *same account.* . . .

But Britain is the parent country, say some. Then the more shame upon her conduct. Even brutes do not devour their young, nor savages make war upon their families; Wherefore, the assertion, if true, turns to her reproach; but it happens not to be true, or only partly so, and the phrase *parent* or *mother country* hath been jesuitically adopted by the King and his parasites, with a low papistical design of gaining an unfair bias on the credulous weakness of our minds. Europe, and not England, is the parent country of America. This new World hath been the asylum for the persecuted lovers of civil and religious liberty from *every part* of Europe. Hither have they fled, not from the tender embraces of the mother, but from the cruelty of the monster; and it is so far true of England, that the same tyranny which drove the first emigrants from home, pursues their descendants still. . . .

Much hath been said of the united strength of Britain and the Colonies, that in conjunction they might bid defiance to the world: But this is mere presumption; the fate of war is uncertain, neither do the expressions mean any thing; for this continent would never suffer itself to be drained of inhabitants, to support the British arms in either Asia, Africa, or Europe.

Besides, what have we to do with setting the world at defiance? Our plan is commerce, and that, well attended to, will secure us the peace and friendship of all Europe; because it is the interest of all Europe to have America a free port. Her trade will always be a protection, and her barrenness of gold and silver secure her from invaders.

I challenge the warmest advocate for reconciliation to show a single advantage that this continent can reap by being connected with Great Britain. I repeat the challenge; not a single advantage is derived. Our corn will fetch its price in any market in Europe, and our imported goods must be paid for by them where we will.

But the injuries and disadvantages which we sustain by that connection, are without number; and our duty to mankind at large, as well as to ourselves, instruct us to renounce the alliance: because, any submission to, or dependance on, Great Britain, tends directly to involve this Continent in European wars and quarrels, and set us at variance with nations who would otherwise seek our friendship, and against whom we have neither anger nor complaint. As Europe is our market for trade, we ought to form no partial connection with any part of it. It is the true interest of America to steer clear of European contentions, which she never can do, while, by her dependance on Britain, she is made the makeweight in the scale of British politics.

Europe is too thickly planted with Kingdoms to be long at peace, and whenever a war breaks out between England and any foreign power, the trade of America goes to ruin, *because of her connection with Britain.* The next war may not turn out like the last, and should it not, the advocates for reconciliation now will be wishing for separation then, because neutrality in that case would be a safer convoy than a man of war. Everything that is right or reasonable pleads for separation. The blood of the slain, the weeping voice of nature cries. 'TIS TIME TO PART. Even the distance at which the Almighty hath placed England and America is a strong and natural proof that the authority of the one over the other, was never the design of Heaven. . . .

If there is any true cause of fear respecting independence, it is because no plan is yet laid down. Men do not see their way out; wherefore, as an opening into that business, I offer the following hints, at the same time modestly affirming that I have no other opinion of them myself than that they may be the means of giving rise to something better. Could the straggling thoughts of individuals be collected, they would frequently form materials for wise and able men to improve into useful matter.

Let the assemblies be annual, with a president only; the representation more equal; their business wholly domestic and subject to the authority of a continental congress.

Let each colony be divided into six, eight, or ten convenient districts, each district to send a proper number of delegates to Congress, so that each colony send at least 30. The whole number in Congress will be at least 390. Each Congress to sit ———— and to choose a president by the following method. When the delegates are met, let a colony be taken from the whole thirteen colonies by lot, after which, let the Congress choose (by ballot) a president from out of the delegates of that province. In the next Congress, let a colony be taken by lot from twelve only, omitting that colony from which the president was taken in the former Congress, and so proceeding on till the whole thirteen shall have had their proper rotation. And in order that nothing may pass into a law but what is satisfactorily just, not less than three-fifths of the Congress to be called a majority. He that will promote discord, under a government so equally formed as this, would have joined Lucifer in his revolt. . . .

But where, say some, is the king of America? I'll tell you, friend, He reigns above, and does not make havoc of mankind like the royal brute of Britain. Yet, that we may not appear to be defective even in earthly honors, let a day be solemnly set apart for proclaiming the charter; let it be brought forth placed on the divine law, the word of God; let a crown be placed thereon, by which the world may know that so far as we approve of monarchy, that in America *the law is king*. For as in absolute governments the king is law, so in free countries the law ought to be king; and there ought to be no other. But lest any ill use should afterward arise, let the crown at the conclusion of the ceremony be demolished and scattered among the people whose right it is.

A government of our own is our natural right: and when a man seriously reflects on the precariousness of human affairs, he will become convinced, that it is infinitely wiser and safer, to form a constitution of our own in a cool deliberate manner, while we have it in our power, than to trust such an interesting event to time and chance. If we omit it now, some Massanello may hereafter arise, who, laying hold of popular disquietudes, may collect together the desperate and the discontented, and by assuming to themselves the powers of government, finally sweep away the liberties of the Continent like a deluge. Should the government of America return again into the hands of Britain, the tottering situation of things will be a temptation for some desperate adventurer to try his fortune; and in such a case, what relief can Britain give? Ere she could hear the news, the fatal business might be done; and ourselves suffering like the wretched Britons under the oppression of the Conqueror. Ye that oppose independence now, ye know not what ye do: ye are opening a door to eternal tyranny, by keeping vacant the seat of government. There are thousands and tens of thousands, who would think it glorious to expel from the Continent, that barbarous and hellish power, which hath stirred up the Indians and the Negroes to destroy us; the cruelty hath a double guilt, it is dealing brutally by us, and treacherously by them.

To talk of friendship with those in whom our reason forbids us to have faith, and our affections wounded thro' a thousand pores instruct us to detest, is madness and folly. Every day wears out the little remains of kindred between us and them; and can there be any reason to hope, that as the relationship expires, the affection will encrease, or that we shall agree better when we have ten times more and greater concerns to quarrel over than ever?

Ye that tell us of harmony and reconciliation, can ye restore to us the time that is past? Can ye give to prostitution its former innocence? neither can ye reconcile Britain and America. The last cord now is broken, the people of England are presenting addresses against us. There are injuries which nature cannot forgive; she would cease to be nature if she did. As well can the lover forgive the ravisher of his mistress, as the Continent forgive the murders of Britain. The Almighty hath implanted in us these unextinguishable feelings for good and wise purposes. They are the Guardians of his Image in our hearts. They distinguish us from the herd of common animals. The social compact would dissolve, and justice be extirpated from the earth, or have only a casual existence were we callous to the touches of affection. The robber and the murderer would often escape unpunished, did not the injuries which our tempers sustain, provoke us into justice.

O! ye that love mankind! Ye that dare oppose not only the tyranny but the tyrant, stand forth! Every spot of the old world is overrun with oppression. Freedom hath been hunted round the Globe. Asia and Africa have long expelled her. Europe regards her like a stranger, and England hath given her warning to depart. O! receive the fugitive, and prepare in time an asylum for mankind.

Source: Thomas Paine, *Common Sense* (Philadelphia, 1776).

DOCUMENT 4: *The True Interest of America Impartially Stated* (Published Anonymously by The Reverend Charles Inglis, March 1776)

Colonists who supported the British during the American Revolution were called loyalists. About 20 percent of the colonists of European ancestry were loyalists. For example, the Reverend Charles Inglis, an Anglican clergyman, was a loyalist who publicly spoke and wrote against American independence. He answered Thomas Paine's *Common Sense* with a pamphlet, *The True Interest of America Impartially Stated.*

In 1777, Rev. Inglis became rector of Trinity Church in New York City. Throughout the Revolutionary War, he wrote essays, published anonymously, against the American cause of independence. He used a pen name, "Papinian," to protect himself against punishment by over-zealous patriots.

Like many other loyalists, Rev. Inglis left America at the end of the Revolutionary War. In 1783 he went to England. Later, Rev. Inglis settled in Nova Scotia, where he became First Bishop of the Church of England in this province of Canada. Rev. Inglis was one of the more than 80,000 loyalists who fled the United States and resettled in Canada.

The excerpt from Rev. Inglis's lengthy reply to Thomas Paine discusses the advantages and disadvantages of deciding against American independence. A primary advantage of union with Britain would be prosperity and peace. What were the other advantages of union with the British, according to Rev. Inglis? A major disadvantage of separation from Britain would be destruction of property and interference with commerce due to war and hostile relations with the British people. What did Rev. Inglis claim would be the other disadvantages of separation from the British Empire? What specific criticisms did he make of Thomas Paine's *Common Sense*? What is your evaluation of Rev. Inglis's case against Paine's *Common Sense*? Does he make an effective reply to Paine's arguments for American independence?

I THINK IT NO DIFFICULT MATTER to point out many advantages which will certainly attend our reconciliation and connection with Great Britain on a firm, constitutional plan. I shall select a few of these; and, that their importance may be more clearly discerned, I shall afterward point out some of the evils which inevitably must attend our separating from Britain and declaring for independency. On each article I shall study brevity.

1. By a reconciliation with Britain, a period would be put to the present calamitous war, by which so many lives have been lost, and so many more must be lost if it continues. This alone is an advantage devoutly to be wished for. This author [Paine] says: "The blood of the slain, the weeping voice of nature cries, 'Tis time to part." I think they cry just the reverse. The blood of the slain, the weeping voice of nature cries: It is time to be reconciled; it is time to lay aside those animosities which have pushed on Britons to shed the blood of Britons; it is high time that those who are connected by the endearing ties of religion, kindred, and country should resume their former friendship and be united in the bond of mutual affection, as their interests are inseparably united.

2. By a reconciliation with Great Britain, peace—that fairest offspring and gift of heaven—will be restored. In one respect peace is like health—we do not sufficiently know its value but by its absence. What uneasiness and anxiety, what evils has this short interruption of peace with the parent state brought on the whole British Empire! Let every man only consult his feelings—I except my antagonist—and it will require no great force of rhetoric to convince him that a removal of those evils and a restoration of peace would be a singular advantage and blessing.

3. Agriculture, commerce, and industry would resume their wonted vigor. At present, they languish and droop, both here and in Britain; and must continue to do so while this unhappy contest remains unsettled.

4. By a connection with Great Britain, our trade would still have the protection of the greatest naval power in the world. England has the advantage, in this respect, of every other state, whether of ancient or modern times. Her insular situation, her nurseries for seamen, the superiority of those seamen above others—these circumstances, to mention no other, combine to make her the first maritime power in the universe—such exactly is the power whose protection we want for our commerce. To suppose, with our author, that we should have no war were we to revolt from England is too absurd to deserve a confutation. I could just as soon set about refuting the reveries of some brainsick enthusiast. Past experience shows that Britain is able to defend our commerce and our coasts; and we have no reason to doubt of her being able to do so for the future.

5. The protection of our trade, while connected with Britain, will not cost us a *fiftieth* part of what it must cost were we ourselves to raise a naval force sufficient for the purpose.

6. While connected with Great Britain, we have a bounty on almost every article of exportation; and we may be better supplied with goods by her than we could elsewhere. What our author says is true, "that our imported goods must be paid for, buy them where we will"; but we may buy them dearer, and of worse quality, in one place than another. The manufactures of Great Britain confessedly surpass any in the world, par-

ticularly those in every kind of metal, which we want most; and no country can afford linens and woolens of equal quality cheaper.

7. When a reconciliation is effected, and things return into the old channel, a few years of peace will restore everything to its pristine state. Emigrants will flow in as usual from the different parts of Europe. Population will advance with the same rapid progress as formerly, and our lands will rise in value.

These advantages are not imaginary but real. They are such as we have already experienced; . . .

Let us now, if you please, take a view of the other side of the question. Suppose we were to revolt from Great Britain, declare ourselves independent, and set up a republic of our own—what would be the consequence? I stand aghast at the prospect; my blood runs chill when I think of the calamities, the complicated evils that must ensue, and may be clearly foreseen—it is impossible for any man to foresee them all. . . .

Supposing then we declared for independency, what would follow? I answer:

1. All our property throughout the continent would be unhinged; the greatest confusion and most violent convulsions would take place. It would not be here as it was in England at the Revolution in 1688. That Revolution was not brought about by a defeasance or disannulling the right of succession. . . . But in case of our revolt, the old constitution would be totally subverted. The common bond that tied us together, and by which our property was secured, would be snapped asunder. It is not to be doubted but our Congress would endeavor to apply some remedy for those evils; but, with all deference to that respectable body, I do not apprehend that any remedy in their power would be adequate, at least for some time. I do not choose to be more explicit; but I am able to support my opinion.

2. What a horrid situation would thousands be reduced to who have taken the oath of allegiance to the King; yet, contrary to their oath as well as inclination, must be compelled to renounce that allegiance or abandon all their property in America! How many thousands more would be reduced to a similar situation, who, although they took not that oath, yet would think it inconsistent with their duty and a good conscience to renounce their sovereign. I dare say these will appear trifling difficulties to our author; but, whatever he may think, there are thousands and thousands who would sooner lose all they had in the world, nay, life itself, than thus wound their conscience. A declaration of independency would infallibly disunite and divide the colonists.

3. By a declaration for independency, every avenue to an accommodation with Great Britain would be closed; the sword only could then decide the quarrel; and the sword would not be sheathed till one had conquered the other.

The importance of these colonies to Britain need not be enlarged on—it is a thing so universally known. The greater their importance is to her, so much the more obstinate will her struggle be not to lose them. The independency of America would, in the end, deprive her of the West Indies, shake her empire to the foundation, and reduce her to a state of the most mortifying insignificance. Great Britain, therefore, must, for her own preservation, risk everything, and exert her whole strength to prevent such an event from taking place. This being the case,

4. Devastation and ruin must mark the progress of this war along the seacoast of America. Hitherto, Britain has not exerted her power. Her number of troops and ships of war here at present is very little more than she judged expedient in time of peace—the former does not amount to 12,000 men—nor the latter to 40 ships, including frigates. Both she and the colonies hoped for and expected an accommodation; neither of them has lost sight of that desirable object. The seas have been open to our ships; and, although some skirmishes have unfortunately happened, yet a ray of hope still cheered both sides that peace was not distant. But, as soon as we declare for independency, every prospect of this kind must vanish. Ruthless war, with all its aggravated horrors, will ravage our once happy land; our seacoasts and ports will be ruined, and our ships taken. Torrents of blood will be spilled, and thousands reduced to beggary and wretchedness. . . .

5. But supposing once more that we were able to cut off every regiment that Britain can spare or hire, and to destroy every ship she can send, that we could beat off any other European power that would presume to intrude upon this continent; yet, a republican form of government would neither suit the genius of the people nor the extent of America. . . .

The Americans are properly Britons. They have the manners, habits, and ideas of Britons; and have been accustomed to a similar form of government. But Britons never could bear the extremes, either of monarchy or republicanism. Some of their kings have aimed at despotism, but always failed. Repeated efforts have been made toward democracy, and they equally failed. Once, indeed, republicanism triumphed over the constitution; the despotism of one person ensued; both were finally expelled. . . . Limited monarchy is the form of government which is most favorable to liberty, which is best adapted to the genius and temper of Britons; although here and there among us a crackbrained zealot for democracy or absolute monarchy may be sometimes found.

Besides the unsuitableness of the republican form to the genius of the people, America is too extensive for it. That form may do well enough for a single city or small territory, but would be utterly improper for such a continent as this. America is too unwieldy for the feeble, dilatory administration of democracy. . . .

Let us only show a disposition to treat or negotiate in earnest—let us fall upon some method to set a treaty or negotiation with Great Britain on foot; and, if once properly begun, there is moral certainty that this unhappy dispute will be settled to the mutual satisfaction and interest of both countries. For my part, I have not the least doubt about it. . . .

But a declaration for independency on the part of America would preclude treaty entirely and could answer no good purpose. We actually have already every advantage of independency, without its inconveniences. By a declaration of independency, we should instantly lose all assistance from our friends in England. It would stop their mouths; for, were they to say anything in our favor, they would be deemed rebels and treated accordingly. . . .

America, till very lately, has been the happiest country in the universe. Blessed with all that nature could bestow with the profusest bounty, she enjoyed, besides, more liberty, greater privileges than any other land. How painful is it to reflect on these things, and to look forward to the gloomy prospects now before us! But it is not too late to hope that matters may mend. By prudent management her former happiness may again return; and continue to increase for ages to come, in a union with the parent state.

However distant humanity may wish the period, yet, in the rotation of human affairs, a period may arrive when (both countries being prepared for it) some terrible disaster, some dreadful convulsion in Great Britain may transfer the seat of empire to this Western Hemisphere—where the British constitution, like the Phoenix from its parent's ashes, shall rise with youthful vigor and shine with redoubled splendor.

But if America should now mistake her real interest—if her sons, infatuated with romantic notions of conquest and empire, ere things are ripe, should adopt this republican's scheme—they will infallibly destroy this smiling prospect. They will dismember this happy country, make it a scene of blood and slaughter, and entail wretchedness and misery on millions yet unborn.

Source: [The Reverend Charles Inglis], *The True Interest of America Impartially Stated* (Philadelphia, 1776).

DOCUMENT 5: Resolution for Independence (June 7, 1776)

Richard Henry Lee of Virginia started the process by which the Continental Congress finally decided for independence and established the United States of America. Lee introduced his "Resolution for Independence" on June 7, 1776. John Adams of Massachusetts seconded Lee's resolution. When Congress voted to approve the resolution on July 2, Adams predicted that the independence of the United States forever would be celebrated on this day. Two days later, on July 4, Congress approved the Declaration of Independence and this day, not July 2, became the official birthday of the United States of America. Nonetheless, Lee's resolution pointed Americans toward independence and confederation.

Only the first of Lee's three statements—the one pertaining to independence—was enacted by Congress on July 2. The other two statements were acted upon later. What was Lee's main point in each of these statements? Why was enactment of Lee's first statement a prerequisite to effective action on the other two statements?

RESOLVED, That these United Colonies are, and of right ought to be, free and independent States, that they are absolved from all allegiance to the British Crown, and that all political connection between them and the State of Great Britain is, and ought to be totally dissolved.

That it is expedient forthwith to take the most effectual measures for forming foreign Alliances.

That a plan of confederation be prepared and transmitted to the respective Colonies for their consideration and approbation.

Source: Worthington C. Ford, ed., *Journals of the Continental Congress,* Vol. 5 (Washington, D.C.: U.S. Government Printing Office, 1904), p. 425.

DOCUMENT 6: Notes on the Debate in Congress on Independence (Thomas Jefferson, June 7–July 4, 1776)

From June 7 until July 4, 1776, the Continental Congress debated the issue of American independence from Britain. Thomas Jefferson recorded the arguments of both sides, those for and against independence, in notes that he wrote during meetings of the Continental Congress. Jefferson noted that some members of Congress, such as John Dickinson, were against declaring independence at this time, even though they saw little opportunity for reconciliation. Who was on this side of the debate? What were their reasons for opposing independence at this time?

Jefferson also recorded the views of congressmen who advocated an immediate declaration of independence, such as John Adams. Who joined Adams on this side of the debate? What were their reasons?

Jefferson generally approved of the Congress's reactions to his draft of the Declaration of Independence. However, he expressed displeasure at the deletion of his condemnation of the slave trade. What did he write about this matter?

Friday, June 7, 1776. The delegates from Virginia moved, in obedience to instructions from their constituents, that the Congress should declare that these United Colonies are and of right ought to be free and independent states; that they are absolved from all allegiance to the British Crown, and that all political connection between them and the state of Great Britain is and ought to be totally dissolved; that measures should be immediately taken for procuring the assistance of foreign powers, and a confederation be formed to bind the colonies more closely together.

The House being obliged to attend at that time to some other business, the proposition was referred to the next day, when the members were ordered to attend punctually at 10 o'clock.

Saturday, June 8. They proceeded to take it into consideration and referred it to a committee of the whole, into which they immediately resolved themselves, and passed that day and Monday, the 10th, in debating on the subject.

It was argued by Wilson, Robert R. Livingston, E. Rutledge, Dickinson, and others:

That, though they were friends to the measures themselves and saw the impossibility that we should ever again be united with Great Britain, yet they were against adopting them at this time;

That the conduct we had formerly observed was wise and proper now, of deferring to take any capital step till the voice of the people drove us into it;

That they were our power, and without them our declarations could not be carried into effect;

That the people of the middle colonies (Maryland, Delaware, Pennsylvania, the Jerseys, and New York) were not yet ripe for bidding adieu to British connection, but that they were fast ripening and in a short time would join in the general voice of America;

That the resolution entered into by this House on the 15th of May for suppressing the exercise of all powers derived from the Crown had shown, by the ferment into which it had thrown these middle colonies, that they had not yet accommodated their minds to a separation from the mother country;

That some of them had expressly forbidden their delegates to consent to such a declaration, and others had given no instructions and, consequently, no powers to give such consent;

That if the delegates of any particular colony had no power to declare such colony independent, certain they were the others could not declare it for them, the colonies being as yet perfectly independent of each other; . . .

On the other side it was urged by J. Adams, Lee, Wythe, and others:

That no gentleman had argued against the policy or the right of separation from Britain, nor had supposed it possible we should ever renew our connection; that they had only opposed its being now declared;

That the question was not whether, by a Declaration of Independence, we should make ourselves what we are not, but whether we should declare a fact which already exists;

That, as to the people or Parliament of England, we had always been independent of them, their restraints on our trade deriving efficacy from our acquiescence only and not from any rights they possessed of imposing them, and that so far our connection had been federal only and was now dissolved by the commencement of hostilities;

That, as to the King, we had been bound to him by allegiance, but that this bond was now dissolved by his assent to the last act of Parliament, by which he declares us out of his protection, and by his levying war on us, a fact which had long ago proved us out of his protection, it being a certain position in law that allegiance and protection are reciprocal, the one ceasing when the other is *withdrawn;* . . .

It appearing in the course of these debates that the colonies of New York, New Jersey, Pennsylvania, Delaware, Maryland, and South Carolina were not yet matured for falling from the parent stem, but that they were fast advancing to that state, it was thought most prudent to wait a while for them, and to postpone the final decision to July 1; but, that this might occasion as little delay as possible, a committee was appointed to prepare a Declaration of Independence. The committee were John Adams, Dr. Franklin, Roger Sherman, Robert R. Livingston, and myself. Committees were also appointed at the same time to prepare a plan of confederation for the colonies, and to state the terms proper to be proposed for foreign alliance. The committee for drawing the Declaration of Independence desired me to do it. It was accordingly done, and, being approved by them, I reported it to the House on Friday, the 28th of June, when it was read and ordered to lie on the table.

On Monday, the 1st of July, the House resolved itself into a committee of the whole and resumed the consideration of the original motion made by the delegates of Virginia, which, being again debated through the day, was carried in the affirmative by the votes of New Hampshire, Connecticut, Massachusetts, Rhode Island, New Jersey, Maryland, Virginia, North Carolina, and Georgia. South Carolina and Pennsylvania voted against it. Delaware had but two members present, and they were divided. The delegates from New York declared they were for it themselves, and were assured their constituents were for it, but that their instructions having been drawn near a twelvemonth before, when reconciliation was still the general object, they were enjoined by them to do nothing which should impede that object. They therefore thought themselves not justifiable in voting on either side and asked leave to withdraw from the question, which was given them. The committee rose and reported their resolution to the House.

Mr. Edward Rutledge of South Carolina then requested the determination might be put off to the next day, as he believed his colleagues, though they disapproved of the resolution, would then join in it for the sake of unanimity. The ultimate question, whether the House would agree to the resolution of the committee, was accordingly postponed to the next day, when it was again moved and South Carolina concurred in voting for it. In the meantime, a third member had come post from the Delaware counties and turned the vote of that colony in favor of the resolution. Members of a different sentiment attending that morning from Pennsylvania also, her vote was changed, so that the whole twelve colonies who were authorized to vote at all gave their voices for it; and within a few days the convention of New York approved of it and thus supplied the void occasioned by the withdrawing of her delegates from the vote.

Congress proceeded the same day to consider the Declaration of Independence, which had been reported and lain on the table the Friday preceding, and on Monday referred to a committee of the whole. The pusillanimous idea that we had friends in England worth keeping terms with still haunted the minds of many. For this reason, those passages which conveyed censures on the people of England were struck out, lest they should give them offense. The clause, too, reprobating the enslaving the inhabitants of Africa was struck out in complaisance to South Carolina and Georgia, who had never attempted to restrain the importation of slaves, and who, on the contrary, still wished to continue it. Our Northern brethren, also, I believe, felt a little tender under those censures; for though their people had very few slaves themselves, yet they had been pretty considerable carriers of them to others.

The debates, having taken up the greater parts of the 2nd, 3rd, and 4th days of July, were, on the evening of the last, closed. The Declaration was reported by the committee, agreed to by the House, and signed by every member present, except Mr. Dickinson.

Source: H. A. Washington, ed., *The Writings of Thomas Jefferson*, Vol. 8 (Washington, D.C.: Taylor & Maury, 1854), pp. 12–26.

DOCUMENT 7: The Declaration of Independence (July 4, 1776)

On July 4, Congress voted for the Declaration of Independence, drafted by Thomas Jefferson, after making minor revisions in the document. The first paragraph of the Declaration explained the document's purpose, which was to justify the separation from Britain. The second paragraph stated a theory of good government generally accepted by Americans, which emphasized popular consent and natural rights of individuals. This theory held that all individuals are equal in their possession of certain "unalienable Rights," which it is the duty of government to protect. These rights were not granted by government. Rather, they were embedded in human nature and, as such, were unconditional possessions of all persons. Therefore, the first purpose of a good government, according to the Declaration of Independence, was to secure these rights. Further, a good government was based on the consent of the governed.

The document included a series of charges or grievances against the British king, which, according to the Americans, justified their withdrawal of loyalty to him. These grievances were examples of actions that violated the criteria for good government stated in the second paragraph of the document. These charges were directed against the king, not Parliament, because the Americans believed they had been tied to Britain only through a common monarch. They persistently had refused to recognize the legitimate authority over them of the Parliament, because they were not represented in this institution.

The final paragraph of the Declaration was an unqualified assertion of sovereignty by the United States of America. It was also an ultimate and unconditional pledge to themselves and the world that they would be free of "all Allegiance to the British Crown."

In the Declaration of Independence Jefferson stated universal criteria for good government. What are these criteria? He also listed grievances against the British king, which exemplified the American view that the British government had not acted in accordance with the criteria for good government. Which items in the list of grievances were the strongest examples used by Jefferson to argue that the British had violated his universal criteria for good government?

In Congress, July 4, 1776,

The unanimous Declaration of the thirteen united States of America,

When in the Course of human events, it becomes necessary for one people to dissolve the political bands which have connected them with another, and to assume among the Powers of the earth, the separate and equal station to which the Laws of Nature and of Nature's God entitle them, a decent respect to the opinions of mankind requires that they should declare the causes which impel them to the separation.

We hold these truths to be self-evident, that all men are created equal, that they are endowed by their Creator with certain unalienable Rights, that among these are Life, Liberty and the pursuit of Happiness. That to secure these rights, Governments are instituted among Men, deriving their just powers from the consent of the governed, That whenever any Form of Government becomes destructive of these ends, it is the Right of the People to alter or to abolish it, and to institute new Government, laying its foundation on such principles and organizing its powers in such form, as to them shall seem most likely to effect their Safety and Happiness. Prudence, indeed, will dictate that Governments long established should not be changed for light and transient causes; and accordingly all experience hath shown, that mankind are more disposed to suffer, while evils are sufferable, than to right themselves by abolishing the forms to which they are accustomed. But when a long train of abuses and usurpations, pursuing invariably the same Object evinces a design to reduce them under absolute Despotism, it is their right, it is their duty, to throw off such Government, and to provide new Guards for their future security.— Such has been the patient sufferance of these Colonies; and such is now the necessity which constrains them to alter their former Systems of Government. The history of the present King of Great Britain is a history of repeated injuries and usurpations, all having in direct object the establishment of an absolute Tyranny over these States. To prove this, let Facts be submitted to a candid world.

He has refused his Assent to Laws, the most wholesome and necessary for the public good.

He has forbidden his Governors to pass Laws of immediate and pressing importance, unless suspended in their operation till his Assent should be obtained; and when so suspended, he has utterly neglected to attend to them.

He has refused to pass other Laws for the accommodation of large districts of people, unless those people would relinquish the right of Representation in the Legislature, a right inestimable to them and formidable to tyrants only.

He has called together legislative bodies at places unusual, uncomfortable, and distant from the depository of their Public Records, for the sole purpose of fatiguing them into compliance with his measures.

He has dissolved Representative Houses repeatedly, for opposing with manly firmness his invasions on the rights of the people.

He has refused for a long time, after such dissolutions, to cause others to be elected; whereby the Legislative Powers, incapable of Annihilation, have returned to the People at large for their exercise; the State remaining in the mean time exposed to all the dangers of invasion from without, and convulsions within.

He has endeavoured to prevent the population of these States; for that purpose obstructing the Laws of Naturalization of Foreigners; refusing to pass others to encourage their migration hither, and raising the conditions of new Appropriations of Lands.

He has obstructed the Administration of Justice, by refusing his Assent to Laws for establishing Judiciary Powers.

He has made Judges dependent on his Will alone, for the tenure of their offices, and the amount and payment of their salaries.

He has erected a multitude of New Offices, and sent hither swarms of Officers to harass our People, and eat out their substance.

He has kept among us, in times of peace, Standing Armies without the Consent of our legislature.

He has affected to render the Military independent of and superior to the Civil Power.

He has combined with others to subject us to a jurisdiction foreign to our constitution, and unacknowledged by our laws; giving his Assent to their acts of pretended legislation:

For quartering large bodies of armed troops among us:

For protecting them, by a mock Trial, from Punishment for any Murders which they should commit on the Inhabitants of these States:

For cutting off our Trade with all parts of the world:

For imposing taxes on us without our Consent:

For depriving us in many cases, of the benefits of Trial by Jury:

For transporting us beyond Seas to be tried for pretended offences:

For abolishing the free System of English Laws in a neighbouring Province, establishing therein an Arbitrary government, and enlarging its Boundaries so as to render it at once an example and fit instrument for introducing the same absolute rule into these Colonies:

For taking away our Charters, abolishing our most valuable Laws, and altering fundamentally the Forms of our Governments:

For suspending our own Legislature, and declaring themselves invested with Power to legislate for us in all cases whatsoever.

He has abdicated Government here, by declaring us out of his Protection and waging War against us.

He has plundered our seas, ravaged our Coasts, burnt our towns, and destroyed the lives of our people.

He is at this time transporting large armies of foreign mercenaries to compleat the works of death, desolation and tyranny, already begun with circumstances of Cruelty & perfidy scarcely paralleled in the most barbarous ages, and totally unworthy the Head of a civilized nation.

He has constrained our fellow Citizens taken Captive on the high Seas to bear Arms against their Country, to become the executioners of their friends and Brethren, or to fall themselves by their Hands.

He has excited domestic insurrections amongst us, and has endeavoured to bring on the inhabitants of our frontiers, the merciless Indian Savages, whose known rule of warfare, is an undistinguished destruction of all ages, sexes and conditions.

In every stage of these Oppressions We have Petitioned for Redress in the most humble terms: Our repeated Petitions have been answered only by repeated injury. A Prince, whose character is thus marked by every act which may define a Tyrant, is unfit to be the ruler of a free People.

Nor have We been wanting in attention to our British brethren. We have warned them from time to time of attempts by their legislature to extend an unwarrantable jurisdiction over us. We have reminded them of the circumstances of our emigration and settlement here. We have appealed to their native justice and magnanimity, and we have conjured them by the ties of our common kindred to disavow these usurpations, which, would inevitably interrupt our connections and correspondence. They too have been deaf to the voice of justice and of consanguinity. We must, therefore, acquiesce in the necessity, which denounces our Separation, and hold them, as we hold the rest of mankind, Enemies in War, in Peace Friends.

We, therefore, the Representatives of the united States of America, in General Congress, Assembled, appealing to the Supreme Judge of the world for the rectitude of our intentions, do, in the Name, and by Authority of the good People of these Colonies, solemnly publish and declare, That these United Colonies are, and of Right ought to be Free and Independent States; that they are Absolved from all Allegiance to the British Crown, and that all political connection between them and the State of Great Britain, is and ought to be totally dissolved; and that as Free and Independent States, they have full Power to levy War, conclude Peace, contract Alliances, establish Commerce, and to do all other Acts and Things which Independent States may of right do. And for the support of this Declaration, with a firm reliance on the Protection of Divine Providence, we mutually pledge to each other our Lives, our Fortunes and our sacred Honor.

JOHN HANCOCK.

New Hampshire
JOSIAH BARTLETT,
WM. WHIPPLE,
MATTHEW THORNTON.

Massachusetts-Bay
SAML. ADAMS,
JOHN ADAMS,
ROBT. TREAT PAINE,
ELBRIDGE GERRY.

Rhode Island
STEP. HOPKINS,
WILLIAM ELLERY.

Connecticut
ROGER SHERMAN,
SAM'EL HUNTINGTON,
WM. WILLIAMS,
OLIVER WOLCOTT.

Georgia
BUTTON GWINNETT,
LYMAN HALL,
GEO. WALTON.

Maryland
SAMUEL CHASE,
WM. PACA,
THOS. STONE,
CHARLES CARROLL of Carrollton.

Virginia
GEORGE WYTHE,
RICHARD HENRY LEE,
TH. JEFFERSON,
BENJA. HARRISON,
THS. NELSON, JR.,
FRANCIS LIGHTFOOT LEE,
CARTER BRAXTON.

New York
WM. FLOYD,
PHIL. LIVINGSTON,
FRANS. LEWIS,
LEWIS MORRIS.

Pennsylvania
ROBT. MORRIS,
BENJAMIN RUSH,
BENJA. FRANKLIN,
JOHN MORTON,
GEO. CLYMER,
JAS. SMITH,
GEO. TAYLOR,
JAMES WILSON,
GEO. ROSS.

Delaware
CAESAR RODNEY,
GEO. READ,
THO. M'KEAN.

North Carolina
WM. HOOPER,
JOSEPH HEWES,
JOHN PENN.

South Carolina
EDWARD RUTLEDGE,
THOS. HEYWARD, JUNR.,
THOMAS LYNCH, JUNR.,
ARTHUR MIDDLETON.

New Jersey
RICHD. STOCKTON,
JNO. WITHERSPOON,
FRAS. HOPKINSON,
JOHN HART,
ABRA. CLARK.

Source: United States Statutes at Large, Vol. 1 (Washington, D.C.: U.S. Government Printing Office, 1845), pp. 1–4.

FURTHER READING

Aldridge, A. O. *Thomas Paine's American Ideology.* Newark: University of Delaware Press, 1984.

Becker, Carl L. *The Declaration of Independence: A Study in the History of Ideas.* New York: Alfred A. Knopf, 1942.

Calhoun, Robert M. *The Loyalists in Revolutionary America, 1760–1781.* New York: Harcourt Brace Jovanovich, 1973.

Flower, Milton E. *John Dickinson: Conservative Revolutionary.* Charlottesville: University of Virginia Press, 1983.

Foner, Eric. *Tom Paine and Revolutionary America.* New York: Oxford University Press, 1976.

Keane, John. *Tom Paine: A Political Life.* Boston: Little, Brown, 1995.

Peterson, Merrill D. *Thomas Jefferson and the New Nation.* New York: Oxford University Press, 1970.

Rakove, Jack N. *The Beginnings of National Politics: An Interpretive History of the Continental Congress.* New York: Alfred A. Knopf, 1979.

Reid, John Phillip. *The Concept of Liberty in the Age of the American Revolution.* Chicago: University of Chicago Press, 1988.

Sheldon, Garrett Ward. *The Political Philosophy of Thomas Jefferson.* Baltimore: Johns Hopkins University Press, 1991.

Wills, Garry. *Inventing America: Jefferson's Declaration of Independence.* Garden City, N.Y.: Doubleday, 1978.

Part II

Making Constitutions for the New American States: Debates on Models of Good Government, 1776–1780

As American soldiers fought the battles of their Revolutionary War, American statesmen made constitutional governments for their new states. The war had broken bonds of political authority that had been built during more than 160 years of British rule in North America. So, American revolutionaries had to face the challenge and opportunity of constructing new political institutions, with new foundations of authority and legitimacy. John Adams of Massachusetts was a primary leader of the movement to make new state governments. Many years later, Adams recorded in his autobiography that "almost every day, I had something to say about advising the States to institute Governments."[1]

Adams presented two resolutions to the Second Continental Congress that promoted new constitutions for the state governments. The first, passed on May 10, 1775, recommended that the American colonies should form new governments. The second, passed on May 15, urged that all forms of authority under the British government should be abolished. These two resolutions, acted upon variously in all the American colonies, were harbingers of their irrevocable separation from the British Empire.

This was the first time, anywhere in the world, that large numbers of people in several contiguous communities (the thirteen colonies) had simultaneously undertaken the deliberate construction of written constitutions to frame their nascent governments. They sought elusive answers to perennial political questions of human communities. What is good government? What are its essential characteristics? How can the essential characteristics of good government be framed by a written constitution? What kind of constitution should be made in order to provide good government for the state?

Thomas Paine, among many others, offered answers to his countrymen on the key questions of this constitutional moment. In *Common Sense,* published in January 1776, Paine made his compelling case for American independence. He also gave advice on the kind of constitutional government that the new independent states should have. Paine recommended government based on a one-house or unicameral legislature. This legislature, directly representative of the voters, would select by majority vote the executive and judicial members of the government, who would be responsible to the legislature. A great believer in democracy, Paine advocated universal manhood suffrage and supremacy in government of the legislature elected by the voters and directly accountable to them. (See Document 3 to examine Paine's words on his model for government in the new American states.) The unknown author of *The People the Best Governors* was one of many who emphasized ideas on good government that were compatible with the views of Tom Paine (see Document 8).

John Adams was a leader of the opposition to Paine's proposed model for government in the American states. After reading *Common Sense,* Adams lauded its author's persuasive argument for American independence, but he rejected Paine's model of government. "This writer," Adams wrote in a letter to a friend (March 10, 1776), "seems to have very inadequate ideas of what is proper and necessary to be done in order to form constitutions for single colonies, as well as a great model of union for the whole."[2] The author of *Common Sense* has "an ignorant notion of a government by one assembly," wrote Adams in another letter to a friend (May 12, 1776). "He is a keen writer but very ignorant of political science."[3]

To counter and defeat ideas like Paine's, John Adams readily offered his views on good government for the new American states. By contrast with Paine, Adams rejected legislative supremacy in favor of separation of powers among three coordinate branches of government—legislative, executive, and judicial—and a system of checks and balances whereby each branch had certain powers to limit or hold in check the powers of the other branches. The chief executive, for example, would have power to veto acts of the legislature, and the legislature would have power to approve the appointments to executive and judicial office of the chief executive. A bicameral or two-house legislature was another facet of Adams's system of separated powers; both houses had to approve proposed legislation, thereby requiring more deliberation and negotiation than would be necessary in a one-house assembly. In the Adams model of government, only men in possession of a certain amount of property or wealth—those with a stake in society—would have the right to vote for representatives in government or to run for public offices.

John Adams wrote *Thoughts on Government,* originally published in April 1776, to advise constitution-makers throughout America about the principles and practices of good government (see Document 9). This widely distributed pamphlet clearly influenced the constitutions of at least seven of the original American states, written from 1776 to 1780: New Jersey, Virginia, North Carolina, Maryland, Delaware, New York, and Massachusetts. The brilliant and influential commentary on good government by Theophilus Parsons, *The Essex Result,* also owed much to Adams's *Thoughts on Government.* (See Document 13 for key excerpts from the lengthy *Essex Result.*)

The differences in American ideas about good government, exemplified by Paine and Adams, were less important than the common civic culture of the colonies. Both Paine and Adams, for example, shared with most Americans a commitment to certain political principles, such as republican government, constitutionalism, popular sovereignty, and individual rights.

Americans generally believed in *republican* government; that is, a government by the people's representatives, with limited terms of office, who should be chosen either directly or indirectly by eligible voters to whom they are accountable. Americans of this era also believed in republican *constitutionalism;* that is, a republican government both empowered and limited by the supreme law of a written constitution. All actions of a constitutional republic should be governed ultimately by the supreme law of a written constitution to provide the rule of law, equally applicable to all citizens of the realm, and should preclude the arbitrary or whimsical acts of rulers.

Paine, Adams, and other American political thinkers were commonly committed to a constitutional republic founded by *popular sovereignty.* That is, the authority and legitimacy of the constitution and the government established under it should stem fully from the consent of the people. Further, all branches of the government—legislative, executive, and judicial—should be based on the sovereignty or the ultimate authority and will of the people.

Finally, Americans fully subscribed to the inherent or natural *rights of individuals* as the ultimate end of a republican constitutional government. There was agreement in America that the primary purpose of government should be protection of the natural rights to life, liberty, and property of all persons of the realm. Certain rights were thought to be natural, because they were presumably rooted in human nature and, therefore, possessed equally by all members of the human species. The Declaration of Independence (Document 7) was the supreme expression of the American founding period on the relationship of good government to the doctrine of natural rights.

In summary, the American consensus on political ideas included the following key ideas. There should be a republican government empowered constitutionally by popular consent to maintain social order, public safety, and carry out other tasks expected of it by the people. This government should be constitutionally limited, by popular consent, to guarantee equally for all persons of the realm their natural rights to life, liberty, and property. These rights, according to the American view taken from Algernon Sidney, John Locke, and similar British thinkers, cannot be granted by the government to anyone. Rather, all human beings inherently possess these rights, and it is the duty of a good constitutional government to protect them. Thus, constitutional limits should be imposed upon the people's representatives in government in order to secure the people's natural rights to life, liberty, and property.

American disagreements about core political principles were conflicts within a consensus on the fundamental worth of republican government, constitutionalism, popular sovereignty, and individual rights. There was disagreement only about the precise meaning and practical application of these principles in the construction and operation of public institutions. So, according to Paine and the anonymous author of *The People the Best Governors* (see Document 8), a good republican government exemplified supremacy of a one-house legislature that would be directly responsible to the popular will. By contrast, John Adams, Theophilus Parsons, and their followers believed that the two-house legislature of a good republican government would share authority with the executive and judiciary in a system of checks and balances of power among three coordinate branches.

From 1776 until 1781, the new American states adopted constitutions for their republican governments, which reflected the general agreement or consensus on core principles and the variations on these principles exemplified by different models of a constitutional republic current at that time. Parts of three state constitutions, their Preambles and Declarations of Rights, are especially noteworthy: The Virginia Declaration of Rights, 1776 (Document 10), the Preamble to the Pennsylvania Constitution of 1776 (Document 11), the Pennsylvania Declaration of Rights (Document 12), the Preamble to the Massachusetts Constitution of 1780 (Document 14), and The Massachusetts Declaration of Rights (Document 15).

The Pennsylvania and Massachusetts documents were the most different of the original American state constitutions. Thomas Paine's ideas were expressed in the Pennsylvania Constitution, and John Adams, a harsh critic of Paine and the Pennsylvania Constitution, was the primary author of the Massachusetts Constitution. Legislative supremacy was carried to an extreme in the Pennsylvania Constitution of

1776. There was a one-house legislature and a plural executive, consisting of a council of thirteen selected by the legislature and accountable to it. So, there was no permanent chief executive or governor, and the executive branch had no power to check and balance the power of the legislature. Further, the judiciary was accountable directly to the legislature. No model of American state government was more at odds with John Adams's *Thoughts on Government* (Document 9). So, Adams despised and severely criticized the Pennsylvania Constitution as foolish and impractical. He particularly worried about the insufficiently restrained power of the majority in the one-house legislature.

In his Massachusetts Constitution of 1780, Adams employed a genuine and practical system of checks and balances among separate branches of government. Like the New York Constitution of 1777, it carefully avoided any tendency toward legislative supremacy. Rather, the Massachusetts Constitution included such limitations on excessive legislative power as a bicameral legislature, an independent executive with power to veto acts of the legislature, and an independent judiciary with the power of judicial review against the other branches of government.

The Adams model prevailed, as state constitutions written after 1780 tended to follow the main features of the Massachusetts Constitution. The original Pennsylvania Constitution was replaced in 1790 when a new frame of government, following the Massachusetts model, was adopted. Another distinction of the Massachusetts Constitution is that it alone, among the original American state constitutions, has never been replaced. It is the world's oldest written constitution in use today.

The Massachusetts Constitution and the New York Constitution of 1777 were the two state constitutions that most influenced the contents of the U.S. Constitution of 1787. Further, the Massachusetts Constitution is important because of the method by which it was drafted and adopted. The people of Massachusetts developed the practice of a constitutional convention, whose members were elected by voters of the state for the single purpose of drafting a constitution. They invented the practice of submitting the document drafted in convention to the people for their ratification or rejection by popular vote. These practices enhanced the image of a constitution as the supreme law, above and beyond the legislative enactments of the government. The Massachusetts method of drafting and ratifying a constitution was a guide to the framers of the U.S. Constitution of 1787, and it has been used by constitution-makers around the world.

Constitution-making in the American states during the Revolutionary War was a laboratory for experimentation in republican government that captured the world's attention. Ever since, political thinkers and actors of different cultures and regions have looked upon the construction, implementation, and revision of the original American state constitutions as a rich source of examples, both positive and negative, on how to establish good government. Further, the ideas, issues, and debates about good government and the best constitution, exemplified by Documents 8–15, have continued on a global scale from the American Revolution to our own times.

NOTES

1. Joseph J. Ellis, *Passionate Sage: The Character and Legacy of John Adams* (New York: W. W. Norton, 1993), p. 41.

2. Charles Francis Adams, ed., *Familiar Letters of John Adams and his Wife Abigail Adams During the Revolution* (Boston: Houghton Mifflin, 1875), p. 146.

3. Page Smith, *John Adams* (Garden City, NY: Doubleday, 1962), p. 240.

DOCUMENT 8: *The People the Best Governors: Or a Plan of Government Founded on the Just Principles of Natural Freedom* **(Published Anonymously in New Hampshire, 1776)**

During 1776, the year of American independence, a remarkable debate began about constitutions and good government for the new American states. Numerous letters, essays, and pamphlets were written and circulated, by Americans with various views, to influence the course of the debate and constitution-making in the states.

An influential publication, published anonymously during the opening phase of this ongoing debate, was probably written by a young man recently arrived in New Hampshire to join the faculty of Dartmouth College. This aspiring professor emphasized representative government directly responsive to the majority will of the people. Further, he advocated universal manhood suffrage and broad access to candidacy for government offices.

The political thought of this anonymous writer tends to agree with the views on government of Thomas Paine expressed in *Common Sense.* These ideas strongly influenced the Pennsylvania Constitution of 1776. According to this author, what are the essential characteristics of good government? Why does he believe the common people to be the best guardians of their own liberty?

. . . Now is the time for the people to be critical in establishing a plan of government: For they are now planting a seed, which will arise with boughs, either extended to shelter the liberty of succeeding ages, or only to skreen the designs of crafty usurpers.

That this short treatise may not be left imperfect, I will only propose, for the consideration of the people, a concise plan, founded on the principles that have been laid down.

It is observed then, in the first place, that the freemen of each incorporated town, through a state, shall chuse by ballot, at an annual meeting, one person respectively, whom they shall think suitable to represent them in a general assembly.

2ndly, That, if the metropolis, and some particular large places, may require an additional number of representatives, it may be granted them by the general assembly as the latter shall think proper.

3rdly, That the general assembly should meet at certain times, twice every year; and, if the state is extensive, there may be two seats of government, in which case the said assembly are to convene at them, once in their turns.

4thly, That the people chuse annually by ballot in their town meetings, a council, consisting of twelve persons, through the government at large, whose business shall be to help in preparing matters for the consideration of the assembly, to assist them with their advice: And lastly, it shall be their duty to inquire into every essential defect in the regulations of government, and to give the people reasonable notice, in a public way, with their opinion respecting the matter.

5thly, That they likewise chuse annually a first executive officer, without any concern in the legislature; but it shall be his duty to transact such occasional business, as the assembly may devolve upon him: And that he be the general commander of the militia, and in these capacities the people; if they please, may stile him a governor—and, in case of his incapacity, a lieutenant, etc. may be appointed as before, to act occasionally in his stead.

6thly, This said governor, with advice of any three of the council, may, at any time, call a special assembly on extraordinary business.

7thly, That the freemen vote annually, in their town meetings respectively, for the judges of the superior court, at large through the government.

8thly, That the judges of the inferior court, attorney's general, probate judges, registrars, etc. be chosen, in manner before mentioned, by the inhabitants of each respective county: And, that the justices of the peace be also chosen by the people of each respective town, in proportion to the representatives.

9thly, That there be one general proxy day agreed upon for the people through the government, to vote for the officers as aforesaid, and that the representatives, likewise, fix upon one day of election, to be annual at which time the votes are to be brought in from the different towns and examined, and the persons for governors, a council, judges, registers, sheriffs, etc. are to be then published through the state.

10thly, That all the resolves of every assembly be conveyed from time to time, by the representatives to each respective town, and there enroled for the inhabitants to see, in order to instruct their said representatives.

11thly, That no person shall hold two public offices in a state, at the same time.

12thly, That no person shall be capable of holding any public office, except he professes a belief of one only invisible God, that governs all things; and that the bible is his revealed word; and that he be also an honest moral man.

13thly, That any freeman through the government may freely enter a complaint of defect or misdemeanour to the general assembly, against any of the executive state officers, and if the assembly think there is just grounds for the said complaint, they may suspend the person so complained of in his office, appoint another for the present in his stead—

but, be obliged to publish in the superior, or county courts, according as the person sustained his said office, their proceeding in that matter, with all their reasons for them; that the people, if they please, may drop the said person or persons, in their next annual election.

14thly, That the assembly may have power to negative any of their members a seat; but, should they do it, be obliged to inform the town or towns, that sent him or them, so negatived, with their reasons for such procedure, that the inhabitants may have an opportunity to chuse another or others, as soon as conveniently may be, which second choice it shall not be in power of the said assembly to negative.

15thly, That the particular town officers be chosen yearly by the inhabitants, as usual; and that each town clerk be the recorder of deeds.

16thly, That any orderly free male of ordinary capacity, and more than 21 years of age, having resided one year in a town, may be a legal voter, during his continuance; but, if he should be absent afterwards steadily more than a year that he should be divested then, of the privilege of voting in said town as if he never had resided there: Provided, he has not a real estate in the aforesaid town of at least one hundred pounds value lawful money.

17thly, That any legal voter shall be capable of holding any office, unless something that has been said to the contrary.

It is a darling principle of freedom, that those who make laws, ought not to execute them: But, notwithstanding, should it be inquired, whether there may be a proper course of appeals, in some important matters, from the superior court to the general assembly, I would answer affirmatively. The cases between man and man, together with their circumstances are so infinite in number, that it is impossible for them all to be specified by the letter of the law. The judges, therefore, in many cases, are obliged not to adhere to the letter, but to put such a construction on matters, as they think most agreeable to the spirit and reason of the law. Now, so far as they are reduced to this necessity, they assume what is in fact the prerogative of the legislature, for those, that made the laws ought to give them a meaning, when they are doubtful. To make then the application: It may happen, that some very important cases may be attended with such circumstances, as are exceptions from the written law, agreeable to the old maxim, *summum jus, summa injusta, extreme right is extreme wrong;* or they may come under doubtful constructions. In either of these instances, the person, that is cast by the verdict, makes his appeal from the court to the general assembly; that they would virtually, in deciding his case, make a regulation, or rather in a legislative capacity, put a lasting construction on the written law, respecting affairs of that particular nature. Thus, by examining the principles of such appeals, we find they imply not that the legislative act in an executive capacity.

Lastly, let every government have an equal weight in the general congress and let the representatives of the respective states be chosen by the people annually by ballot, in their stated town meetings; the votes to be carried in, and published at the appointed election, as with respect to a governor, council, etc. in manner aforesaid; and the assemblies of the respective states may have power to instruct the said representatives from time to time; as they shall think proper.

It appears that the forms of government, that have hitherto been proposed since the breach with Great-Britain, by the friends of the American states, have been rather too arbitrary. The people are now contending for freedom, and would to God they might not only obtain but likewise keep it in their own hands. I own myself a friend to a popular government, have freely submitted my reasons upon it. And although the plan here proposed, might not ever been adapted as yet, nevertheless those as free, have alone secured the liberties of former ages; and a just notion of them has guarded the people against the sly insinuations and proposals of those, of more arbitrary turn, whose schemes have a tendency to deprive mankind of their natural rights.

FINIS.

Source: Frederick Chase, *A History of Dartmouth College and the Town of Hanover* (Cambridge, Mass.: J. Wilson, 1891), pp. 655–57.

DOCUMENT 9: *Thoughts on Government: Applicable to the Present State of the American Colonies* (In a Letter from a Gentleman [John Adams] to His Friend, April 1776)

John Adams of Massachusetts, the author of *Thoughts on Government,* was a highly respected member of the Second Continental Congress. Other leaders looked to him for advice on constitutional principles and practices, because he was a widely recognized master of the classical and contemporary literature on political thought. Thus, it was not unusual that his colleague in Congress, Richard Henry Lee of Virginia, asked Adams for ideas on a model state government, which could guide constitution-making in Virginia and other American colonies on the verge of independent statehood.

Adams responded to Lee in a letter, November 15, 1775, which emphasized twin principles: separation of powers and a system of checks and balances. He wrote that governments exercise three kinds of power: legislative, executive, and judicial. He insisted that only by separating, balancing, and limiting these powers could tyranny be checked and freedom secured for the people under the government's authority.

As American independence became imminent, other colleagues in Congress also approached Adams for advice on constitution-making in their states, such as John Penn and William Hooper of North Carolina. Adams responded by drafting and circulating an essay, *Thoughts on Government,* which elaborated his brief letter to Richard Henry Lee. Adams hoped his pamphlet would counter and refute the model of government set forth by Thomas Paine in *Common Sense* and by his potentially influential followers, such as the anonymous author of *The People the Best Governors* (see Document 8). Adams emphasized the importance of the purposes of government. Why? What, according to Adams should be the purpose of a good government?

Adams was particularly opposed to constitutional plans based on a single assembly. His preference for a bicameral legislature was part of his constitutional plan of separated powers with checks and balances as the means to the end of a properly limited government. Further, Adams stressed that a good government should be conducted by the rule of law rather than the whims of rulers. This "empire of laws" would be the key to fairness and justice in a free government.

What were Adams's arguments for a bicameral legislature? Why, according to Adams, was good government necessarily based on separation of powers with checks and balances? Explain his proposed system of separated powers. What were key examples of his proposed system of checks and balances? Why did he advocate the necessity of an independent judiciary? Finally, why did Adams emphasize the rule of law in government and society?

My dear Sir,

If I was equal to the task of forming a plan for the government of a colony, I should be flattered with your request, and very happy to comply with it; because, as the divine science of politics is the science of social happiness, and the blessings of society depend entirely on the constitutions of government, which are generally institutions that last for many generations, there can be no employment more agreeable to a benevolent mind than a research after the best.

Pope flattered tyrants too much when he said,

> "For forms of government let fools contest,
> That which is best administered is best."

Nothing can be more fallacious than this. But poets read history to collect flowers, not fruits; they attend to fanciful images, not the effects of social institutions. Nothing is more certain, from the history of nations and nature of man, than that some forms of government are better fitted for being well administered than others.

We ought to consider what is the end of government, before we determine which is the best form. Upon this point all speculative politicians will agree, that the happiness of society is the end of government, as all divines and moral philosophers will agree that the happiness of the individual is the end of man. From this principle it will follow, that the form of government which communicates ease, comfort, security, or, in one word, happiness, to the greatest number of persons, and in the greatest degree, is the best. . . .

The foundation of every government is some principle or passion in the minds of the people. The noblest principles and most generous affections in our nature, then, have the fairest chance to support the noblest and most generous models of government. . . .

There is no good government but what is republican. That the only valuable part of the British constitution is so; because the very definition of a republic is "an empire of laws, and not of men." That, as a republic is the best of governments, so that particular arrangement of the powers of society, or, in other words, that form of government which is best contrived to secure an impartial and exact execution of the laws, is the best of republics.

Of republics there is an inexhaustible variety, because the possible combinations of the powers of society are capable of innumerable variations.

As good government is an empire of laws, how shall your laws be made? In a large society, inhabiting an extensive country, it is impossible that the whole should assemble to make laws. The first necessary step, then, is to depute power from the many to a few of the most wise and good. But by what rules shall you choose your representatives? Agree upon the number and qualifications of persons who shall have the benefit of choosing, or annex this privilege to the inhabitants of a certain extent of ground.

The principal difficulty lies, and the greatest care should be employed in constituting this representative assembly. It should be in miniature an exact portrait of the people at large. It should think, feel, reason and act like them. That it may be the interest of this assembly to do strict justice at all times, it should be an equal representation, or, in other words, equal interests among the people should have equal interests in it. Great care should be taken to effect this, and to prevent unfair, partial, and corrupt elections. Such regulations, however, may be better made in times of greater tranquillity than the present; and they will spring up themselves naturally, when all the powers of government come to be in the hands of the people's friends. At present, it will be safest to proceed in all established modes, to which the people have been familiarized by habit.

A representation of the people in one assembly being obtained, a question arises, whether all the powers of government, legislative, executive, and judicial, shall be left in this body? I think a people cannot be long free, nor ever happy, whose government is in one assembly. My reasons for this opinion are as follow:—

1. A single assembly is liable to all the vices, follies, and frailties of an individual; subject to fits of humor, starts of passion, flights of enthusiasm, partialities, or prejudice, and consequently productive of hasty results and absurd judgments. And all these errors ought to be corrected and defects supplied by some controlling power.

2. A single assembly is apt to be avaricious, and in time will not scruple to exempt itself from burdens, which it will lay, without compunction, on its constituents.

3. A single assembly is apt to grow ambitious, and after a time will not hesitate to vote itself perpetual. This was one fault of the Long Parliament; but more remarkably of Holland, whose assembly first voted themselves from annual to septennial, then for life, and after a course of years, that all vacancies happening by death or otherwise, should be filled by themselves, without any application to constituents at all.

4. A representative assembly, although extremely well qualified, and absolutely necessary, as a branch of the legislative, is unfit to exercise

the executive power, for want of two essential properties, secrecy and despatch.

5. A representative assembly is still less qualified for the judicial power, because it is too numerous, too slow, and too little skilled in the laws.

6. Because a single assembly, posed of all the powers of government, would make arbitrary laws for their own interest, execute all laws arbitrarily for their own interest, and adjudge all controversies in their own favor.

But shall the whole power of legislation rest in one assembly? Most of the foregoing reasons apply equally to prove that the legislative power ought to be more complex; to which we may add, that if the legislative power is wholly in one assembly, and the executive in another, or in a single person, these two powers will oppose and encroach upon each other, until the contest shall end in war, and the whole power, legislative and executive, be usurped by the strongest.

The judicial power, in such case, could not mediate, or hold the balance between the two contending powers, because the legislative would undermine it. And this shows the necessity, too, of giving the executive power a negative upon the legislative, otherwise this will be continually encroaching upon that.

To avoid these dangers, let a distinct assembly be constituted, as a mediator between the two extreme branches of the legislature, that which represents the people, and that which is vested with the executive power.

Let the representative assembly then elect by ballot, from among themselves or their constituents, or both, a distinct assembly, which, for the sake of perspicuity, we will call a council. It may consist of any number you please, say twenty or thirty, and should have a free and independent exercise of its judgment, and consequently a negative voice in the legislature.

These two bodies, thus constituted, and made integral parts of the legislature, let them unite, and by joint ballot choose a governor, who, after being stripped of most of those badges of domination, called prerogatives, should have a free and independent exercise of his judgment, and be made also an integral part of the legislature. This, I know, is liable to objections; and, if you please, you may make him only president of the council, as in Connecticut. But as the governor is to be invested with the executive power, with consent of council, I think he ought to have a negative upon the legislative. If he is annually elective, as he ought to be, he will always have so much reverence and affection for the people, their representatives and counsellors, that, although you give him an independent exercise of his judgment, he will seldom use it in opposition to the two houses, except in cases the public utility of which would be conspicuous; and some such cases would happen.

In the present exigency of American affairs, when, by an act of Parliament, we are put out of the royal protection, and consequently discharged from our allegiance, and it has become necessary to assume government for our immediate security, the governor, lieutenant-governor, secretary, treasurer, commissary, attorney-general, should be chosen by joint ballot of both houses. And these and all other elections, especially of representatives and counsellors, should be annual, there not being in the whole circle of the sciences a maxim more infallible than this, "where annual elections end, there slavery begins."

These great men, in this respect, should be, once a year,

> "Like bubbles on the sea of matter borne,
> They rise, they break, and to that sea return."

This will teach them the great political virtues of humility, patience, and moderation, without which every man in power becomes a ravenous beast of prey.

This mode of constituting the great offices of state will answer very well for the present; but if by experiment it should be found inconvenient, the legislature may, at its leisure, devise other methods of creating them, by elections of the people at large, as in Connecticut, or it may enlarge the term for which they shall be chosen to seven years, or three years, or for life, or make any other alterations which the society shall find productive of its ease, its safety, its freedom, or, in one word, its happiness.

A rotation of all offices, as well as of representatives and counsellors, has many advocates, and is contended for with many plausible arguments. It would be attended, no doubt, with many advantages; and if the society has a sufficient number of suitable characters to supply the great number of vacancies which would be made by such a rotation, I can see no objection to it. These persons may be allowed to serve for three years, and then be excluded three years, or for any longer or shorter term.

Any seven or nine of the legislative council may be made a quorum, for doing business as a privy council, to advise the governor in the exercise of the executive branch of power, and in all acts of state.

The governor should have the command of the militia and of all your armies. The power of pardons should be with the governor and council.

Judges, justices, and all other officers, civil and military, should be nominated and appointed by the governor, with the advice and consent of council, unless you choose to have a government more popular; if you do, all officers, civil and military, may be chosen by joint ballot of both houses; or, in order to preserve the independence and importance of each house, by ballot of one house, concurred in by the other. Sheriffs should be chosen by the freeholders of counties; so should registers of deeds and clerks of counties.

All officers should have commissions, under the hand of the governor and seal of the colony.

The dignity and stability of government in all its branches, the morals of the people, and every blessing of society depend so much upon an upright and skillful administration of justice, that the judicial power ought to be distinct from both the legislative and executive, and independent upon both, that so it may be a check upon both, as both should be checks upon that. The judges, therefore, should be always men of learning and experience in the laws, of exemplary morals, great patience, calmness, coolness, and attention. Their minds should not be distracted with jarring interests; they should not be dependent upon any man, or body of men. To these ends, they should hold estates for life in their offices; or, in other words, their commissions should be during good behavior, and their salaries ascertained and established by law. For misbehavior, the grand inquest of the colony, the house of representatives, should impeach them before the governor and council, where they should have time and opportunity to make their defence; but, if convicted, should be removed from their offices, and subjected to such other punishment as shall be proper.

A militia law, requiring all men, or with very few exceptions besides cases of conscience, to be provided with arms and ammunition, to be trained at certain seasons; and requiring counties, towns, or other small districts, to be provided with public stocks of ammunition and entrenching utensils, and with some settled plans for transporting provisions after the militia, when marched to defend their country against sudden invasions; and requiring certain districts to be provided with field-pieces, companies of matrosses, and perhaps some regiments of light-horse, is always a wise institution, and, in the present circumstances of our country, indispensable.

Laws for liberal education of youth, especially of the lower class of people, are so extremely wise and useful, that, to a humane and generous mind, no expense for this purpose would be thought extravagant. . . .

A constitution founded on these principles introduces knowledge among the people, and inspires them with a conscious dignity becoming freemen; a general emulation takes place, which causes good humor, sociability, good manners, and good morals to be general. That elevation of sentiment inspired by such a government, makes the common people brave and enterprising. That ambition which is inspired by it makes them sober, industrious, and frugal. You will find among them some elegance, perhaps, but more solidity; a little pleasure, but a great deal of business; some politeness, but more civility. If you compare such a coun-

try with the regions of domination, whether monarchical or aristocrati-
cal, you will fancy yourself in Arcadia or Elysium.

If the colonies should assume governments separately, they should be
left entirely to their own choice of the forms; and if a continental constitution should be formed, it should be a congress, containing a fair and
adequate representation of the colonies, and its authority should sacredly
be confined to those cases, namely, war, trade, disputes between colony
and colony, the post-office, and the unappropriated lands of the crown,
as they used to be called.

These colonies, under such forms of government, and in such a union,
would be unconquerable by all the monarchies of Europe.

You and I, my dear friend, have been sent into life at a time when the
greatest lawgivers of antiquity would have wished to live. How few of
the human race have ever enjoyed an opportunity of making an election
of government, more than of air, soil, or climate, for themselves or their
children! When, before the present epocha, had three millions of people
full power and a fair opportunity to form and establish the wisest and
happiest government that human wisdom can contrive? I hope you will
avail yourself and your country of that extensive learning and indefati-
gable industry which you possess, to assist her in the formation of the
happiest governments and the best character of a great people....

Source: Charles F. Adams, ed., *The Works of John Adams,* Vol. 4 (Boston: Little,
Brown, 1856), pp. 194–99.

DOCUMENT 10: The Virginia Declaration of Rights (June 12, 1776)

Virginia was prominent among the first group of six states to adopt a constitution. The task of constitution-making was assigned to a twenty-eight-man committee, which was appointed by a Convention, whose members were elected by Virginia's voters to govern the colony in the absence of British authority.

The constitutional committee's first achievement was a Declaration of Rights, written primarily by George Mason, and submitted to the Convention on May 27, 1776. It was passed unanimously on June 11, and then the Convention turned its attention to drafting a plan of government, the body of the constitution, which would be placed after the document on rights. The Virginia Declaration of Rights was an extraordinary statement of the natural rights doctrine, which held that all persons, by virtue of their membership in the human species, possessed equally certain rights. Governments could not claim to be the source of these rights because they are rooted in human nature, and they could not legitimately deprive people of them. Rather, the primary purpose of a good government was to secure these rights for people living under its authority. Among the natural rights proclaimed in this document are freedom of speech, religious liberty, and certain legal protections for persons accused of crimes. Further, the ideas of limited government and the rule of law pervade the document.

The Virginia Constitution was not as distinguished as the Declaration of Rights, which preceded it. The Virginia Constitution reflected common patterns of the original American state constitution. For example, it provided for a bicameral legislature, whose members were elected by eligible voters of the state. The governor, or chief executive, was selected by the legislature in a government designed for legislative supremacy, which was typical of the early state constitutions; the only exceptions were New York's 1777 Constitution and Massachusetts's 1780 Constitution.

The Virginia Declaration of Rights influenced similar statements of rights that preceded six other state constitutions, including the states of Pennsylvania and Massachusetts. Further, the federal Bill of Rights, adopted in 1791, was based on the Virginia Declaration of Rights. Finally, Sections I, II, and III of the Virginia Declaration of Rights clearly influenced the immortal phrases of Thomas Jefferson in the Declaration of Independence, written several weeks later (see Document 7).

Compare the opening sections of the Virginia Declaration of Rights and the American Declaration of Independence (see Document 7). What were the similarities in wording and political principles of the two documents? How did both documents exemplify the doctrine of natural rights? What fundamental freedoms of individuals were proclaimed by the Virginia Declaration of Rights?

A Declaration of Rights made by the Representatives of the good People of Virginia, assembled in full and free Convention, which rights to pertain to them and their posterity as the basis and foundation of government.

I. That all men are by nature equally free and independent, and have certain inherent rights, of which, when they enter into a state of society, they cannot by any compact, deprive or divest their posterity; namely, the enjoyment of life and liberty with the means of acquiring and possessing property, and pursuing and obtaining happiness and safety.

II. That all power is vested in, and consequently derived from, the people; that magistrates are their trustees and servants, and at all times amendable to them.

III. That government is, or ought to be, instituted for the common benefit, protection and security of the people, nation, or community; of all the various modes and forms of government, that is best which is capable of producing the greatest degree of happiness and safety, and is most effectually secured against the danger of maladministration; and that, when a government shall be found inadequate or contrary hath an indubitable, unalienable and indefeasible right to reform, alter or abolish it, in such manner as shall be judged most conducive to the public weal.

IV. That no man, or set of men, are entitled to exclusive or separate emoluments or privileges from the community but in consideration of public services, which not being descendible, neither ought the offices of magistrate, legislator, or judge to be hereditary.

V. That the legislative, executive and judicial powers should be separate and distinct; and that the members thereof may be restrained from oppression, by feeling and participating the burdens of the people, they should, at fixed periods, be reduced to a private station, return into that body from which they were originally taken, and the vacancies be supplied by frequent, certain and regular elections, in which all, or any part of the former members to be again eligible or ineligible, as the laws shall direct.

VI. That all elections ought to be free, and that all men having sufficient evidence of permanent common interest with, and attachment to the community have the right of suffrage, and cannot be taxed, or deprived of their property for public uses, without their own consent, or that of their representatives so elected, nor bound by any law to which they have not in like manner assented, for the public good.

VII. That all power of suspending laws, or the execution of laws, by any authority, without consent of the representatives of the people, is injurious to their rights, and ought not to be exercised.

VIII. That in all capital or criminal prosecutions, a man hath a right to demand the cause and nature of his accusation, to be confronted with the accusers and witnesses, to call for evidence in his favor, and to speedy trial by an impartial jury of twelve men of his vicinage, without whose unanimous consent he cannot be found guilty; nor can he be compelled to give evidence against himself; that no man be deprived of his liberty, except by the law of the land or the judgment of his peers.

IX. That excessive bail ought not to be required, nor excessive fines imposed, nor cruel and unusual punishments inflicted.

X. That general warrants, whereby an officer or messenger may be commanded to search suspected places without evidence of a fact committed, or to seize any person or persons not named, or whose offence is not particularly described and supported by evidence, are grievous and oppressive, and ought not to be granted.

XI. That in controversies respecting property, and in suits between man and man, the ancient trial by jury of twelve men is preferable to any other, and ought to be held sacred.

XII. That the freedom of the press is one of the great bulwarks of liberty, and can never be restrained but by despotic governments.

XIII. That a well regulated militia, composed of the body of the people, trained to arms, is the proper, natural, and safe defence of a free State; that standing armies in time of peace should be avoided as dangerous to liberty; and that in all cases the military should be under strict subordination to, and governed by, the civil power.

XIV. That the people have a right to uniform government; and therefore, that no government separate from or independent of the government of Virginia, ought to be erected or established within the limits thereof.

XV. That no free government, or the blessing of liberty, can be preserved to any people, but by a firm adherence to justice, moderation, temperance, frugality and virtue, and by a frequent recurrence to fundamental principles.

XVI. That religion, or the duty which we owe to our Creator, and the manner of discharging it, can be directed only by reason and conviction, not by force or violence; and therefore all men are equally entitled to the free exercise of religion, according to the dictates of conscience; and that it is the duty of all to practice Christian forbearance, love and charity towards each other.

Source: Francis N. Thorpe, ed., *The Federal and State Constitutions, Colonial Charters, and Other Organic Laws of the States, Territories, and Colonies Now or Heretofore Forming the United States of America*, Vol. 7 (Washington, D.C.: U.S. Government Printing Office, 1909), pp. 3812–14.

DOCUMENT 11: Preamble to the Pennsylvania Constitution (August 1776)

The Preamble was the front piece to the Pennsylvania Declaration of Rights and Frame of Government, or Constitution, which follow it. This Preamble expressed the purposes and foundations of good government, which presumably were to be fulfilled by the constitutional government to be established for the state. Common ideas of the American founding period are highlighted, such as natural rights, popular sovereignty, and government limited by law. Further, the security and happiness of the people are proclaimed as important purposes of good government.

According to this Preamble, what were the purposes or ends of good government? What were the foundations of good government? To what extent did this Preamble agree with the opening sections of the Virginia Declaration of Rights (Document 10) and the Declaration of Independence (Document 7)? To what extent did this Preamble agree with John Adams's ideas on the purposes and foundations of good government (see Document 9)?

WHEREAS all government ought to be instituted and supported for the security and protection of the community as such, and to enable the individuals who compose it to enjoy their natural rights, and the other blessings which the Author of existence has bestowed upon man; and whenever these great ends of government are not obtained, the people have a right, by common consent to change it, and take such measures as to them may appear necessary to promote their safety and happiness. AND WHEREAS the inhabitants of this commonwealth have in consideration of protection only, heretofore acknowledged allegiance to the king of Great Britain; and the said king has not only withdrawn that protection, but commenced, and still continues to carry on, with unabated vengeance, a most cruel and unjust war against them, employing therein, not only the troops of Great Britain, but foreign mercenaries, savages and slaves, for the avowed purpose of reducing them to a total and abject submission to the despotic domination of the British parliament, with many other acts of tyranny, (more fully set forth in the declaration of Congress) whereby all allegiance and fealty to the said king and his successors, are dissolved and at an end, and all power and authority derived from him ceased in these colonies. AND WHEREAS it is absolutely necessary for the welfare and safety of the inhabitants of said colonies, that they be henceforth free and independent States, and that just, permanent, and proper forms of government exist in every part of them, derived from and founded on the authority of the people only, agreeable to the directions of the honourable American Congress. We, the representatives of the freemen of Pennsylvania, in general convention met, for the express purpose of framing such a government, confessing the goodness of the great Governor of the universe (who alone knows to what degree of earthly happiness mankind may attain, by perfecting the arts of government) in permitting the people of this State, by common consent, and without violence, deliberately to form for themselves such just rules as they shall think best, for governing their future society; and being fully convinced, that it is our indispensable duty to establish such original principles of government, as will best promote the general happiness of the people of this State, and their posterity, and provide for future improvements, without partiality for, or prejudice against any particular class, sect, or denomination of men whatever, do, by virtue of the authority vested in use by our constituents, ordain, declare, and establish, the following *Declaration of Rights* and *Frame of Government*, to be the CONSTITUTION of this commonwealth, and to remain in force therein for ever, unaltered, except in such articles as shall hereafter on experience be found to require improvement, and which shall by the same authority of the people, fairly delegated as this frame of government directs, be amended or improved for the more effectual obtaining and securing the great end and design of all government, herein before mentioned.

Source: Francis N. Thorpe, ed., *The Federal and State Constitutions, Colonial Charters, and Other Organic Laws of the States, Territories, and Colonies Now or Heretofore Forming the United States of America,* Vol. 5 (Washington, D.C.: U.S. Government Printing Office, 1909), p. 3081.

DOCUMENT 12: Pennsylvania Declaration of Rights (August 1776)

Thomas Paine was one of the four principal authors of the Pennsylvania Declaration of Rights and Frame of Government or Constitution. So, it is not surprising that these documents reflect his ideas on government expressed in *Common Sense* (see Document 3). The Declaration of Rights, however, was also influenced by George Mason's Virginia Declaration of Rights (Document 10). A notable difference from the Virginia Declaration is the greater liberality of the Pennsylvania document. For example, the Pennsylvania Declaration of Rights uniquely guarantees freedom of speech among its list of natural rights. No other state Declaration of Rights guaranteed this particular right to liberty, which had never before appeared in any constitutional document. What other examples of rights can be found in the Pennsylvania Declaration that are *not* included in the Virginia Declaration of Rights? To what extent is the Pennsylvania Declaration of Rights similar to or different from the Virginia Declaration of Rights?

A DECLARATION OF THE RIGHTS OF THE INHABITANTS OF THE COMMONWEALTH, OR STATE OF PENNSYLVANIA

I. That all men are born equally free and independent, and have certain natural, inherent and inalienable rights, amongst which are, the enjoying and defending life and liberty, acquiring, possessing and protecting property, and pursuing and obtaining happiness and safety.

II. That all men have a natural and unalienable right to worship Almighty God according to the dictates of their own consciences and understanding: And that no man ought or of right can be compelled to attend any religious worship, or erect or support any place of worship, or maintain any ministry, contrary to, or against, his own free will and consent: Nor can any man, who acknowledges the being of a God, be justly deprived or abridged of any civil right as a citizen, on account of his religious sentiments or peculiar mode of religious worship: And that no authority can or ought to be vested in, or assumed by any power whatever, that shall in any case interfere with, or in any manner controul, the right of conscience in the free exercise of religious worship.

III. That the people of this State have the sole, exclusive and inherent right of governing and regulating the internal police of the same.

IV. That all power being originally inherent in, and consequently derived from, the people; therefore all officers of government, whether legislative or executive, are their trustees and servants, and at all times accountable to them.

V. That government is, or ought to be, instituted for the common benefit, protection and security of the people, nation or community; and not for the particular emolument or advantage of any single man, family, or sett of men, who are a part only of that community; And that the community hath an indubitable, unalienable and indefeasible right to reform, alter, or abolish government in such manner as shall be by that community judged most conducive to the public weal.

VI. That those who are employed in the legislative and executive business of the State, may be restrained from oppression, the people have a right, at such periods as they may think proper, to reduce their public officers to a private station, and supply the vacancies by certain and regular elections.

VII. That all elections ought to be free; and that all free men having a sufficient evident common interest with, and attachment to the community, have a right to elect officers, or to be elected into office.

VIII. That every member of society hath a right to be protected in the enjoyment of life, liberty and property, and therefore is bound to contribute his proportion towards the expence of that protection, and yield his personal service when necessary, or an equivalent thereto: But no part of a man's property can be justly taken from him, or applied to public uses, without his own consent, or that of his legal representatives: Nor can any man who is conscientiously scrupulous of bearing arms, be justly compelled thereto, if he will pay such equivalent, nor are the people bound by any laws, but such as they have in like manner assented to, for their common good.

IX. That in all prosecutions for criminal offences, a man hath a right to be heard by himself and his council, to demand the cause and nature of his accusation, to be confronted with the witnesses, to call for evidence in his favour, and a speedy public trial, by an impartial jury of the country, without the unanimous consent of which jury he cannot be found guilty; nor can he be compelled to give evidence against himself; nor can any man be justly deprived of his liberty except by the laws of the land, or the judgment of his peers.

X. That the people have a right to hold themselves, their houses, papers, and possessions free from search and seizure, and therefore warrants without oaths or affirmations first made, affording a sufficient foundation for them, and whereby any officer or messenger may be commanded or required to search suspected places, or to seize any person or persons, his or their property, not particularly described, are contrary to that right, and ought not to be granted.

XI. That in controversies respecting property, and in suits between man and man, the parties have a right to trial by jury, which ought to be held sacred.

XII. That the people have a right to freedom of speech, and of writing, and publishing their sentiments; therefore the freedom of the press ought not to be restrained.

XIII. That the people have a right to bear arms for the defence of themselves and the state; and as standing armies in the time of peace are dangerous to liberty, they ought not to be kept up; And that the military should be kept under strict subordination to, and governed by, the civil power.

XIV. That a frequent recurrence to fundamental principles, and a firm adherence to justice, moderation, temperance, industry, and frugality are absolutely necessary to preserve the blessings of liberty, and keep a government free: The people ought therefore to pay particular attention to these points in the choice of officers and representatives, and have a right to exact a due and constant regard to them, from their legislatures and magistrates, in the making and executing such laws as are necessary for the good government of the state.

XV. That all men have a natural inherent right to emigrate from one state to another that will receive them, or to form a new state in vacant countries, or in such countries as they can purchase, whenever they think that thereby they may promote their own happiness.

XVI. That the people have a right to assemble together, to consult for their common good, to instruct their representatives, and to apply to the legislature for redress of grievances, by address, petition, or remonstrance.

Source: Francis N. Thorpe, ed., *The Federal and State Constitutions, Colonial Charters, and Other Organic Laws of the States, Territories, and Colonies Now or Heretofore Forming the United States of America,* Vol. 5 (Washington, D.C.: U.S. Government Printing Office, 1909) pp. 3082–83.

DOCUMENT 13: *The Essex Result* (Theophilus Parsons, Newburyport, Massachusetts, 1778)

In 1778, the Massachusetts General Court (the state's legislature) drafted a Constitution for state government and submitted it to the people in their town meetings for their approval or rejection. The people overwhelmingly rejected the document.

Later that year, several towns of Essex County, in the northeast part of Massachusetts, elected delegates to a convention, where they deliberated upon defects of the rejected Constitution of 1778 and the characteristics of good government. A summary of ideas with which the delegates agreed was written by Theophilus Parsons, a young lawyer of Newburyport, who later became Chief Justice of the Supreme Judicial Court of Massachusetts. Parsons's report, known as *The Essex Result,* was a brilliant synopsis of ideas on good government along the lines of John Adam's *Thoughts on Government.* In concert with Adam's pamphlet, *The Essex Result* greatly influenced the successful Massachusetts Constitution of 1780. Parsons emphasized ideas such as the natural rights doctrine, popular sovereignty, separation of powers with checks and balances, limited government, and the rule of law based on a written constitution.

What, according to *The Essex Result,* are the essential characteristics of good government? According to this document, why should there be separation of powers among three coordinate branches of government with checks and balances of powers? According to *The Essex Result,* why should a good government be limited by the rule of law in a written constitution? Do you agree?

... Was it asked, what is the best form of government for the people of the Massachusetts-Bay? we confess it would be a question of infinite importance: and the man who could truly answer it, would merit a statue of gold to his memory, and his fame would be recorded in the annals of late posterity, with unrivalled lustre. The question, however, must be answered, and let it have the best answer we can possibly give it. Was a man to mention a despotic government, his life would be a just forfeit to the resentments of an affronted people. Was he to hint monarchy, he would deservedly be hissed off the stage, and consigned to infamy. A republican form is the only one consonant to the feelings of the generous and brave Americans. Let us now attend to those principles, upon which all republican governments, who boast any degree of political liberty, are founded, and which must enter into the spirit of a FREE republican constitution. For all republics are not FREE.

All men are born equally free. The rights they possess at their births are equal, and of the same kind. Some of those rights are alienable, and may be parted with for an equivalent. Others are unalienable and inherent, and of that importance, that no equivalent can be received in exchange. . . .

It has been observed, that each individual parts with the power of controuling his natural alienable rights, only when the good of the whole requires it, he therefore has remaining, after entering into political society, all his unalienable natural rights, and a part also of his alienable natural rights, provided the good of the whole does not require the sacrifice of them. Over the class of unalienable rights the supreme power hath no controul, and they ought to be clearly defined and ascertained in a BILL of RIGHTS, previous to the ratification of any constitution. The bill of rights should also contain the equivalent every man receives, as a consideration for the rights he has surrendered. This equivalent consists principally in the security of his person and property, and is also unassailable by the supreme power: for if the equivalent is taken back, those natural rights which were parted with to purchase it, return to the original proprietor, as nothing is more true, than that ALLEGIANCE AND PROTECTION ARE RECIPROCAL.

The committee also proceeded to consider upon what principles, and in what manner, the supreme power of the state thus composed of the powers of the several individuals thereof, may be formed, modelled, and exerted in a republic, so that every member of the state may enjoy political liberty. This is called by some, *the ascertaining of the political law of the state.* Let it now be called *the forming of a constitution.* . . .

Before we proceed further, it must be again considered, and kept always in view, that we are not attempting to form a temporary constitution, one adjusted only to our present circumstances. We wish for one founded upon such principles as will secure to us freedom and happiness, however our circumstances may vary. . . .

The supreme power is considered as including the legislative, judicial, and executive powers. . . .

A little attention to the subject will convince us, that these three powers ought to be in different hands, and independent of one another, and so ballanced, and each having that check upon the other, that their independence shall be preserved—If the three powers are united, the government will be absolute, *whether these powers are in the hands of one or a large number.* The same party will be the legislator, accuser, judge and executioner; and what probability will an accused person have of an acquittal, however innocent he may be, when his judge will be also a party.

If the legislative and judicial powers are united, the maker of the law will also interpret it; and the law may then speak a language, dictated by the whims, the caprice, or the prejudice of the judge, with impunity to him—And what people are so unhappy as those, whose laws are uncertain. It will also be in the breast of the judge, when grasping after his prey, to make a retrospective law, which shall bring the unhappy offender within it; and this also he can do with impunity—The subject can have no peaceable remedy—The judge will try himself, and an acquittal is the certain consequence. He has it also in his power to enact any law, which may shelter him from deserved vengeance.

Should the executive and legislative powers be united, mischiefs the most terrible would follow. The executive would enact those laws it pleased to execute, and no others—The judicial power would be set aside as inconvenient and tardy—The security and protection of the subject would be a shadow—The executive power would make itself absolute, and the government end in a tyranny—Lewis the eleventh of France, by cunning and treachery compleated the union of the executive and legislative powers of that kingdom, and upon that union established a system of tyranny. France was formerly under a free government.

The assembly or representatives of the united states of Holland, exercise the executive and legislative powers, and the government there is absolute.

Should the executive and judicial powers be united, the subject would then have no permanent security of his person and property. The executive power would interpret the laws and bend them to his will; and, as he is the judge, he may leap over them by artful constructions, and gratify, with impunity, the most rapacious passions. Perhaps no cause in any state has contributed more to promote internal convulsions, and to stain the scaffold with it's best blood, than this unhappy union. And it is an union which the executive power in all states, hath attempted to form: if that could not be compassed, to make the judicial power dependent upon it. Indeed the dependence of any of these powers upon either of the others, which in all states has always been attempted by one or the other of them, has so often been productive of such calamities, and of the shedding of such oceans of blood, that the page of history seems to be one continued tale of human wretchedness.

The following principles now seem to be established.

1. That the supreme power is limited, and cannot controul the unalienable rights of mankind, nor resume the equivalent (that is, the security of person and property) which each individual receives, as a consideration for the alienable rights he parted with in entering into political society.

2. That these unalienable rights, and this equivalent, are to be clearly

defined and ascertained in a BILL OF RIGHTS, previous to the ratification of any constitution.

3. That the supreme power should be so formed and modelled, as to exert the greatest possible power, wisdom, and goodness.

4. That the legislative, judicial, and executive powers, are to be lodged in different hands, that each branch is to be independent, and further, to be so ballanced, and be able to exert such checks upon the others, as will preserve it from a dependence on, or an union with them.

5. That government can exert the greatest power when its supreme authority is vested in the hands of one or a few.

6. That the laws will be made with the greatest wisdom, and best intentions, when men, of all the several classes in the state concur in the enacting of them.

7. That a government which is so constituted, that it cannot afford a degree of political liberty nearly equal to all it's members, is not founded upon principles of freedom and justice, and where any member enjoys no degree of political liberty, the government, so far as it respects him, is a tyranny, for he is controuled by laws to which he has never consented.

8. That the legislative power of a state hath no authority to controul the natural rights of any of its members, unless the good of the whole requires it.

9. That a majority of the state is the only judge when the general good does require it.

10. That where the legislative power of the state is so formed, that a law may be enacted by the minority, each member of the state does not enjoy political liberty. And

11. That in a free government, a law affecting the person and property of its members, is not valid, unless it has the consent of a majority of the members, which majority should include those, who hold a major part of the property in the state. . . .

Source: Theophilus Parsons, Jr., ed., *Memoir of Theophilus Parsons* (Boston, 1859), pp. 359–402.

DOCUMENT 14: Preamble to the Massachusetts Constitution (1780)

This Preamble precedes the Massachusetts Declaration of Rights (see Document 15) and the Massachusetts Frame of Government or Constitution. It sets forth the ends or purposes of good government. Further, it describes premises of the "social compact" by which the people of Massachusetts consented to this constitution as the supreme law of the state. According to this social compact, the people collectively agreed with each individual of the society, and each individual agreed with the whole society, that all will be governed for the common good by the supreme law of the constitution. Thus, all powers of the government were founded on the consent of the governed.

According to this Preamble, what are the purposes of good government? To what extent are the ends of government in this Preamble similar to those proclaimed in the opening section of the Virginia Declaration of Rights (Document 10), the Preamble to the Pennsylvania Constitution (Document 11), and the Declaration of Independence (Document 7)? According to this Preamble, what are the characteristics of the social compact by which the people of Massachusetts agreed to this constitution?

PREAMBLE

THE end of the institution, maintenance and administration of government, is to secure the existence of the body-politic; to protect it; and to furnish the individuals who compose it, with the power of enjoying, in safety and tranquility, their natural rights, and the blessings of life: And whenever these great objects are not obtained, the people have a right to alter the government, and to take measures necessary for their safety, prosperity and happiness.

THE body-politic is formed by a voluntary association of individuals: It is a social compact, by which the whole people covenants with each citizen, and each citizen with the whole people, that all shall be governed by certain laws for the common good. It is the duty of the people, therefore, in framing a Constitution of Government, to provide for an equitable mode of making laws, as well as for an impartial interpretation, and a faithful execution of them; that every man may, at all times, find his security in them.

WE, therefore, the people of Massachusetts, acknowledging, with grateful hearts, the goodness of the Great Legislator of the Universe, in affording us, in the course of His providence, an opportunity, deliberately and peaceably, without fraud, violence or surprise, of entering into an original, explicit, and solemn compact with each other; and of forming a new Constitution of Civil Government, for ourselves and posterity; and devoutly imploring His direction in so interesting a design, DO agree upon, ordain and establish, the following *Declaration of Rights, and Frame of Government,* as the CONSTITUTION of the COMMONWEALTH of MASSA-CHUSETTS.

Source: The Journal of the Convention for Framing a Constitution of Government for the State of Massachusetts-Bay (Boston, 1832), p. 222.

DOCUMENT 15: The Massachusetts Declaration of Rights (1780)

In September 1779, John Adams had an opportunity to apply his *Thoughts on Government* to the making of a state constitution. He was a delegate to the Constitutional Convention of Massachusetts. Earlier in 1779, the people of the state had voted to have this convention and had elected delegates to it. At the Convention, Adams was named to a three-man committee, with Samuel Adams and James Bowdoin, to draft a Declaration of Rights and Frame of Government or Constitution. Adams took on this task for the committee and submitted a draft of his work to the Convention, which approved it with minor changes on March 2, 1789. The people of the state, voting in their town meetings, ratified the Declaration of Rights and Frame of Government on June 15, 1780, and the Constitution was implemented on October 25, 1780.

This Declaration of Rights owed much to the Virginia Declaration, as did the other original state Declaration of Rights. For example, as with the Virginia Declaration of Rights, this document stressed the natural rights doctrine, separation of powers, legal protections for the rights of persons accused of crimes, and the rule of law. Compare this document (see below) with the Virginia and Pennsylvania Declarations (Documents 10 and 12). To what extent is it similar to these documents? What significant differences distinguish the Massachusetts Declaration of Rights from the Virginia and Pennsylvania Declarations? Which of the three documents is more liberal in its provision for individual rights to liberty?

A Declaration of the Rights of the Inhabitants of
the Commonwealth of Massachusetts

ART. I.—ALL men are born free and equal, and have certain natural, essential, and unalienable rights; among which may be reckoned the right of enjoying and defending their lives and liberties; that of acquiring, possessing, and protecting property; in fine, that of seeking and obtaining their safety and happiness.

II.—IT is the right as well as the duty of all men in society, publicly, and at stated seasons, to worship the SUPREME BEING, the great creator and preserver of the universe. And no subject shall be hurt, molested, or restrained, in his person, liberty, or estate, for worshipping GOD in the manner and season most agreeable to the dictates of his own conscience;

or for his religious profession or sentiments; provided he doth not disturb the public peace, or obstruct others in their religious worship.

III.—AS the happiness of a people, and the good order and preservation of civil government, essentially depend upon piety, religion and morality; and as these cannot be generally diffused through a community, but by the institution of the public worship of GOD, and of public instructions in piety, religion and morality: Therefore, to promote their happiness and to secure the good order and preservation of their government, the people of this Commonwealth have a right to invest their legislature with power to authorize and require, the several towns, parishes, precincts, and other bodies-politic, or religious societies, to make suitable provision, at their own expense, for the institution of the public worship of GOD, and for the support and maintenance of public protestant teachers of piety, religion and morality, in all cases where such provision shall not be made voluntarily.

AND the people of this Commonwealth have also a right to, and do, invest their legislature with authority to enjoin upon all the subjects an attendance upon the instructions of the public teachers aforesaid, at stated times and seasons, if there be any on whose instructions they can conscientiously and conveniently attend.

PROVIDED notwithstanding, that the several towns, parishes, precincts, and other bodies-politic, or religious societies, shall, at all times, have the exclusive right of electing their public teachers, and of contracting with them for their support and maintenance.

AND all monies paid by the subject to the support of public worship, and of the public teachers aforesaid, shall, if he require it, be uniformly applied to the support of the public teacher or teachers of his own religious sect of denomination, provided there be any on whose instructions he attends: otherwise it may be paid towards the support of the teacher or teachers of the parish or precinct in which the said monies are raised.

AND every denomination of christians, demeaning themselves peaceably, and as good subjects of the Commonwealth, shall be equally under the protection of the law: And no subordination of any one sect or denomination to another shall ever be established by law.

IV.—THE people of this Commonwealth have the sole and exclusive right of governing themselves as a free, sovereign, and independent state; and do, and forever hereafter shall, exercise and enjoy every power, jurisdiction, and right, which is not, or may not hereafter, be by them expressly delegated to the United States of America, in Congress assembled.

V.—ALL power residing originally in the people, and being derived from them, the several magistrates and officers of government, vested with authority, whether legislative, executive, or judicial, are their substitutes and agents, and are at all times accountable to them.

VI.—NO man, nor corporation, or association of men, have any other title to obtain advantages, or particular and exclusive privileges, distinct from those of the community, than what arises from the consideration of services rendered to the public; and this title being in nature neither hereditary, nor transmissible to children, or descendants, or relations by blood, the idea of a man born a magistrate, lawgiver, or judge, is absurd and unnatural.

VII.—GOVERNMENT is instituted for the common good; for the protection, safety, prosperity and happiness of the people; and not for the profit, honor, or private interest of any one man, family, or class of men: Therefore the people alone have an incontestible, unalienable, and indefeasible right to institute government; and to reform, alter, or totally change the same, when their protection, safety, prosperity and happiness require it.

VIII.—IN order to prevent those, who are vested with authority, from becoming oppressors, the people have a right, at such periods and in such manner as they shall establish by their frame of government, to cause their public officers to return to private life; and to fill up vacant places by certain and regular elections and appointments.

IX.—ALL elections ought to be free; and all the inhabitants of this Commonwealth, having such qualifications as they shall establish by their frame of government, have an equal right to elect officers, and to be elected, for public employments.

X.—EACH individual of the society has a right to be protected by it in the enjoyment of his life, liberty and prosperity, according to standing laws. He is obliged, consequently, to contribute his share to the expense of this protection; to give his personal service, or an equivalent, when necessary: But no part of the property of any individual, can, with justice, be taken from him, or applied to public uses without his own consent, or that of the representative body of the people: In fine, the people of this Commonwealth are not controllable by any other laws, than those to which their constitutional representative body have given their consent. And whenever the public exigencies require, that the property of any individual should be appropriated to public uses, he shall receive a reasonable compensation therefor.

XI.—EVERY subject of the Commonwealth ought to find a certain remedy, by having recourse to the laws, for all injuries or wrongs which he may receive in his person, property, or character. He ought to obtain right and justice freely, and without being obliged to purchase it; completely, and without any denial; promptly, and without delay; conformably to the laws.

XII.—NO subject shall be held to answer for any crime or offence, until the same is fully and plainly, substantially and formally, described to him; or be compelled to accuse, or furnish evidence against himself. And every subject shall have a right to produce all proofs, that may be favorable to him; to meet the witnesses against him face to face, and to be fully heard in his defence by himself, or his council, at his election. And no subject shall be arrested, imprisoned, despoiled, or deprived of his property, immunities, or privileges, put out of the protection of the law, exiled, or deprived of his life, liberty, or estate; but by the judgment of his peers, or the laws of the land.

AND the legislature shall not make any law, that shall subject any person to a capital or infamous punishment, excepting for the government of the army and navy, without trial by jury.

XIII.—IN criminal prosecution, the verification of facts in the vicinity where they happen, is one of the greatest securities of the life, liberty, and property of the citizen.

XIV.—EVERY subject has a right to be secure from all unreasonable searches, and seizures of his person, his houses, his papers, and all his possessions. All warrants, therefore, are contrary to this right, if the cause or foundation of them be not previously supported by oath or affirmation; and if the order in the warrant to a civil officer, to make search in suspected places, or to arrest one or more suspected persons, or to seize their property, be not accompanied with a special designation of the persons or objects of search, arrest, or seizure: and no warrant ought to be issued but in cases, and with the formalities, prescribed by the laws.

XV.—IN all controversies concerning property, and in all suits between two or more persons, except in cases in which it has heretofore been otherways used and practiced, the parties have a right to a trial by jury; and this method of procedure shall be held sacred, unless, in causes arising on the high-seas, and such as relate to mariners wages, the legislature shall hereafter find it necessary to alter it.

XVI.—THE liberty of the press is essential to the security of freedom in a state: it ought not, therefore, to be restrained in this Commonwealth.

XVII.—THE people have a right to keep and to bear arms for the common defence. And as in time of peace armies are dangerous to liberty, they ought not to be maintained without the consent of the legislature; and the military power shall always be held in an exact subordination to the civil authority, and be governed by it.

XVIII.—A FREQUENT recurrence to the fundamental principles of the constitution, and a constant adherence to those of piety, justice, moderation, temperance, industry, and frugality, are absolutely necessary to preserve the advantages of liberty, and to maintain a free government: The people ought, consequently, to have a particular attention to all those principles, in the choice of their officers and representatives: And they have a right to require of their law-givers and magistrates, an exact and constant observance of them, in the formation and execution of the laws necessary for the good administration of the Commonwealth.

XIX.—THE people have a right, in an orderly and peaceable manner, to assemble to consult upon the common good; give instructions to their representatives; and to request of the legislative body, by the way of addresses, petitions, or remonstrances, redress of the wrongs done them, and of the grievances they suffer.

XX.—THE power of suspending the laws, or the execution of the laws, ought never to be exercised but by the legislature, or by authority derived from it, to be exercised in such particular cases only as the legislature shall expressly provide for.

XXI.—THE freedom of deliberation, speech and debate, in either house of the legislature, is so essential to the rights of the people, that it cannot be the foundation of any accusation or prosecution, action or complaint, in any other court or place whatsoever.

XXII.—THE legislature ought frequently to assemble for the redress of grievances, for correcting, strengthening, and confirming the laws, and for making new laws, as the common good may require.

XXIII.—NO subsidy, charge, tax, impost, or duties, ought to be established, fixed, laid, or levied, under any pretext whatsoever, without the consent of the people, or their representatives in the legislature.

XXIV.—LAWS made to punish for actions done before the existence of such laws, and which have not been declared crimes by preceding laws, are unjust, oppressive, and inconsistent with the fundamental principles of a free government.

XXV.—NO subject ought, in any case, or in any time, to be declared guilty of treason or felony by the legislature.

XXVI.—NO magistrate or court of law shall demand excessive bail or sureties, impose excessive fines, or inflict cruel or unusual punishments.

XXVII.—IN time of peace no soldier ought to be quartered in any house without the consent of the owner; and in time of war such quarters ought not to be made but by the civil magistrate, in a manner ordained by the legislature.

XXVIII.—NO person can in any case be subjected to law-martial, or to any penalties or pains, by virtue of that law, except those employed in the army or navy, and except the militia in actual service, but by authority of the legislature.

XXIX.—IT is essential to the preservation of the rights of every individual, his life, liberty, property and character, that there be an impartial interpretation of the laws, and administration of justice. It is the right of every citizen to be tried by judges as free, impartial and independent as the lot of humanity will admit. It is therefore not only the best policy, but for the security of the rights of the people, and of every citizen, that the judges of the supreme judicial court should hold their offices as long as they behave themselves well; and that they should have honorable salaries ascertained and established by standing laws.

XXX.—IN the government of this Commonwealth, the legislative department shall never exercise the executive and judicial powers, or either of them: The executive shall never exercise the legislative and judicial powers, or either of them: The judicial shall never exercise the legislative and executive powers, or either of them: to the end it may be a government of laws and not of men.

Source: The Journal of the Convention for Framing a Constitution of Government for the State of Massachusetts-Bay (Boston, 1832), pp. 225–49.

FURTHER READING

Adams, Willi Paul. *The First American Constitutions.* Chapel Hill: University of North Carolina Press, 1980.

Ellis, Joseph J. *Passionate Sage: The Character and Legacy of John Adams.* New York: W. W. Norton and Company, 1993.

Lutz, Donald S. *The Origins of American Constitutionalism.* Baton Rouge: Louisiana State University Press, 1988.

Morgan, Edmund S. *Inventing the People: The Rise of Popular Sovereignty in England and America.* New York: W. W. Norton and Company, 1988.

Peters, Ronald M., Jr. *The Massachusetts Constitution of 1780: A Social Compact.* Amherst: University of Massachusetts Press, 1978.

Schechter, Stephen L., and Richard B. Bernstein, eds. *New York and the Union: Contributions to the American Constitutional Experience.* Albany: New York State Commission on the Bicentennial of the United States Constitution, 1990.

Selsam, J. Paul. *The Pennsylvania Constitution of 1776: A Study in Revolutionary Democracy.* New York: Octagon Books, 1971.

Sutton, Robert P. *Revolution to Secession: Constitution Making in the Old Dominion.* Charlottesville: University of Virginia Press, 1989.

Wood, Gordon S. *The Creation of the American Republic, 1776–1787.* Chapel Hill: University of North Carolina Press, 1969.

Zuckert, Michael P. *Natural Rights and the New Republicanism.* Princeton, New Jersey: Princeton University Press, 1994.

Part III

Problems of Equality and Liberty in the New American States, 1776–1792

Americans were the first people ever to found a nation on abstract principles, such as the equal right to liberty of all persons. The Declaration of Independence expressed a commonly held American ideal in its proclamation that "all men are created equal" in their possession of "certain unalienable Rights" to "Life, Liberty, and the pursuit of Happiness." Thus, the Declaration expressed the doctrine of natural rights, the belief that certain rights belong equally to all persons by virtue of their common human nature.

In line with the Declaration's ideals, the American states appeared to be havens of equality and liberty in a world largely hostile or indifferent to such principles. Nowhere else in the world of the 1770s and 1780s—*not* in Europe, Asia, or Africa—were certain political liberties as widespread as in the new American states. In 1780, for example, more men had the right to vote and hold public office in America than in any other country. And Americans generally enjoyed effective legal protection for such rights as freedom of conscience, freedom of the press, and freedom to own property, which most of the world's people could not even imagine.

There were, however, embarrassing contradictions of freedom and equality in the new American states. At the moment of the adoption of the Declaration of Independence, for example, slavery existed in all thirteen states—states whose leaders vowed to "pledge to each other our Lives, our Fortunes, and our sacred Honor" in their struggle for human equality and liberty. Further, women suffered legal and habitual discrimination, as did free men of the lower socioeconomic classes.

The American institution of slavery was the largest and most perplexing contradiction of American ideals. In 1776, more than 20 percent of the new nation's population was African American, either imported by force to work as slaves or descended from those brought from Africa by slave traders. Free African Americans comprised less than 1 percent of the population. In 1790, the year of the first federal census of the country's population, nearly four million people were counted as inhabitants of the United States of America. About 700,000 of them were African Americans, and no more than 50,000 of those were free.

Most slaves lived in five southern states that also included free African Americans: Maryland (103,036 slaves and 8,043 free), Virginia (292,627 slaves and 12,866 free), North Carolina (100,783 slaves and 5,041 free), South Carolina (107,094 slaves and 1,801 free), and Georgia (29,264 slaves and 398 free). By contrast, there were very few or no slaves in the five New England states, where free African Americans outnumbered those in bondage: New Hampshire (157 slaves and 630 free), Vermont (no slaves and 269 free), Massachusetts (no slaves and 5,369 free), Rhode Island (958 slaves and 3,484 free), and Connecticut (2,648 slaves and 2,771 free). The slave and free African-American population of the four middle states was: New York (21,193 slaves and 4,682 free), New Jersey (11,423 slaves and 2,762 free), Pennsylvania (3,707 slaves and 6,531 free), and Delaware (8,887 slaves and 3,899 free).

All American state constitutions were based on the idea of natural rights, but only that of Vermont, admitted to the Union in 1791, prohibited slavery. The natural rights doctrine, however, was a beacon for appeals by black and white Americans to abolish slavery. Early in 1777, free African Americans of Boston appealed to the government of Massachusetts to abolish slavery in the name of the natural right to freedom enjoyed by all persons, which was acknowledged in the Declaration of Independence. This petition (Document 18) was ignored, but only four years later, in the 1781 case of *Brom and Bett v. John Ashley* (decided by the Inferior Court of Common Pleas of Great Barrington, Massachusetts), the plaintiff argued successfully that Article I of the 1780 Massachusetts Declaration of Rights applied to blacks as well as whites. Thus, slavery should not be legal under a constitution that declares "All men are born free and equal, and have certain natural, essential, and unalienable rights." Two years later, in the case of *Commonwealth v. Nathaniel Jennison* (1783), the Massachusetts Superior Court declared that Quock Walker, a slave of Nathaniel Jennison, should be free, because slavery violated Article I of the Commonwealth's Declaration of Rights (see Document 19). Quock Walker's lawyer, Levi Lincoln, based his case on the premise that slavery was illegal under natural law and the consequent natural right to liberty of all persons. Walker's attorney asked: "Is it not a law of nature that all men are equal and free? Is it not the law of nature, the law of

God? Is not the law of God then against slavery?"[1] Further, Walker's counsel pointed to Article I of the Massachusetts Declaration of Rights as a constitutional example of natural law, which invalidated the institution of slavery. So, he concluded, Nathaniel Jennison had no right to keep Quock Walker as his slave.

In 1780, Pennsylvania became the first state to pass a law providing for the gradual abolition of slavery. Other northern states followed this example, so that by the turn of the century, slavery was on the way to extinction in this region. Not so in the South, however, where slavery remained entrenched, despite regular protests against it by Christian ministers, state and federal officials, and African-American leaders.

From 1776 through the 1790s, numerous antislavery sermons were preached by Christian ministers, such as James Dana, pastor of the First Congregational Church of New Haven, Connecticut (see Document 23). Like other sermons of this type, this piece by the Reverend Dana appealed to the natural rights doctrine to justify his case against slavery.

A remarkable protest against slavery was a letter sent in 1791 to Thomas Jefferson, then secretary of state under President George Washington. The letter writer was a brilliant free black man, Benjamin Banneker, who achieved distinction as a surveyor, mathematician, astronomer, and author of almanacs (see Document 24, Banneker's letter, and Document 25, two responses by Thomas Jefferson). Banneker followed an irrefutable line of argument in his appeal to the natural rights doctrine and constitutional statements about civil liberties and equality before the law. The numerous antislavery speeches and petitions, such as those by James Dana and Benjamin Banneker, provide evidence of discomfort and disgust among many white and black Americans about a deplorable institution that violated the country's highest ideals.

Although many public speakers and writers protested vigorously and continuously against unjust treatment of black Americans, there were no notable public statements during the founding era in support of civil and political rights for women. White women, like blacks of both sexes, suffered legal discrimination. Except in New Jersey until 1807, American women could neither vote nor hold government offices. Further, women throughout the American states were not allowed to make binding contracts, sue in court, or serve on juries. Any money or land a woman possessed became the property of her spouse after she married.

Abigail Adams expressed the private concerns of at least some American women about their inferior legal status in a now-famous letter to her husband John in which she pleaded with him to "Remember the Ladies" during his participation in the Continental Congress (see Document 16). John Adams replied frivolously to his wife's letter that "we know better than to repeal our masculine systems."[2] She replied that "I cannot say that I think you very generous to the ladies, for whilst you are proclaiming peace and good will to Men, Emancipating all Nations, you insist upon retaining an absolute power over Wives."[3] According to her biographer, Phyllis Lee Levin, Abigail Adams in her private letters to John "had launched unwittingly the timeless campaign for women's rights."[4] But this campaign would be left to a future time, because during Abigail's era, it was not possible. Nowhere in the world of the late eighteenth century, not even in revolutionary America, was there public recognition of equal rights for women.

John Adams revealed his very serious reservations about any expansion of political rights for women in a letter to James Sullivan (see Document 17). John Adams's opinions about limitations on the political liberties of women and lower class or unpropertied males were typical of his time.

Virtually outside the American revolutionaries' concerns about human rights were more than 200,000 so-called Indians or Native Americans who lived east of the Mississippi River. Most white Americans looked upon the eighty-five Native American nations within the United States as obstacles in their way, occupying land that they wanted. Conflict about rights to the use of land was the unresolvable issue between the Indians and the other Americans.

Native Americans were dismayed to learn that the British had granted away their territory in the 1783 Treaty of Paris, which ended the American War of Independence. They soon confronted agents of Congress who informed them that Native Americans were subject to the authority and territorial claims of the U.S. government. Many Native-American leaders petitioned the state and federal governments for help in retaining their land against the claims of settlers (see Document 22). These petitions, however, were ineffective means for redress of grievances for people whose rights were not recognized by the new state and federal governments.

While white Americans tended to agree about their new nation's claims to land occupied by Native Americans, they disagreed about church–state relations. A central issue in several states was whether the state government could or should provide support for religious institutions. The constitutions of Massachusetts, New Hampshire, Connecticut, Maryland, Georgia, and South Carolina clearly sanctioned government support, on a nonpreferential basis, for Christian religions. The constitutions of Virginia, North Carolina, and New Jersey provided for free exercise of religion or freedom of conscience, but they did not clearly prohibit nondiscriminatory support by the government for the several Christian denominations of each state. So, an issue was raised about separation of church and state: Could the state government raise taxes for the specific purpose of supporting nonpreferentially the various Christian denominations of the state? In 1784–1785, this issue came to a head in Virginia.

Patrick Henry, Virginia's most popular politician, proposed that the General Assembly enact a tax law to provide public support equally and non-preferentially for religious education to be conducted by all Christian churches of the state. It seemed that a majority in the state supported Henry's bill, including such luminaries as Richard Henry Lee and George Washington. James Madison, however, opposed Henry's bill, because he feared that any kind of governmental support of religion was a dangerous intrusion into a private matter, which should be free of entanglement with the state.

Madison penned a fifteen-point protest against Henry's bill, called a Memorial and Remonstrance Against Religious Assessments, and circulated this petition among the people of Virginia (see Document 20). Madison's fifteen "remonstrances" or protests, a compelling argument for complete separation of church and state as a necessary protection of religious liberty, helped to sway public opinion against Henry's bill, and the General Assembly set it aside without a vote in October 1785.

In the wake of this political victory, Madison proposed that the Virginia General Assembly enact the Virginia Statute for Religious Freedom, written by Thomas Jefferson (see Document 21), who was serving abroad as the U.S. diplomatic representative to the French government. Jefferson's statute passed on January 16, 1786, thereby lawfully providing for complete religious liberty in Virginia, including freedom from government coercion to support religious institutions, which were left free to function without interference, positive or negative, from the state government. These two documents, Madison's Memorial and Remonstrance Against Religious Assessments and Jefferson's Virginia Statute for Religious Freedom, pointed the way to eventual separation of church and state in all the American states. (Massachusetts was the last one to comply, when it disestablished the state government from the church in 1833.) Finally, these documents authored by Madison and Jefferson became foundations for the two clauses on religious liberty in the First Amendment to the U.S. Constitution, ratified in 1791.

Vexing problems of liberty and equality loomed large in the new American states during and immediately after the Revolution. They pertained to the denial of rights for some Americans (e.g., blacks, women, and Native Americans), which had been proclaimed in the new nation's founding documents as the unalienable possession of all persons. Further, there was the issue of church–state separation as a protection for the fullest enjoyment of religious liberty by all Americans, including minority religious groups with unpopular beliefs and practices. Public discussions and protests about these various problems of liberty and equality, exemplified by Documents 16–25, led eventually to an expansion of the rights and liberties of all Americans.

NOTES

1. "Brief of Levi Lincoln," *Belknap Papers of Collections of the Massachusetts Historical Society*, 5th Series, Vol. 3 (Boston, 1877), pp. 438–42.

2. Phyllis Lee Levin, *Abigail Adams: A Biography* (New York: St. Martin's Press, 1987), p. 83.

3. Ibid., p. 84.

4. Ibid., p. 81.

DOCUMENT 16: Letter to John Adams (Abigail Adams, March 31, 1776)

The rights of women were *not* on the political agenda of Americans fighting for independence from the British. No prominent American of the founding era publicly challenged the legal and traditional supremacy of men over women in a new nation committed to the principles of equal rights.

In a now famous personal letter to her husband, Abigail Adams revealed her private concern about the rights of women. As John Adams and other members of the Continental Congress were preparing to declare independence from Britain, Abigail Adams implored her husband to "Remember the Ladies"—their rights to liberty and claims to equality before the law. Abigail Adams argued against any type of unlimited power as a temptation to tyranny. She feared that the power of men over women, unless limited by law, would be an invitation to tyranny.

John Adams replied flippantly, "Depend upon it, we know better than to repeal our masculine systems. Although . . . in Practice, you know, We are the subjects. We have only the name of Masters, and rather than give up this, which would completely subject Us to the Despotism of the Petticoat, I hope General Washington, and all our brave Heroes would fight" (April 14, 1776).

What is the main political idea of Abigail Adams's letter? Upon what principles does Abigail Adams base her main idea? How do her principles compare with those of American revolutionaries in their conflict with the British government?

Braintree, March 31, 1776

I wish you would ever write me a Letter half as long as I write you; and tell me if you may where your Fleet are gone? What sort of Defence Virginia can make against our common Enemy? Whether it is so situated as to make an able Defence? Are not the Gentery Lords and the common people vassals, are they not like the uncivilized Natives Britain represents us to be? I hope their Rifle Men who have shown themselves very savage and even Blood thirsty; are not a specimen of the Generality of the people.

I am willing to allow the Colony great merit for having produced a Washington but they have been shamefully duped by a Dunmore.

I have sometimes been ready to think that the passion for Liberty cannot be Equally Strong in the Breasts of those who have been accustomed to deprive their fellow Creatures of theirs. Of this I am certain that it is not founded upon that generous and christian principal of doing to others as we would that others should do unto us. . . .

I long to hear that you have declared an independancy—and by the way in the new Code of Laws which I suppose it will be necessary for you to make I desire you would Remember the Ladies, and be more generous and favourable to them than your ancestors. Do not put such unlimited power into the hands of the Husbands. Remember all Men would be tyrants if they could. If particuliar care and attention is not paid to the Ladies we are determined to foment a Rebellion, and will not hold ourselves bound by any Laws in which we have no voice, or Representation.

That your Sex are Naturally Tyrannical is a Truth so thoroughly established as to admit of no dispute, but such of you as wish to be happy willingly give up the harsh title of Master for the more tender and endearing one of Friend. Why then, not put it out of the power of the vicious and the Lawless to use us with cruelty and indignity with impunity. Men of Sense in all Ages abhor those customs which treat us only as the vassals of your Sex. Regard us then as Beings placed by providence under your protection and in immitation of the Supreme Being make use of that power only for our happiness.

Source: Charles Francis Adams, ed., *Familiar Letters of John Adams and His Wife Abigail Adams, During the Revolution* (Boston: Houghton Mifflin, 1876), pp. 148–50.

DOCUMENT 17: Letter to James Sullivan (John Adams, May 26, 1776)

John Adams responded playfully to his wife's letter about women's rights (see Document 16). Not so when he replied to James Sullivan, a member of the Massachusetts General Court, who had written to Adams in May 1776 to seek his advice about the desirability of extending the right to vote to disenfranchised people, such as women and men without property. Adams opposed extension of political rights to people without the means to be independent stakeholders.

In this letter to Mr. Sullivan, Adams expressed views held by most Americans of his time, including a majority of the revolutionary leaders. Like most men of his time and place, Adams supported a republican form of government, which involved the consent and participation of the people (see Document 9). But Adams was concerned about who should participate in politics and public affairs, and the justifications for their participation. Adams's position on participation excluded women and men without property. Why? How did Adams justify this position about who should or should not vote? What hope or opportunity to improve their political status did Adams hold out to people without the right to vote or hold public office?

To James Sullivan

Philadelphia, 26 May 1776

. . . Our worthy friend, Mr. Gerry, has put into my hands a letter from you, of the sixth of May, in which you consider the principles of representation and legislation, and give us hints of some alterations, which you seem to think necessary, in the qualification of voters.

I wish, Sir, I could possibly find time to accompany you, in your investigation of the principles upon which a representative assembly stands, and ought to stand, and in your examination whether the practice of our colony has been conformable to those principles. But, alas! Sir, my time is so incessantly engrossed by the business before me, that I cannot spare enough to go through so large a field; and as to books, it is not easy to obtain them here; nor could I find a moment to look into them, if I had them.

It is certain, in theory, that the only moral foundation of government is, the consent of the people. But to what an extent shall we carry this principle? Shall we say that every individual of the community, old and young, male and female, as well as rich and poor, must consent, expressly, to every act of legislation? No, you will say, this is impossible. How, then, does the right arise in the majority to govern the minority, against their will? Whence arises the right of the men to govern the women, without their consent? Whence the right of the old to bind the young, without theirs?

But let us first suppose that the whole community, of every age, rank, sex, and condition, has a right to vote. This community is assembled. A motion is made, and carried by a majority of one voice. The minority will not agree to this. Whence arises the right of the majority to govern, and the obligation of the minority to obey?

From necessity, you will say, because there can be no other rule.

But why exclude women?

You will say, because their delicacy renders them unfit for practice and experience in the great businesses of life, and the hardy enterprises of war, as well as the arduous cares of state. Besides, their attention is so much engaged with the necessary nurture of their children, that nature has made them fittest for domestic cares. And children have not judgment or will of their own. True. But will not these reasons apply to others? Is it not equally true, that men in general, in every society, who are wholly destitute of property, are also too little acquainted with public affairs to form a right judgment, and too dependent upon other men to have a will of their own? If this is a fact, if you give to every man who has no property, a vote, will you not make a fine encouraging provision for corruption, by your fundamental law? Such is the frailty of the human heart, that very few men who have no property, have any judgment of their own. They talk and vote as they are directed by some man of property, who has attached their minds to his interest.

Upon my word, Sir, I have long thought an army a piece of clockwork, and to be governed only by principles and maxims, as fixed as any in mechanics; and, by all that I have read in the history of mankind, and in authors who have speculated upon society and government, I am much inclined to think a government must manage a society in the same manner; and that this is machinery too.

Harrington has shown that power always follows property. This I believe to be as infallible a maxim in politics, as that action and reaction are equal, is in mechanics. Nay, I believe we may advance one step farther, and affirm that the balance of power in a society, accompanies the balance of property in land. The only possible way, then, of preserving the balance of power on the side of equal liberty and public virtue, is to make the acquisition of land easy to every member of society; to make a division of the land into small quantities, so that the multitude may be possessed of landed estates. If the multitude is possessed of the balance of real estate, the multitude will have the balance of power, and in that case the multitude will take care of the liberty, virtue, and interest of the multitude, in all acts of government.

I believe these principles have been felt, if not understood, in the Massachusetts Bay, from the beginning; and therefore I should think that wisdom and policy would dictate in these times to be very cautious of making alterations. Our people have never been very rigid in scrutinizing into the qualifications of voters, and I presume they will not now begin to be so. But I would not advise them to make any alteration in the laws, at present, respecting the qualifications of voters.

Your idea that those laws which affect the lives and personal liberty of all, or which inflict corporal punishment, affect those who are not qualified to vote, as well as those who are, is just. But so they do women, as well as men; children, as well as adults. What reason should there be for excluding a man of twenty years eleven months and twenty-seven days old, from a vote, when you admit one who is twenty-one? The reason is, you must fix upon some period in life, when the understanding and will of men in general, is fit to be trusted by the public. Will not the same reason justify the state in fixing upon some certain quantity of property, as a qualification?

The same reasoning which will induce you to admit all men who have no property, to vote, with those who have, for those laws which affect the person, will prove that you ought to admit women and children; for, generally speaking, women and children have as good judgments, and as independent minds, as those men who are wholly destitute of property; these last being to all intents and purposes as much dependent upon others, who will please to feed, clothe, and employ them, as women are upon their husbands, or children on their parents.

As to your idea of proportioning the votes of men, in money matters, to the property they hold, it is utterly impracticable. There is no possible way of ascertaining, at any one time, how much every man in a community is worth; and if there was, so fluctuating is trade and property, that this state of it would change in half an hour. The property of the whole community is shifting every hour, and no record can be kept of the changes.

Society can be governed only by general rules. Government cannot accommodate itself to every particular case as it happens, nor to the circumstances of particular persons. It must establish general comprehensive regulations for cases and persons. The only question is, which general rule will accommodate most cases and most persons.

Depend upon it, Sir, it is dangerous to open so fruitful a source of controversy and altercation as would be opened by attempting to alter the qualifications of voters; there will be no end of it. New claims will arise; women will demand a vote; lads from twelve to twenty-one will think their rights not enough attended to; and every man who has not a farthing, will demand an equal voice with any other, in all acts of state. It tends to confound and destroy all distinctions, and prostrate all ranks to one common level.

Source: Charles Francis Adams, ed., *The Works of John Adams, Second President of the United States with a Life of the Author,* Vol. 9 (Boston: Little, Brown, 1856), pp. 375–78.

DOCUMENT 18: Petition Against Slavery to the General Court of Massachusetts (January 13, 1777)

African Americans took seriously the eloquent words about natural rights and equal justice in the Declaration of Independence and other public documents of the revolutionary era. They agreed with the prevailing belief in the United States that natural rights were the common possession of all humans. They could not, therefore, be given by the government to the people, who naturally possessed them. Further, the government could not reasonably deny these natural rights to any person. They noted that slave holders and supporters of slavery also believed that unalienable rights were superior to any man-made law and charged them with hypocrisy, unless they renounced slavery.

Acting on their pro-rights views, a group of free African Americans in Massachusetts petitioned their new state government to abolish slavery in the name of the ideals of the American Revolution. What arguments against slavery did these petitioners present to the General Court of Massachusetts?

To the Honorable Counsel & House of Representatives for the State of Massachusetts Bay in General Court Assembled, January 13, 1777.

THE PETITION OF A GREAT NUMBER of blacks detained in a state of slavery in the bowels of a free and Christian country humbly shows that your petitioners apprehend that they have in common with all other men a natural and unalienable right to that freedom which the Great Parent of the universe has bestowed equally on all mankind and which they have never forfeited by any compact or agreement whatever. But they were unjustly dragged by the hand of cruel power from their dearest friends and some of them even torn from the embraces of their tender parents, from a populous, pleasant, and plentiful country and in violation of laws of nature and of nations and in defiance of all the tender feelings of humanity, brought here either to be sold like beasts of burden and, like them, condemned to slavery for life—among a people professing the mild religion of Jesus; a people not insensible of the secrets of rational being, nor without spirit to resent the unjust endeavors of others to reduce them to a state of bondage and subjection. Your Honor need not be informed that a life of slavery like that of your petitioners, deprived of every social privilege of everything requisite to render life tolerable, is far worse then nonexistence.

In imitation of the laudable example of the good people of these states, your petitioners have long and patiently awaited the event of petition after petition presented by them to the legislative body of this state, and cannot but with grief reflect that their success has been but too similar. They cannot but express their astonishment that it has never been considered that every principle from which America has acted in the course of their unhappy difficulties with Great Britain pleads stronger than a thousand arguments in favor of your petitioners.

They therefore humbly beseech Your Honors to give this petition its due weight and consideration, and cause an act of legislation to be passed whereby they may be restored to the enjoyments of that which is the natural right of all men, and that their children, who were born in this land of liberty, may not be held as slaves after they arrive at the age of twenty-one years. So may the inhabitants of this state, no longer chargeable with the inconsistency of acting themselves the part which they condemn and oppose in others, be prospered in their present glorious struggle for liberty and have those blessings for themselves.

Source: Collections, Massachusetts Historical Society, 5th Series, Vol. 3 (Boston, 1877), pp. 436–37.

DOCUMENT 19: Quock Walker's Case (1783)

Quock Walker's case, heard by Judge C. J. Cushing in the Superior Court of Massachusetts, was a mortal blow against slavery in Massachusetts, which had been in serious decline ever since the start of the American War of Independence. The case was initiated by Quock Walker, whom Nathaniel Jennison claimed as his slave. Jennison had assaulted Walker in the process of reclaiming him from a white family with whom Walker was living as a free man. Walker charged Jennison with criminal assault. Jennison defended his actions by claiming that he was merely punishing a disobedient slave, not assaulting a free man with rights. The official name given to this case was *Commonwealth [of Massachusetts] v. Jennison.*

Jennison was judged guilty of assault against Walker, who was declared a free man. In his opinion on this case, Judge Cushing held that the institution of slavery should be illegal in Massachusetts, because it violated Article I of the state's Declaration of Rights (Document 15), which stated unequivocally the doctrine of natural rights as applicable unconditionally and equally to all persons.

What was Cushing's response to Quock Walker's complaint against Jennison? To what extent does the Superior Court's response agree with the 1777 petition by free African Americans to the General Court of Massachusetts (see Document 18)?

As TO THE DOCTRINE OF SLAVERY and the right of Christians to hold Africans in perpetual servitude, and sell and treat them as we do our horses and cattle, that (it is true) has been heretofore countenanced by the province laws formerly, but nowhere is it expressly enacted or established. It has been a usage—a usage which took its origin from the practice of some of the European nations, and the regulations of British government respecting the then colonies, for the benefit of trade and wealth. But whatever sentiments have formerly prevailed in this particular or slid in upon us by the example of others, a different idea has taken place with the people of America, more favorable to the natural rights of mankind, and to that natural, innate desire of liberty, which with heaven (without regard to color, complexion, or shape of noses) . . . has inspired all the human race. And upon this ground our constitution of government, by which the people of this commonwealth have solemnly bound themselves, sets out with declaring that all men are born free and equal—and that every subject is entitled to liberty, and to have it guarded by the laws, as well as life and property—and in short is totally repugnant to the idea of being born slaves. This being the case, I think the idea of slavery is inconsistent with our own conduct and constitution; and there can be no such thing as perpetual servitude of a rational creature, unless his liberty is forfeited by some criminal conduct or given up by personal consent or contract.

Verdict: Guilty.

Source: Proceedings of the Massachusetts Historical Society, Vol. 3 (Boston, 1791), p. 294.

DOCUMENT 20: Memorial and Remonstrance Against Religious Assessments (James Madison, June 20, 1785)

James Madison of Orange County, Virginia was a staunch supporter of the individual's rights to freedom from unjust or unnatural coercion by the state. He was particularly committed to the cause of religious liberty, and he believed separation of church and state to be a necessary condition of this fundamental freedom. So, in 1784–1785, as a member of the Virginia General Assembly, he led opposition to a bill that would have levied a tax on Virginians "to restore and propagate the holy Christian religion" through financial support of Christian clergymen.

Madison certainly was not opposed to the needs and mission of organized religion. Rather, he believed these needs and this mission should be addressed in the private sphere of society, free of entanglement with and possible coercion by government. Madison's Memorial and Remonstrance was written to arouse statewide opposition to the proposed law on religious assessments, and it succeeded. The General Assembly set aside this bill in October 1785, in response to an outpouring of public opposition.

Madison presented fifteen distinct arguments against the proposed tax to support nonpreferentially all Christian denominations of the state. He argued that religion should neither be promoted nor interfered with by the government because it was the individual's natural right freely to exercise it in accord with his or her conscience.

According to Madison, why would the proposed tax law in support of religious education have a harmful effect on the rights and liberties of individuals? Why, according to Madison, would this proposed law not be necessary for the well-being of the state government and society? Why would it even be harmful to the government and society? How did Madison use the doctrine of natural rights to support his position in this Memorial and Remonstrance?

To The Honorable The General Assembly of
The Commonwealth Of Virginia.
A Memorial and Remonstrance.

We, the subscribers, citizens of the said Commonwealth, having taken into serious consideration, a Bill printed by order of the last Session of General Assembly, entitled "A Bill establishing a provision for Teachers of the Christian Religion," and conceiving that the same, if finally armed with the sanctions of a law, will be a dangerous abuse of power, are bound as faithful members of a free State, to remonstrate against it, and to declare the reasons by which we are determined. We remonstrate against the said Bill,

1. Because we hold it for a fundamental and undeniable truth, "that Religion or the duty which we owe to our Creator and the Manner of discharging it, can be directed only by reason and conviction, not by force or violence." The Religion then of every man must be left to the conviction and conscience of every man; and it is the right of every man to exercise it as these may dictate. This right is in its nature an unalienable right. It is unalienable; because the opinions of men, depending only on the evidence contemplated by their own minds, cannot follow the dictates of other men: It is unalienable also; because what is here a right towards men, is a duty towards the Creator. It is the duty of every man to render to the Creator such homage, and such only, as he believes to be acceptable to him. This duty is precedent both in order of time and degree of obligation, to the claims of Civil Society. . . . We maintain therefore that in matters of Religion, no man's right is abridged by the institution of Civil Society, and that Religion is wholly exempt from its cognizance. True it is, that no other rule exists, by which any question which may divide a Society, can be ultimately determined, but the will of the majority; but it is also true, that the majority may trespass on the rights of the minority.

2. Because if religion be exempt from the authority of the Society at large, still less can it be subject to that of the Legislative Body. The latter are but the creatures and vicegerents of the former. Their jurisdiction is both derivative and limited: it is limited with regard to the co-ordinate departments, more necessarily is it limited with regard to the constituents. The preservation of a free government requires not merely, that the metes and bounds which separate each department of power may be invariably maintained; but more especially, that neither of them be suffered to overleap the great Barrier which defends the rights of the people. The Rulers who are guilty of such an encroachment, exceed the commission from which they derive their authority, and are Tyrants. The People who submit to it are governed by laws made neither by themselves, nor by an authority derived from them, and are slaves.

3. Because, it is proper to take alarm at the first experiment on our liberties. We hold this prudent jealousy to be the first duty of citizens, and one of [the] noblest characteristics of the late Revolution. . . . Who does not see that the same authority which can establish Christianity, in exclusion of all other Religions, may establish with the same ease any particular sect of Christians, in exclusion of all other Sects? That the same authority which can force a citizen to contribute three pence only of his

property for the support of any one establishment, may force him to conform to any other establishment in all cases whatsoever?

4. Because, the bill violates that equality which ought to be the basis of every law, and which is more indispensible, in proportion as the validity or expediency of any law is more liable to be impeached. If "all men are by nature equally free and independent," all men are to be considered as entering into Society on equal conditions; as relinquishing no more, and therefore retaining no less, one than another, of their natural rights. Above all are they to be considered as retaining an "*equal* title to the free exercise of Religion according to the dictates of conscience." Whilst we assert for ourselves a freedom to embrace, to profess and to observe the Religion which we believe to be of divine origin, we cannot deny an equal freedom to those whose minds have not yet yielded to the evidence which has convinced us. If this freedom be abused, it is an offence against god, not against man: To God, therefore, not to men, must an account of it be rendered. As the Bill violates equality by subjecting some to peculiar burdens; so it violates the same principle, by granting to others peculiar exemptions. . . .

5. Because the bill implies either that the Civil Magistrate is a competent Judge of Religious truth; or that he may employ Religion as an engine of Civil policy. The first is an arrogant pretension falsified by the contradictory opinions of Rulers in all ages, and throughout the world: The second an unhallowed perversion of the means of salvation.

6. Because the establishment proposed by the Bill is not requisite for the support of the Christian Religion. To say that it is, is a contradiction to the Christian Religion itself; for every page of it disavows a dependence on the powers of this world: it is a contradiction to fact; for it is known that this Religion both existed and flourished, not only without the support of human laws, but in spite of every opposition from them; and not only during the period of miraculous aid, but long after it had been left to its own evidence, and the ordinary care of Providence: Nay, it is a contradiction in terms; for a Religion not invented by human policy, must have pre-existed and been supported, before it was established by human policy. It is moreover to weaken in those who profess this Religion a pious confidence in its innate excellence, and the patronage of its Author; and to foster in those who still reject it, a suspicion that its friends are too conscious of its fallacies, to trust it to its own merits.

7. Because experience witnesseth that ecclesiastical establishments, instead of maintaining the purity and efficacy of Religion, have had a contrary operation. . . .

8. Because the establishment in question is not necessary for the Support of Civil Government. If it be urged as necessary for the support of Civil Government only as it is a means of supporting Religion, and it be

not necessary for the latter purpose, it cannot be necessary for the former. . . .

9. Because the proposed establishment is a departure from that generous policy, which, offering an asylum to the persecuted and oppressed of every Nation and Religion, promised a lustre to our country, and an accession to the number of its citizens. . . .

10. Because, it will have a like tendency to banish our Citizens. The allurements presented by other situations are every day thinning their number. To superadd a fresh motive to emigration, by revoking the liberty which they now enjoy, would be the same species of folly which has dishonoured and depopulated flourishing kingdoms.

11. Because, it will destroy that moderation and harmony which the forbearance of our laws to intermeddle with Religion, has produced amongst its several sects. Torrents of blood have been spilt in the old world, by vain attempts of the secular arm to extinguish Religious discord, by proscribing all difference in Religious opinions. Time has at length revealed the true remedy. Every relaxation of narrow and rigorous policy, wherever it has been tried, has been found to assuage the disease. The American Theatre has exhibited proofs, that equal and compleat liberty, if it does not wholly eradicate it, sufficiently destroys its malignant influence on the health and prosperity of the State. . . .

12. Because, the policy of the bill is adverse to the diffusion of the light of Christianity. The first wish of those who enjoy this precious gift, ought to be that it may be imparted to the whole race of mankind. Compare the number of those who have as yet received it with the number still remaining under the dominion of false Religions; and how small is the former! Does the policy of the Bill tend to lessen the disproportion? No; it at once discourages those who are strangers to the light of [revelation] from coming into the Region of it; and countenances, by example the nations who continue in darkness, in shutting out those who might convey it to them. Instead of levelling as far as possible, every obstacle to the victorious progress of truth, the Bill with an ignoble and unchristian timidity would circumscribe it, with a wall of defence, against the encroachments of error.

13. Because attempts to enforce by legal sanctions, acts obnoxious to so great a proportion of Citizens, tend to enervate the laws in general, and to slacken the bands of Society. If it be difficult to execute any law which is not generally deemed necessary or salutary, what must be the case where it is deemed invalid and dangerous? and what may be the effect of so striking an example of impotency in the Government, on its general authority.

14. Because a measure of such singular magnitude and delicacy ought not to be imposed, without the clearest evidence that it is called for by a majority of citizens: and no satisfactory method is yet proposed by

which the voice of the majority in this case may be determined, or its influence secured. . . .

15. Because, finally, "the equal right of every citizen to the free exercise of his Religion according to the dictates of conscience" is held by the same tenure with all our other rights. If we recur to its origin, it is equally the gift of nature; if we weigh its importance, it cannot be less dear to us; if we consult the Declaration of those rights which pertain to the good people of Virginia, as the "basis and foundation of government," it is enumerated with equal solemnity, or rather studied emphasis. . . .

Source: Gaillard Hunt, ed., *The Writings of James Madison,* Vol. 2 (New York: G. P. Putnam's Sons, 1910), pp. 183–91.

DOCUMENT 21: The Virginia Statute for Religious Freedom (Thomas Jefferson, January 16, 1786)

Thomas Jefferson, a friend and neighbor of James Madison in the piedmont region of Virginia, drafted a bill to buttress and extend the principle of religious liberty expressed in Section XVI of the 1776 Virginia Declaration of Rights. This proposed statute was introduced to the Virginia General Assembly in 1779, but it languished without adequate support for six years, until James Madison promoted its passage in the wake of his successful campaign against a proposed law that would have levied taxes for the nonpreferential support of the state's various Christian denominations.

Jefferson's bill became law in January 1786, and Virginia moved to the forefront of American states in the cause of religious liberty. Jefferson's statute is introduced by a preamble, Section I, and followed by a concluding statement, Section III. The preamble is a profound argument for freedom of expression, with particular emphasis on every person's inherent right to free exercise of religious belief. According to Jefferson, government should be prohibited by law from interfering with a person's natural right to freedom of expression, which is the intent of Section II, the statute. Section III states that the individual's right to religious liberty does not come from government; rather, it is a natural right of individuals, based in human nature, that supersedes the power of government.

How did Jefferson use the natural rights doctrine in Sections I and III to justify this statute? Compare Section II, the statute, with Section XVI of the Virginia Declaration of Rights (see Document 10). How did Jefferson's statute support and expand upon the protections for religious liberty expressed in the Virginia Declaration of Rights?

I. Whereas Almighty God hath created the mind free; that all attempts to influence it by temporal punishments or burthens, or by civil incapacitations, tend only to beget habits of hypocrisy and meanness, and are a departure from the plan of the Holy author of our religion, who being Lord both of body and mind, yet chose not to propagate it by coercions on either, as was in his Almighty power to do; that the impious presumption of legislators and rulers, civil as well as ecclesiastical, who being themselves but fallible and uninspired men, have assumed dominion over the faith of others, setting up their own opinions and modes of thinking as the only true and infallible, and as such endeavouring to impose them on others, hath established and maintained false religions over the greatest part of the world, and through all time; that to compel a man to furnish contributions of money for the propagation of opinions which he disbelieves, is sinful and tyrannical; that even the forcing him to support this or that teacher of his own religious persuasion, is depriving him of the comfortable liberty of giving his contributions to the particular pastor, whose morals he would make his pattern, and whose powers he feels most persuasive to righteousness, and is withdrawing from the ministry those temporary rewards, which proceeding from an approbation of their personal conduct, are an additional incitement to earnest and unremitting labours for the instruction of mankind; that our civil rights have no dependence on our religious opinions, any more than our opinions in physics or geometry; that therefore the proscribing any citizen as unworthy the public confidence by laying upon him an incapacity of being called to offices of trust and emolument, unless he profess or renounce this or that religious opinion, is depriving him injuriously of those privileges and advantages to which in common with his fellow-citizens he has a natural right; that it tends only to corrupt the principles of that religion it is meant to encourage, by bribing with a monopoly of worldly honours and emoluments, those who will externally profess and conform to it; that though indeed these are criminal who do not withstand such temptation, yet neither are those innocent who lay the bait in their way; that to suffer the civil magistrate to intrude his powers into the field of opinion, and to restrain the profession or propagation of principles on supposition of their ill tendency, is a dangerous fallacy, which at once destroys all religious liberty, because he being of course judge of that tendency will make his opinions the rule of judgment, and approve or condemn the sentiments of others only as they shall square with or differ from his own; that it is time enough for the rightful purposes of civil government, for its officers to interfere when principles break out into overt acts against peace and good order; and finally, that truth is great and will prevail if left to herself, that she is the proper and sufficient antagonist to error, and has nothing to fear from the conflict, unless by human interposition disarmed of her natural weapons, free argument and debate, errors ceasing to be dangerous when it is permitted freely to contradict them:

II. *Be it enacted by the General Assembly,* That no man shall be compelled to frequent or support any religious worship, place or ministry whatsoever, nor shall be enforced, restrained, molested, or burthened in his body or goods, nor shall otherwise suffer on account of his religious opinions or belief; but that all men shall be free to profess, and by argument to maintain, their opinions in matters of religion, and that the same shall in no wise diminish, enlarge, or affect their civil capacities.

III. And though we well know that this Assembly, elected by the people for the ordinary purposes of legislation only, have no power to re-strain the acts of succeeding Assemblies, constituted with powers equal to our own, and that therefore to declare this act to be irrevocable would be of no effect in law; yet we are free to declare, and do declare, that the rights hereby asserted are of the natural rights of mankind, and that if any act shall be hereafter passed to repeal the present, or to narrow its operation, such act will be an infringement of natural right.

Source: W. W. Hening, ed., *Statutes at Large of Virginia,* Vol. 12 (Richmond, Va.: Samuel Shepherd, 1836), pp. 84–86.

DOCUMENT 22: Letter from Three Seneca Leaders to President George Washington (1790)

During the period following the American War of Independence, many Native-American leaders sent petitions to executives and legislators of the federal and state governments of the United States. Their purpose was to express grievances and protests against loss of their lands in the aftermath of the 1783 Treaty of Paris, which ended the American War of Independence and recognized U.S. sovereignty in territories claimed by various Native-American nations.

One of these nations, the Seneca, was the largest tribe of the Iroquois federation. They inhabited land in upper New York State west of Seneca Lake. Three Seneca leaders—Big Tree, Cornplanter, and Half-Town—sent a letter of complaint to President Washington about threats to their possession of traditional Seneca territory. They argued that the King of England had no right to cede their land by treaty to the United States of America. Further, they appealed to the president of the United States to treat them justly and to refrain from abusing them because they were too weak to resist.

What grievances did the Seneca leaders express to President Washington? What reasons did they use to justify their protests?

Father: The voice of the Seneca nations speaks to you; the great counsellor, in whose heart the wise men of all the *thirteen fires* [13 U.S. states] have placed their wisdom. It may be very small in your ears, and we, therefore, entreat you to hearken with attention; for we are able to speak of things which are to us very great.

When your army entered the country of the Six Nations, we called you the *town destroyer;* to this day, when your name is heard, our women look behind them and turn pale, and our children cling close to the necks of their mothers.

When our chiefs returned from Fort Stanwix, and laid before our council what had been done there, our nation was surprised to hear how great a country you had compelled them to give up to you, without your paying to us any thing for it. Every one said, that your hearts were yet swelled with resentment against us for what had happened during the war, but that one day you would consider it with more kindness. We asked each other, *What have we done to deserve such severe chastisement?*

Father: when you kindled your 13 fires separately, the wise men assembled at them told us that you were all brothers; the children of one great father, who regarded the red people as his children. They called us brothers, and invited us to his protection. They told us that he resided beyond the great water where the sun first rises; and that he was a king whose power no people could resist, and that his goodness was as bright as the sun. What they said went to our hearts. We accepted the invitation, and promised to obey him. What the Seneca nation promises, they faithfully perform. When you refused obedience to that king, he commanded us to assist his beloved men in making you sober. In obeying him, we did no more than yourselves had led us to promise. We were deceived; but your people teaching us to confide in that king, had helped to deceive us; and we now appeal to your breast. *Is all the blame ours?*

Father: when we saw that we had been deceived, and heard the invitation which you gave us to draw near to the fire you had kindled, and talk with you concerning peace, we made haste towards it. You told us you could crush us to nothing; and you demanded from us a great country, as the price of that peace which you had offered to us: *as if our want of strength had destroyed our rights.* Our chiefs had felt your power, and were unable to contend against you, and they therefore gave up that country. What they agreed to has bound our nation, but your anger against us must by this time be cooled, and although our strength is not increased, nor your power become less, we ask you to consider calmly— *Were the terms dictated to us by your commissioners reasonable and just? . . .*

Father: you have said that we were in your hand, and that by closing it you could crush us to nothing. Are you determined to crush us? If you are, tell us so; that those of our nation who have become your children, and have determined to die so, may know what to do. In this case, one chief has said, he would ask you to put him out of his pain. Another, who will not think of dying by the hand of his father, or his brother, has said he will retire to the Chataughque, eat of the fatal root, and sleep with his fathers in peace.

All the land we have been speaking of belonged to the Six Nations. No part of it ever belonged to the king of England, and he could not give it to you.

Hear us once more. At Fort Stanwix we agreed to deliver up those of our people who should do you any wrong, and that you might try them and punish them according to your law. We delivered up two men accordingly. But instead of trying them according to your law, the lowest of your people took them from your magistrate, and put them immediately to death. It is just to punish the murder with death; but the Senecas will not deliver up their people to men who disregard the treaties of their own nation.

Source: Samuel G. Drake, *Biography and History of the Indians of North America* (Boston: Antiquarian Institute, 1837), pp. 609–11.

DOCUMENT 23: A Sermon Against Slavery (The Reverend James Dana, September 9, 1791)

Many Christian ministers spoke out from the pulpit against the institution of slavery and the slave trade. One of the most prominent antislavery preachers was James Dana, who in 1791 was pastor of the First Congregational Church of New Haven, Connecticut. He preached several antislavery sermons, which were published and widely distributed. Rev. Dana argued that slavery was a violation of God's commandments and the rights of individuals stated in the laws of the American states and based in human nature. He claimed that the practice of slavery contradicted the principles of both Christianity and free government.

How did Rev. Dana use Christian doctrine to argue against slavery? What connection did he make between Christian doctrine and the natural rights doctrine?

... Our late warfare was expressly founded on such principles as these: "All men are created equal: They are endowed by their Creator with certain unalienable rights; among these are life, liberty, and the pursuit of happiness." Admitting these just principles, ... the Africans are our brethren. And, according to the principles of our religion, they are *children of the free-woman as well as we.* This instructs us, *that God is no respecter of persons, or of nations—hath put no difference between Jew and Greek, barbarian and Scythian.* In Christ Jesus, in whom it was foretold "all nations shall be blessed," those "who sometimes were far off, are brought nigh, and have access by one Spirit unto the Father." So that they "are no more strangers and foreigners, but fellow-citizens with the saints, and of the household of God." The heathen will all be given him for his inheritance, and the uttermost parts of the earth for a possession.

Why then should we treat our African brethren as the elder son in the parable treated the younger, offended at the compassion of their common parent towards him? Why place them in a situation incapable of recovery from their lost state? their state of moral death? Did Jesus come to redeem us from the worst bondage? Shall his disciples then enslave those whom he came to redeem from slavery? who are the purchase of his blood? Is this *doing to others,* as he hath commanded, *whatsoever we would that they should do to us?* Is it to *love our neighbour as ourselves?*

On a view of the wretched servitude of the Africans, some may suspect, that they must have been *sinners above all men, because they suffer such things.* This way of reasoning, however common, our Lord has reproved—particularly in the instance of the blind man; of those who were slain by the fall of the tower in Siloam; and of those whose blood Pilate mingled with the public sacrifices. All mankind are *the offspring of God.* His government over them is parental. Children may have the fullest proof that the government of their father is not capricious and tyrannic, but most wise and kind: At the same time, they cannot explain many parts of it; but unreservedly submit to his pleasure, having the fullest confidence in his superior wisdom, his paternal care and affection.

That such as have been educated in slavish principles, justify and practise slavery, may not seem strange. Those who profess to understand and regard the principles of liberty should cheerfully unite to abolish slavery.

Our middle and northern states have prohibited any further importation of slaves. South-Carolina passed a prohibitory act for a limited time. Consistently with the federal constitution the traffic may be stopped in seventeen years; and a duty of ten dollars may be laid on every slave now imported. By an act of the legislature of Connecticut, all blacks and mulattoes born within the state from March 1784, will be manumitted at the age of 25 years. The act of Pennsylvania liberates them at the age of twenty eight years. Such provision hath been made for the gradual abolition of slavery in the United States. . . .

The revolution in the United States hath given free course to the principles of liberty. One ancient kingdom, illuminated by these principles, and actuated by the spirit of liberty, hath established a free constitution. The spirit will spread, and shake the throne of despotic princes. Neither an habit of submission to arbitrary rule in church and state, nor the menaced interference of neighboring kingdoms, could prevent, or counterwork, a revolution, propitious in its aspect on the rights of other nations, and of mankind. No combination of European potentates can impede the progress of freedom. The time is hastening, when their subjects will not endure to be told, that no government shall exist in any nation but such as provides for the perpetuation of absolute monarchy, and the transmission of it to the families in present possession. The time is hastening, when no monarch in Europe shall tell his subjects, *Your silver and your gold are mine.*

The present occasion will be well improved, if we set ourselves to banish all slavish principles, and assert our liberty as men, citizens and Christians. We have all one Father: He will have all his offspring to be saved. We are disciples of one master: He will finally *gather together in one the children of God.* Let us unite in carrying into effect the purpose of the Saviour's appearance. This was to give *peace and good will to man,* and thus bring *glory to God on high.* . . .

Source: James Dana, *The African Slave Trade: A Discourse Before the Connecticut Society for the Promotion of Freedom* (New Haven: Thomas and Samuel Green, 1791).

DOCUMENT 24: Letter to Thomas Jefferson (Benjamin Banneker, August 19, 1791)

Benjamin Banneker, a free African American, lived on his farm in Baltimore County, Maryland. Descended from free grandparents and parents who were also farmers and property owners in Baltimore County, he was able to develop extraordinary talents as an inventor, engineer, mathematician, surveyor of land, and writer of published works.

In 1791, Banneker worked with his neighbor, Andrew Ellicott, to survey and establish boundaries for the District of Columbia and the new national capital. In August of that same year, he sent a letter to Thomas Jefferson, the U.S. secretary of state, with a prepublication copy of an almanac he had written. This volume was the first of several annual almanacs produced by Banneker to provide useful information on agriculture, astronomy, mathematics, and various other subjects.

In his letter to Jefferson, Banneker appealed to the secretary of state and author of the Declaration of Independence to denounce slavery and racial discrimination against black Americans. He appealed to the natural rights doctrine to justify his arguments for equality and against slavery and racial discrimination. Further, he pointed to his intellectual achievements to demonstrate the capabilities of a free black person.

What reasons did Banneker present to Jefferson to influence him to oppose slavery and support the rights of black people? How did Banneker use the doctrine of natural rights to justify his position and persuade Jefferson to agree with him?

Maryland, Baltimore County,
Near Ellicott's Lower Mills August 19th, 1791.
Thomas Jefferson Secretary of State.

Sir, I am fully sensible of the greatness of that freedom which I take with you on the present occasion; a liberty which Seemed to me Scarcely allowable, when I reflected on that distinguished, and dignifyed station in which you Stand; and the almost general prejudice and prepossession which is so previlent in the world against those of my complexion.

I suppose it is a truth too well attested to you, to need a proof here, that we are a race of Beings who have long laboured under the abuse and censure of the world, that we have long been looked upon with an eye of contempt, and that we have long been considered rather as brutish than human, and Scarcely capable of mental endowments.

Sir, I hope I may Safely admit, in consequence of that report which hath reached me, that you are a man far less inflexible in Sentiments of this nature, than many others; that you are measurably friendly and well disposed towards us, and that you are willing and ready to Lend your aid and assistance to our relief from those many distresses and numerous calamities to which we are reduced.

Now, Sir, if this is founded in truth, I apprehend you will readily embrace every opportunity to eradicate that train of absurd and false ideas and oppinions which so generally prevail with respect to us, and that your Sentiments are concurrent with mine, which are that one universal Father hath given being to us all, and that he hath not only made us all of one flesh, but that he hath also without partiality afforded us all the Same Sensations, and endued us all with the same faculties, and that however variable we may be in Society or religion, however diversified in Situation or colour, we are all of the Same Family, and Stand in the Same relation to him.

Sir, if these are Sentiments of which you are fully persuaded, I hope you cannot but acknowledge, that it is the indispensible duty of those who maintain for themselves the rights of human nature, and who profess the obligations of Christianity, to extend their power and influence to the relief of every part of the human race, from whatever burthen or oppression they may unjustly labour under; and this I apprehend a full conviction of the truth and obligation of these principles should lead all to.

Sir, I have long been convinced, that if your love for yourSelves and for those inesteemable laws which preserve to you the rights of human nature, was founded on Sincerity, you could not but be Solicitous, that every Individual of whatsoever rank or distinction, might with you equally enjoy the blessings thereof, neither could you rest Satisfyed, short of the most active diffusion of your exertions, in order to their promotion from any State of degradation, to which the unjustifyable cruelty and barbarism of men may have reduced them.

Sir I freely and Chearfully acknowledge, that I am of the African race, and, in that colour which is natural to them of the deepest dye; and it is under a Sense of the most profound gratitude to the Supreme Ruler of the universe, that I now confess to you, that I am not under that State of tyrannical thraldom, and inhuman captivity, to which too many of my brethren are doomed; but that I have abundantly tasted of the fruition of those blessings which proceed from that free and unequalled liberty with which you are favoured and which I hope you will willingly allow you have received from the immediate Hand of that Being from whom proceedeth every good and perfect gift.

Sir, Suffer me to recall to your mind that time in which the Arms and tyranny of the British Crown were exerted with every powerful effort, in order to reduce you to a State of Servitude; look back I intreat you on the variety of dangers to which you were exposed, reflect on that time in which every human aid appeared unavailable, and in which even hope and fortitude wore the aspect of inability to the Conflict, and you cannot but be led to a Serious and grateful Sense of your miraculous and providential preservation; You cannot but acknowledge, that the present freedom and tranquillity which you enjoy you have mercifully received, and that it is the peculiar blessing of Heaven.

This, Sir, was a time in which you clearly saw into the injustice of a State of Slavery, and in which you had Just apprehensions of the horrors of its condition, it was now Sir, that your abhorrence thereof was so excited, that you publickly held forth this true and invaluable doctrine, which is worthy to be recorded and remembered in all Succeeding ages. "We hold these truths to be Self evident, that all men are created equal, and that they are endowed by their creator with certain inalienable rights, that amongst these are life, liberty, and the persuit of happiness."

Here, Sir, was a time in which your tender feelings for your selves engaged you thus to declare, you were then impressed with proper ideas of the great valuation of liberty, and the free possession of those blessings to which you were entitled by nature; but Sir how pitiable is it to reflect, that altho you were so fully convinced of the benevolence of the Father of mankind, and of his equal and impartial distribution of those rights and privileges which he had conferred upon them, that you should at the Same time counteract his mercies, in detaining by fraud and violence so numerous a part of my brethren under groaning captivity and cruel oppression, that you should at the Same time be found guilty of that most criminal act, which you professedly detested in others, with respect to yourselves.

Sir, I suppose that your knowledge of the situation of my brethren is too extensive to need a recital here; neither shall I presume to prescribe methods by which they may be relieved, otherwise than by recommending to you, and all others, to wean yourselves from those narrow prejudices which you have imbibed with respect to them, and as Job proposed to his friends "Put your Souls in their Souls' stead," thus shall your hearts be enlarged with kindness and benevolence towards them, and thus shall you need neither the direction of myself or others in what manner to proceed herein.

And now, Sir, altho my Sympathy and affection for my brethren hath caused my enlargement thus far, I ardently hope that your candour and generosity will plead with you in my behalf, when I make known to you, that it was not originally my design; but that having taken up my pen in order to direct to you as a present, a copy of an Almanack which I have calculated for the Succeeding year, I was unexpectedly and unavoidably led thereto.

This calculation, Sir, is the production of my arduous study, in this my advanced Stage of life; for having long had unbounded desires to become Acquainted with the Secrets of nature, I have had to gratify my curiosity herein thro my own assiduous application to Astronomical Study, in which I need not to recount to you the many difficulties and disadvantages which I have had to encounter.

And altho I had almost declined to make my calculation for the ensuing year, in consequence of that time which I had allotted therefor being taking up at the Federal Territory by the request of Mr. Andrew Ellicott, yet finding myself under Several engagements to printers of this state to whom I had communicated my design, on my return to my place of residence, I industriously apply'd myself thereto, which I hope I have accomplished with correctness and accuracy, a copy of which I have taken the liberty to direct to you, and which I humbly request you will favourably receive, and altho you may have the opportunity of perusing it after its publication, yet I chose to send it to you in manuscript previous thereto, that thereby you might not only have an earlier inspection, but that you might also view it in my own hand writing.

And now Sir, I Shall conclude and Subscribe my Self with the most profound respect,

Your most Obedient humble Servant
Benjamin Banneker.

Source: Universal Asylum and Columbian Magazine, Vol. 2 (October 1792), pp. 222–24.

DOCUMENT 25: Letters to Benjamin Banneker and to the Marquis de Condorcet (Thomas Jefferson, August 30, 1791)

Thomas Jefferson, a slave owner, received Benjamin Banneker's letter on August 26 and replied to him four days later. Jefferson was impressed by the high quality of Banneker's almanac and sent it to the Marquis de Condorcet, a French scholar. He appeared to recognize that unjust treatment and the deplorable conditions of life in slavery had prevented most black Americans from opportunities to develop their talents. The example of Banneker's extraordinary intellectual achievements seemed to influence his feelings favorably about the capabilities of black Americans. However, Jefferson did not free his slaves or persuade other Virginians to abolish this odious institution. What evidence can be found in Jefferson's letters that Banneker had favorably influenced his views about the capabilities and rights of African Americans?

Philadelphia. Aug. 30, 1791

[To Benjamin Banneker]

Sir,–I thank you sincerely for your letter of the 19th instant and for the Almanac it contained. No body wishes more than I do to see such proofs as you exhibit, that nature has given to our black brethren, talents equal to those of the other colors of men, and that the appearance of a want of them is owing merely to the degraded condition of their existence, both in Africa & America. I can add with truth, that no body wishes more ardently to see a good system commenced for raising the condition both of their body & mind to what it ought to be, as fast as the imbecility of their present existence, and other circumstances which cannot be neglected, will admit. I have taken the liberty of sending your Almanac to Monsieur de Condorcet, Secretary of the Academy of Sciences at Paris, and member of the Philanthropic society, because I considered it as a document to which your whole colour had a right for their justification against the doubts which have been entertained of them. I am with great esteem, Sir Your most obed^t humble serv^t.

Philadelphia. Aug. 30, 1791

To the Marquis de Condorcet

Dear Sir, . . . I am happy to be able to inform you that we have now in the United States a Negro, the son of a black man born in Africa, and of a black woman born in the United States, who is a very respectable mathematician. I procured him to be employed under one of our chief directors in laying out the new federal city on the Potowmac, & in the intervals of his leisure, while on that work, he made an Almanac for the next year, which he sent me in his own hand writing, & which I inclose to you. I have seen very elegant solutions of Geometrical problems by him. Add to this that he is a very worthy & respectable member of society. He is a free man. I shall be delighted to see these instances of moral eminence so multiplied as to prove that the want of talents observed in them is merely the effect of their degraded condition, and not proceeding from any difference in the structure of the parts on which intellect depends. . . .

Present my affectionate respects to Madame de Condorcet, and accept yourself assurances of the sentiments of esteem & attachment which I have the honour to be Dear Sir your most obed^t & most humble serv^t.

Source: Paul L. Ford, ed., *The Writings of Thomas Jefferson,* Vol. 5 (New York: G. P. Putnam's Sons, 1895), pp. 377–78.

FURTHER READING

Alley, Robert S., ed. *James Madison on Religious Liberty.* Buffalo, N.Y.: Prometheus Books, 1985.

Bedini, Silvio A. *The Life of Benjamin Banneker.* New York: Charles Scribner's Sons, 1972.

Berlin, Ira, and Ronald Hoffman. *Slavery and Freedom in the Age of the American Revolution.* Charlottesville: University of Virginia Press, 1983.

Curry, Thomas J. *The First Freedoms: Church and State in America to the Passage of the First Amendment.* New York: Oxford University Press, 1986.

Levin, Phyllis Lee. *Abigail Adams: A Biography.* New York: St. Martin's Press, 1987.

Merrell, James H. "Indians and the New Republic," *The Blackwell Encyclopedia of the American Revolution,* edited by Jack P. Greene and J. R. Pole. Cambridge, Mass.: Basil Blackwell, 1992, pp. 392–98.

Nash, Gary. *Race and Revolution.* Madison, Wisc.: Madison House, 1990.

Norton, Mary Beth. *Liberty's Daughters: The Revolutionary Experience of American Women, 1750–1800.* Boston: Little, Brown, 1980.

Peterson, Merril D., and Robert Vaughan, eds. *The Statute for Religious Liberty: Its Evolution and Consequences in American History.* Cambridge: Cambridge University Press, 1988.

Pole, J. R. *The Pursuit of Equality in American History,* 2nd Ed. Berkeley: University of California Press, 1993, pp. 1–131.

Part IV

The Crisis of Government Under the Articles of Confederation, 1781–1787

After receiving Richard Henry Lee's resolution for independence on June 7, 1776 (see Document 5), the Continental Congress turned to the task of constituting officially and formally a government for the soon-to-be independent United States of America. A committee of thirteen members was appointed to draft Articles of Confederation for the imminent union of the American states. John Dickinson of Pennsylvania assumed leadership of the committee and became the principal writer of the Articles.

Dickinson's draft was submitted to Congress before July 4, 1776, when Congress approved its Declaration of Independence (see Document 7). However, Dickinson did not attend sessions of Congress after July 4, so he was not there to defend provisions of his draft against critics.

Thomas Burke of North Carolina became a leader of the delegates who wanted to protect the powers and authority of the thirteen states within the Confederation. Burke argued that Dickinson's draft of the Articles of Confederation assigned too much power to the Congress and reserved too little power to the states. He pointed to Article III of the Dickinson draft, which provided, "Each colony shall retain and enjoy as much of its present Laws, Rights and Customs as it may think fit, and reserve to itself the sole and exclusive regulation and Government of its internal Police, in all Matters that shall not interfere with the Articles at this Confederation."[1]

Burke and his followers deemed this proposed article an unacceptable limitation on the states, which they held to be the sovereign and supreme entities of the union. Burke offered the following replacement for Dickinson's proposed Article III, to which the Continental Congress assented as Article II of the final and official version of the Articles of

Confederation: "Each State retains its sovereignty, freedom and independence, and every power, jurisdiction, and right, which is not by this confederation expressly delegated to the United States, in Congress assembled."

Burke's successful modification of Dickinson's draft significantly moved the locus of primary power in this union to the states and away from the Congress of the United States. Other elements of the final draft (see Document 26) also made Congress weak, which led ultimately to the Articles of Confederation being replaced by the U.S. Constitution at the Constitutional Convention in 1787. For instance, the Congress lacked power to enforce its acts. Further, it could request, but not command, states to pay taxes to support the Confederation. Finally, it was often difficult for Congress to act, because the approval of nine states was required for decisions on particularly important matters. Unanimity, the approval of all thirteen states, was required for amendments to the Articles of Confederation.

Of course, unanimous agreement of the states was required to ratify the Articles and institute government under them, which did not happen until 1781, four years after the final draft had been produced. The largest obstacle to ratification was the reluctance of states with territorial claims in the western region of the country (e.g., Virginia, New York, and Massachusetts) to yield their claims to the Congress of the Confederation. Several small states without western land claims refused to ratify the Articles of Confederation until the claims were yielded by such states as Virginia and New York.

Finally, on September 6, 1780, the Continental Congress passed a resolution "that the unappropriated lands that may be ceded or relinquished to the United States by any particular States . . . shall be disposed of for the common benefit of the United States, and be settled and formed into distinct republican States, which shall become members of the Federal Union, and shall have the same rights of sovereignty, freedom and independence, as the other States."[2] Virginia, then, formally yielded to the United States its vast western land claims north and west of the Ohio River in the Virginia Act of Cession. Other states with western land claims eventually followed Virginia's example. Following this resolution of the western land claims issue, Maryland, the last recalcitrant state, ratified the Articles, and they took effect on March 1, 1781.

The grandest achievement of government under the Articles of Confederation was its negotiation in 1783 of the Treaty of Paris, which officially ended the American War of Independence. In addition to its formal recognition of an independent United States of America, the British yielded their claims to vast western territories across the Appalachian Mountains as far as the Mississippi River.

The remaining great work of Congress under the Articles of Confederation was its enactment of laws for organizing, distributing, settling, and governing the lands of the vast Northwest Territory, which had become its undisputed responsibility after the Treaty of Paris. Thomas Jefferson of Virginia drafted and Congress enacted the Ordinances of 1784 and 1785, which were preliminary plans for dividing, selling, and governing the western lands.

The Ordinance of 1785 provided for surveying the land systematically into townships that would measure six miles square. They would be divided by north-south and east-west lines surveyed at intervals of one mile, so that thirty-six sections would be created in each township. In each township, section 16 was to be set aside to provide funds for public schools. Sections 8, 11, 26, and 27 would be reserved for use by the U.S. government. Remaining land in each township would be sold at public auction for at least $1 per acre, and the buyer would receive a deed for the land officially recorded in the government's land office. Soon after passage of the Ordinance of 1785, surveyors were in eastern Ohio to lay out townships under the direction of Thomas Hutchins, Geographer of the United States.

The way was opened for purchase and settlement of the first segment of the Northwest Territory. But to make this way to the west safe and secure, workable governments had to be established in the western territories. Members of Congress were not satisfied with provisions for territorial government in the Ordinance of 1784, so they passed in 1787 the Northwest Ordinance (see Document 34). It provided a process for moving through three stages of territorial government to a petition for statehood, on equal terms with the other states, and promised that not less than three nor more than five states would be created out of the area north and west of the Ohio River. Further, the Northwest Ordinance included six Articles of Compact that guaranteed certain natural rights of individuals to the inhabitants of the territory, and prohibited slavery. These Articles of Compact, modeled on state declarations of rights, were a bill of rights for the Northwest Territory; there was not an equivalent document for the United States until ratification in 1791 of the federal Bill of Rights.

Five states were eventually made from the Northwest Territory (Ohio in 1803, Indiana in 1816, Illinois in 1818, Michigan in 1837, and Wisconsin in 1848). A small part of the original Northwest Territory was included within the boundaries of Minnesota, which became a state in 1858. The 1787 Northwest Ordinance eventually became the model by which thirty-one of the fifty American states advanced from territorial status to equal statehood in the United States of America.

The Northwest Ordinance bound westward-moving settlers to the United States with guarantees of equal citizenship and self-government—a remarkable development in an era when most people of the world were ruled by tyrants, and when dependent territories were held by ruling powers only as exploited colonies. Thus, 150 years after enactment of the Northwest Ordinance, Franklin D. Roosevelt wrote, "The principles therein embodied served as the highway, broad and safe, over which poured the westward march of our civilization. On this plan was the United States built."[3]

As the Northwest Ordinance was being enacted in the summer of 1787, however, the Congress was living its last days under a moribund Articles of Confederation. It would soon be replaced by new institutions of government under the U.S. Constitution, being drafted in Philadelphia while the Continental Congress met in New York.

From its inception in 1781, government under the Articles of Confederation was fatally flawed. Alexander Hamilton of New York was among the first to point out publicly that, "The fundamental defect is a want of power in Congress." He argued, "The idea of an uncontrollable sovereignty in each state over its internal police will defeat the other powers given to Congress, and make our union feeble and precarious."[4] George Washington agreed with Hamilton's criticisms, and emphatically proclaimed his own charges against the Articles of Confederation in a letter sent to all the governors of the American states (see Document 27).

Hamilton, Washington, and many other leaders agreed that the Articles of Confederation had to be revised or replaced to provide the kind of government needed by the United States (see the letter by John Jay of New York to George Washington, Document 29, and Washington's reply, Document 30). Some prominent Americans, however, disagreed with the criticism of the Articles and argued against hasty revisions of them. Richard Henry Lee, for example, argued against drastic changes in government in a letter to Samuel Adams of Massachusetts (see Document 28). Was the U.S. government really inadequate and in need of drastic and immediate change?

The movement for constitutional change gained momentum in the letter part of 1786 at an extraordinary gathering known as the Annapolis Convention. It was organized by James Madison of Virginia, who persuaded his state government to invite representatives from all thirteen states to discuss mutual problems and "such commercial regulations [as] may be necessary to their common interest and their permanent harmony."[5]

Only five states sent delegates to the Annapolis Convention: Delaware, New Jersey, New York, Pennsylvania, and Virginia, which was a big disappointment. But James Madison and Alexander Hamilton of New York decided to make the most of this situation. They spent four days, September 11–14, discussing their next moves to improve the government of the United States. They formally expressed their recommendations to the thirteen state governments and the Continental Congress in a report drafted for the Annapolis Convention by Alexander Hamilton (see Document 31).

The key provision of Hamilton's report was the request that Congress call another convention of the states to meet in Philadelphia in May 1787, which would decide how to revise the Articles of Confederation to make the U.S. government "adequate to the exigencies of the Union." Thus, the conditions were created for convening the fateful meeting in Philadelphia that wrote the Constitution of 1787. On February 21, 1787, Congress responded favorably, if reluctantly, to Hamilton's petition from Annapolis.

During the latter part of 1786, Americans suffered acutely from an economic depression. These hard times increased the mounting pressures for constitutional reform. Then, an explosive event, known as Shays's Rebellion, erupted in Massachusetts and pushed many reluctant reformers into the camp of Hamilton, Madison, and other advocates of political change.

Debt-ridden farmers of western Massachusetts, especially burdened by the economic depression, rallied around Daniel Shays, a captain of the Continental Army during the recent revolutionary war. Shays led an uprising to close the courts that enforced debt collections and to prompt changes in government.

Shays's Rebellion was suppressed easily by the superior fire power of the Massachusetts militia, but it created an appearance of national crisis that compelled many Americans to join the movement to revise or replace the Articles of Confederation. George Washington, for example, expressed the opinion of many Americans when he wrote, "We are fast verging to anarchy and confusion."[6]

Thomas Jefferson, following American events from abroad (he served in Paris as the American Minister to the French government), was not as alarmed as Washington. He down-played the significance of Shays's Rebellion in letters to two Virginians, Edward Carrington and James Madison (see Documents 32 and 33).

If Shays's Rebellion had been an isolated event, then Jefferson's benign view of it might have prevailed. But it sparked a flurry of unrest in several states, where impoverished debtors physically resisted both private bill collectors and public tax collectors. In South Carolina, for example, debt-ridden farmers riotously shut down the Camden Courthouse. Maryland's Charles County Courthouse was similarly attacked and its business disrupted. And so it went, here and there, to the point of raising public anxiety and compelling public action for constitutional change, which was conducted by the Constitutional Convention at Philadelphia in the summer of 1787.

The government under the Articles of Confederation deserved limited praise for its few significant achievements, such as the highly successful negotiations of peace with Britain, signified by the 1783 Treaty of Paris, and its western land policies codified in the Land Ordinance of 1785 and the Northwest Ordinance of 1787. On balance, however, its deficiencies, rooted in the Articles of Confederation, were too great to overcome, at least in the short run. Both the achievements and the deficiencies are revealed in Documents 26–34, which point the way toward the fundamental constitutional reform achieved at the Philadelphia Convention of 1787, a true turning point in the political history of America and the world.

NOTES

1. Richard B. Morris, *The Forging of the Union, 1781–1787* (New York: Harper and Row, 1987), p. 84.

2. Worthington C. Ford, ed., *Journals of the Continental Congress, 1774–1789*, Vol. 18 (Washington, D.C.: U.S. Government Printing Office, 1910), p. 915.

3. Harlow Lindley, Norris F. Schneider, Milo F. Quaife, and George J. Blazier, *History of the Ordinance of 1787 and the Old Northwest Territory* (Marietta, Ohio: Northwest Territory Celebration Commission, 1937), p. 79.

4. Harold C. Syrett, et al., *The Papers of Alexander Hamilton*, Vol. 2 (New York: Columbia University Press, 1979), p. 400.

5. Morris, *The Forging of the Union*, p. 251.

6. Ibid., p. 266.

DOCUMENT 26: The Articles of Confederation (1781)

The Articles of Confederation, the first constitution of the United States, was drafted in November 1777, ratified in February 1781, and superseded in June 1788 by ratification of a new federal Constitution. A preamble, pledging "perpetual union" of the thirteen sovereign states, introduced thirteen Articles, which specified the terms of Union, institutions of government, powers granted and denied to government, and procedures for conducting government.

The Articles established a unicameral legislative body, the Congress, to represent and act for this confederation of thirteen sovereign states, which "expressly delegated" only a few "sole and exclusive" powers "to the United States in Congress assembled." The powers of Congress pertained mostly to the international relations or foreign affairs of these United States. What were the main powers of Congress (see Article IX)?

Congress could make decisions by majority vote of the states, with each state, regardless of the size of its delegation, possessing one vote. Decision-making on a few very important matters required agreement by a super majority of nine states. Which matters of government required this super majority for decision-making (see Articles IX and X)? Congress was limited in its exercise of certain powers, such as raising money to pay expenses of the Confederation. In what other ways was the power of Congress limited or impeded?

Most powers of government under the Articles of Confederation were reserved to the thirteen sovereign states (see Articles II and III). What do these articles indicate about the powers of the states relative to the powers of Congress? What limitations were placed upon state powers (see Article VI)? What does Article VI indicate about the locus of power between the states and the Congress of the Confederation?

To all to whom these Presents shall come, we the under signed Delegates of the States affixed to our Names, send greeting.

Whereas the Delegates of the United States of America, in Congress assembled, did, on the 15th day of November, in the Year of Our Lord One thousand Seven Hundred and Seventy seven, and in the Second Year of the Independence of America, agree to certain articles of Confederation and perpetual Union between the States of Newhampshire, Massachusetts-bay, Rhodeisland and Providence Plantations, Connecticut, New York, New Jersey, Pennsylvania, Delaware, Maryland, Virginia, North-Carolina, South-Carolina, and Georgia in the words following, viz. "Articles of Confederation and perpetual Union between the states of Newhampshire, Massachusetts-bay, Rhodeisland and Providence Plantations, Connecticut, New-York, New-Jersey, Pennsylvania, Delaware, Maryland, Virginia, North-Carolina, South-Carolina and Georgia.

ARTICLE I. The Stile of this confederacy shall be "The United States of America."

ARTICLE II. Each state retains its sovereignty, freedom, and independence, and every Power, Jurisdiction and right, which is not by this confederation expressly delegated to the United States, in Congress assembled.

ARTICLE III. The said states hereby severally enter into a firm league of friendship with each other, for their common defence, the security of their Liberties, and their mutual and general welfare, binding themselves to assist each other, against all force offered to, or attacks made upon them, or any of them, on account of religion, sovereignty, trade, or any other pretence whatever.

ARTICLE IV. The better to secure and perpetuate mutual friendship and intercourse among the people of the different states in this union, the free inhabitants of each of these states, paupers, vagabonds and fugitives from justice excepted, shall be entitled to all privileges and immunities of free citizens in the several states; and the people of each state shall have free ingress and regress to and from any other state, and shall enjoy therein all the privileges of trade and commerce, subject to the same duties, impositions and restrictions as the inhabitants thereof respectively, provided that such restriction shall not extend so far as to prevent the removal of property imported into any state, to any other state, of which the Owner is an inhabitant; provided also that no imposition, duties or restriction shall be laid by any state, on the property of the united states, or either of them.

If any Person guilty of, or charged with treason, felony, or other high misdemeanor in any state, shall flee from Justice, and be found in any of the united states, he shall, upon demand of the Governor or executive power, of the state from which he fled, be delivered up and removed to the state having jurisdiction of his offence.

Full faith and credit shall be given in each of these states to the records, acts and judicial proceedings of the courts and magistrates of every other state.

ARTICLE V. For the more convenient management of the general interests of the united states, delegates shall be annually appointed in such manner as the legislature of each state shall direct, to meet in Congress on the first Monday in November, in every year, with a power reserved to each state, to recal its delegates, or any of them, at any time within the year, and to send others in their stead, for the remainder of the Year.

No state shall be represented in Congress by less than two, nor by more than seven Members; and no person shall be capable of being a delegate for more than three years in any term of six years; nor shall any person, being a delegate, be capable of holding any office under the united states, for which he, or another for his benefit receives any salary, fees or emolument of any kind.

Each state shall maintain its own delegates in a meeting of the states, and while they act as members of the committee of the states.

In determining questions in the united states in Congress assembled, each state shall have one vote.

Freedom of speech and debate in Congress shall not be impeached or questioned in any Court, or place out of Congress, and the members of congress shall be protected in their persons from arrests and imprisonments, during the time of their going to and from, and attendance on congress, except for treason, felony, or breach of the peace.

ARTICLE VI. No state, without the Consent of the united states in congress assembled, shall send any embassy to, or receive any embassy from, or enter into any conference, agreement, alliance or treaty with any King prince or state; nor shall any person holding any office of profit or trust under the united states, or any of them, accept of any present, emolument, office or title of any kind whatever from any king, prince or foreign state; nor shall the united states in congress assembled, or any of them, grant any title of nobility.

No two or more states shall enter into any treaty, confederation or alliance whatever between them, without the consent of the united states in congress assembled, specifying accurately the purposes for which the same is to be entered into, and how long it shall continue.

No state shall lay any imposts or duties, which may interfere with any stipulations in treaties, entered into by the united states in congress assembled, with any king, prince or state, in pursuance of any treaties already proposed by congress, to the courts of France and Spain.

No vessels of war shall be kept up in time of peace by any state, except such number only, as shall be deemed necessary by the united states in congress assembled, for the defence of such state, or its trade; nor shall any body of forces be kept up by any state, in time of peace, except such number only, as in the judgment of the united states, in congress assembled, shall be deemed requisite to garrison the forts necessary for the defence of such state; but every state shall always keep up a well regulated and disciplined militia, sufficiently armed and accoutred, and shall provide and constantly have ready for use, in public stores, a due number of field pieces and tents, and a proper quantity of arms, ammunition and camp equipage.

No state shall engage in any war without the consent of the united states in congress assembled, unless such state be actually invaded by enemies, or shall have received certain advice of a resolution being formed by some nation of Indians to invade such state, and the danger is so imminent as not to admit of a delay till the united states in congress assembled can be consulted: nor shall any state grant commissions to any ships or vessels of war, nor letters of marque or reprisal, except it be after a declaration of war by the united states in congress assembled, and then only against the kingdom or state and the subjects thereof, against which war has been so declared, and under such regulations as shall be established by the united states in congress assembled, unless such state be infested by pirates, in which case vessels of war may be fitted out for that occasion, and kept so long as the danger shall continue, or until the united states in congress assembled, shall determine otherwise.

ARTICLE VII. When land-forces are raised by any state for the common defence, all officers of or under the rank of colonel, shall be appointed by the legislature of each state respectively, by whom such forces shall be raised, or in such manner as such state shall direct, and all vacancies shall be filled up by the State which first made the appointment.

ARTICLE VIII. All charges of war, and all other expences that shall be incurred for the common defence or general welfare, and allowed by the united states in congress assembled, shall be defrayed out of a common treasury, which shall be supplied by the several states in proportion to the value of all land within each state, granted to or surveyed for any Person, as such land and the buildings and improvements thereon shall be estimated according to such mode as the united states in congress assembled, shall from time to time direct and appoint.

The taxes for paying that proportion shall be laid and levied by the authority and direction of the legislatures of the several states within the time agreed upon by the united states in congress assembled.

ARTICLE IX. The united states in congress assembled, shall have the sole and exclusive right and power of determining on peace and war, except in the cases mentioned in the sixth article—of sending and receiving ambassadors—entering into treaties and alliances, provided that no treaty of commerce shall be made whereby the legislative power of the respective states shall be restrained from imposing such imposts and duties on foreigners as their own people are subjected to, or from prohibiting the exportation or importation of any species of goods or commodities, whatsoever—of establishing rules for deciding in all cases, what captures on land or water shall be legal, and in what manner prizes taken by land or naval forces in the service of the united states shall be divided or appropriated—of granting letters of marque and reprisal in times of peace—appointing courts for the trial of piracies and felonies committed on the high seas and establishing courts for receiving and determining finally appeals in all cases of captures, provided that no member of congress shall be appointed a judge of any of the said courts.

The united states in congress assembled shall also be the last resort on appeal in all disputes and differences now subsisting or that hereafter may arise between two or more states concerning boundary, jurisdiction or any other cause whatever; which authority shall always be exercised in the manner following. Whenever the legislative or executive authority or lawful agent of any state in controversy with another shall present a petition to congress stating the matter in question and praying for a hearing, notice thereof shall be given by order of congress to the legislative or executive authority of the other state in controversy, and a day assigned for the appearance of the parties by their lawful agents, who shall then be directed to appoint by joint consent, commissioners or judges to constitute a court for hearing and determining the matter in question: but if they cannot agree, congress shall name three persons out of each of the united states, and from the list of such persons each party shall alternately strike out one, the petitioners beginning, until the number shall be reduced to thirteen; and from that number not less than seven, nor more than nine names as congress shall direct, shall in the presence of congress be drawn out by lot, and the persons whose names shall be so drawn or any five of them, shall be commissioners or judges, to hear and finally determine the controversy, so always as a major part of the judges who shall hear the cause shall agree in the determination: and if either party shall neglect to attend at the day appointed, without showing reasons, which congress shall judge sufficient, or being present shall refuse to strike, the congress shall proceed to nominate three persons out of each state, and the secretary of congress shall strike in behalf of such party absent or refusing; and the judgment and sentence of the court to be appointed, in the manner before prescribed, shall be final and conclusive; and if any of the parties shall refuse to submit to the authority of such court, or to appear or defend their claim or cause, the court shall nevertheless proceed to pronounce sentence, or judgment, which shall in like manner be final and decisive, the judgment or sentence and other proceedings being in either case transmitted to congress, and lodged among the acts of congress for the security of the parties concerned: provided that every commissioner, before he sits in judgment, shall take an oath to be administered by one of the judges of the supreme or superior court of the state, where the cause shall be tried, "well and truly to hear and determine the matter in question, according to the best of his judgment, without favour, affection or hope of reward:" provided also, that no state shall be deprived of territory for the benefit of the united states.

All controversies concerning the private right of soil claimed under different grants of two or more states, whose jurisdictions as they may respect such lands, and the states which passed such grants are adjusted, the said grants or either of them being at the same time claimed to have originated antecedent to such settlement of jurisdiction, shall on the petition of either party to the congress of the united states, be finally determined as near as may be in the same manner as is before prescribed for deciding disputes respecting territorial jurisdiction between different states.

The united states in congress assembled shall also have the sole and exclusive right and power of regulating the alloy and value of coin struck by their own authority, or by that of the respective states—fixing the standard of weights and measures throughout the united states—regulating the trade and managing all affairs with the Indians, not members of any of the states, provided that the legislative right of any state within its own limits be not infringed or violated—establishing or regulating post-offices from one state to another, throughout all the united states, and exacting such postage on the papers passing thro' the same as may be requisite to defray the expences of the said office—appointing all officers of the land forces, in the service of the united states, excepting regimental officers—appointing all the officers of the naval forces, and commissioning all officers whatever in the service of the united states—making rules for the government and regulation of the said land and naval forces, and directing their operations.

The united states in congress assembled shall have authority to appoint a committee, to sit in the recess of congress, to be denominated "A Committee of the States," and to consist of one delegate from each state; and to appoint such other committees and civil officers as may be necessary for managing the general affairs of the united states under their direction—to appoint one of their number to preside, provided that no person be allowed to serve in the office of president more than one year in any term of three years; to ascertain the necessary sums of money to be raised for the service of the united states, and to appropriate and apply the same for defraying the public expenses—to borrow money, or emit bills on the credit of the united states, transmitting every half year to the respective states an account of the sums of money so borrowed or emitted,—to build and equip a navy—to agree upon the number of land forces, and to make requisitions from each state for its quota, in proportion to the number of white inhabitants in such state; which requisition shall be binding, and thereupon the legislature of each state shall appoint the regimental officers, raise the men and cloath, arm and equip them in a soldier like manner, at the expence of the united states; and the officers and men so cloathed, armed and equipped shall march to the place appointed, and within the time agreed on by the united states in congress assembled: But if the united states in congress assembled shall, on consideration of circumstances judge proper that any state should not raise men, or should raise a smaller number than its quota, and that any other state should raise a greater number of men than the quota thereof, such extra number shall be raised, officered, cloathed, armed and equipped in the same manner as the quota of such state, unless the legislature of such state shall judge that such extra number cannot be safely spared out of the same, in which case they shall raise officer, cloath, arm and equip as many of such extra number as they judge can be safely spared. And the officers and men so cloathed, armed and equipped, shall march to the place appointed, and within the time agreed on by the united states in congress assembled.

The united states in congress assembled shall never engage in a war, nor grant letters of marque and reprisal in time of peace, nor enter into any treaties or alliances, nor coin money, nor regulate the value thereof, nor ascertain the sums and expences necessary for the defence and welfare of the united states, or any of them, nor emit bills, nor borrow money on the credit of the united states, nor appropriate money, nor agree upon the number of vessels of war, to be built or purchased, or the number of land or sea forces to be raised, nor appoint a commander in chief of the army or navy, unless nine states assent to the same: nor shall a question on any other point, except for adjourning from day to day be determined, unless by the votes of a majority of the united states in congress assembled.

The congress of the united states shall have power to adjourn to any time within the year, and to any place within the united states, so that no period of adjournment be for a longer duration than the space of six Months, and shall publish the Journal of their proceedings monthly, except such parts thereof relating to treaties, alliances or military operations, as in their judgment require secrecy; and the yeas and nays of the delegates of each state on any question shall be entered on the Journal, when it is desired by any delegate; and the delegates of a state, or any of them, at his or their request shall be furnished with a transcript of the said Journal, except such parts as are above excepted, to lay before the legislatures of the several states.

ARTICLE X. The committee of the states, or any nine of them, shall be authorized to execute, in the recess of congress, such of the powers of congress as the united states in congress assembled, by the consent of nine states, shall from time to time think expedient to vest them with; provided that no power be delegated to the said committee, for the exercise of which, by the articles of confederation, the voice of nine states in the congress of the united states assembled is requisite.

ARTICLE XI. Canada acceding to this confederation, and joining in the measures of the united states, shall be admitted into, and entitled to all the advantages of this union: but no other colony shall be admitted into the same, unless such admission be agreed to by nine states.

ARTICLE XII. All bills of credit emitted, monies borrowed and debts contracted by, or under the authority of congress, before the assembling of the united states, in pursuance of the present confederation, shall be deemed and considered as a charge against the united states, for payment and satisfaction whereof the said united states, and the public faith are hereby solemnly pledged.

ARTICLE XIII. Every state shall abide by the determinations of the united states in congress assembled, on all questions which by this confederation are submitted to them. And the Articles of this confederation shall be inviolably observed by every state, and the union shall be perpetual; nor shall any alteration at any time hereafter be made in any of them; unless such alteration be agreed to in a congress of the united states, and be afterwards confirmed by the legislatures of every state.

And Whereas it hath pleased the Great Governor of the World to incline the hearts of the legislatures we respectively represent in congress, to approve of, and to authorize us to ratify the said articles of confederation and perpetual union. Know Ye that we the undersigned delegates, by virtue of the power and authority to us given for that purpose, do by these presents, in the name and in behalf of our respective constituents, fully and entirely ratify and confirm each and every of the said articles of confederation and perpetual union, and all and singular the matters and things therein contained: And we do further solemnly plight and engage the faith of our respective constituents, that they shall abide by the determinations of the united states in congress assembled, on all questions, which by the said confederation are submitted to them. And that the articles thereof shall be inviolably observed by the states we respectively represent, and that the union shall be perpetual. In Witness whereof we have hereunto set our hands in Congress. Done at Philadelphia in the state of Pennsylvania the ninth day of July, in the Year of our Lord one Thousand seven Hundred and Seventy-eight, and in the third year of the independence of America.

Josiah Bartlett, John Wentworth, junr August 8th, 1778,	On the part & behalf of the State of New Hampshire.
John Hancock, Samuel Adams, Elbridge Gerry, Francis Dana, James Lovell, Samuel Holten,	On the part and behalf of the State of Massachusetts Bay.
William Ellery, Henry Marchant, John Collins,	On the part and behalf of the State of Rhode-Island and Providence Plantations.
Roger Sherman, Samuel Huntington, Oliver Wolcott, Titus Hosmer, Andrew Adams,	On the part and behalf of the State of Connecticut.
Jas Duane, Fra: Lewis, Wm Duer, Gouvr Morris,	On the part and behalf of the State of New York.
Jno Witherspoon, Nathl Scudder,	On the Part and in Behalf of the State of New Jersey, November 26th, 1778.
Robert Morris, Daniel Roberdeau, Jon. Bayard Smith, William Clingar, Joseph Reed, 22d July, 1778,	On the part and behalf of the State of Pennsylvania.

Thos McKean,
   Febr 22d, 1779,
John Dickinson,
   May 5th, 1779,
Nicholas Van Dyke,
	On the part &
	behalf of the
	State of
	Delaware.

John Hanson, March 1, 1781, Daniel Carroll, do	On the part and behalf of the State of Maryland.
Richard Henry Lee, John Banister, Thomas Adams, Jno Harvie, Francis Lightfoot Lee,	On the Part and Behalf of the State of Virginia.

John Penn, July 21st, 1778, Corns Harnett, Jno Williams,	}	On the part and behalf of the State of North Carolina.
Henry Laurens, William Henry Drayton, Jno Mathews, Richd Hutson, Thos Heyward, junr.	}	On the part and on behalf of the State of South Carolina.
Jno Walton, 24th July, 1778, Edwd Telfair, Edwd Langworthy,	}	On the part and behalf of the State of Georgia

Source: Worthington C. Ford, ed., *Journals of the Continental Congress, 1774–1789,* Vol. 19 (Washington, D.C.: U.S. Government Printing Office, 1904), pp. 214–20.

DOCUMENT 27: Circular Letter to the State Governors (George Washington, June 8, 1783)

George Washington, the great general and hero of the American War of Independence, worried about the future of the Confederation for which he had successfully fought. Thus, as one of his last actions as commander of the United States Army, General Washington wrote a letter to the governors of the thirteen states to warn them about defects of the Articles of Confederation and the dire consequences that could result from failure to repair the flaws in government. According to Washington, there was a great need to increase the powers and duties of the central government in relationship to the state governments. He believed the very existence of the United States was at risk.

What recommendations did Washington make for repairing the defects in government? What negative consequences did he predict, unless the problems of government were quickly solved?

. . . There are four things, which I humbly conceive, are essential to the well being, I may even venture to say, to the existence of the United States as an Independent Power:

1st. An indissoluble Union of the States under one Federal Head.

2dly. A Sacred regard to Public Justice.

3dly. The adoption of a proper Peace Establishment, and

4thly. The prevalence of that pacific and friendly Disposition, among the People of the United States, which will induce them to forget their local prejudices and policies, to make those mutual concessions which are requisite to the general prosperity, and in some instances, to sacrifice their individual advantages to the interest of the Community.

These are the Pillars on which the glorious Fabrick of our Independency and National Character must be supported; Liberty is the Basis, and whoever would dare to sap the foundation, or overturn the Structure, under whatever specious pretexts he may attempt it, will merit the bitterest execration, and the severest punishment which can be inflicted by his injured Country.

On the three first Articles I will make a few observations, leaving the last to the good sense and serious consideration of those immediately concerned.

Under the first head, altho' it may not be necessary or proper for me in this place to enter into a particular disquisition of the principles of the Union, and to take up the great question which has been frequently agitated, whether it be expedient and requisite for the States to delegate a larger proportion of Power to Congress, or not, Yet it will be a part of my duty, and that of every true Patriot, to assert without reserve, and to insist upon the following positions, That unless the States will suffer Congress to exercise those prerogatives, they are undoubtedly invested with by the Constitution, every thing must very rapidly tend to Anarchy and confusion, That it is indispensable to the happiness of the individual States, that there should be lodged somewhere, a Supreme Power to regulate and govern the general concerns of the Confederated Republic, without which the Union cannot be of long duration. That there must be a faithfull and pointed compliance on the part of every State, with the late proposals and demands of Congress, or the most fatal consequences will ensue, That whatever measures have a tendency to dissolve the Union, or contribute to violate or lessen the Sovereign Authority, ought to be considered as hostile to the Liberty and Independency of America, and the Authors of them treated accordingly, and lastly, that unless we can be enabled by the concurrence of the States, to participate of the fruits of the Revolution, and enjoy the essential benefits of Civil Society, under a form of Government so free and uncorrupted, so happily guarded against the danger of oppression, as has been devised and adopted by the Articles of Confederation, it will be a subject of regret, that so much blood and treasure have been lavished for no purpose, that so many sufferings have been encountered without a compensation, and that so many sacrifices have been made in vain. Many other considerations might here be adduced to prove, that without an entire conformity to the Spirit of the Union, we cannot exist as an Independent Power; it will be sufficient for my purpose to mention but one or two which seem to me of the greatest importance. It is only in our united Character as an Empire, that our Independence is acknowledged, that our power can be regarded, or our Credit supported among Foreign Nations. The Treaties of the European Powers with the United States of America, will have no validity on a dissolution of the Union. We shall be left nearly in a state of Nature, or we may find by our own unhappy experience, that there is a natural and necessary progression, from the extreme of anarchy to the extreme of Tyranny; and that arbitrary power is most easily established on the ruins of Liberty abused to licentiousness.

Source: John C. Fitzpatrick, ed., *The Writings of George Washington from the Original Manuscript Sources, 1745–1799*, Vol. 26 (Washington, D.C.: U.S. Government Printing Office, 1931), pp. 483–96.

DOCUMENT 28: Letter to Samuel Adams (Richard Henry Lee, March 14, 1785)

Richard Henry Lee of Virginia, president (presiding officer) of the Congress in 1785, had served in the Continental Congress from its inception in 1784 and drafted the Resolution for Independence enacted on July 2, 1776. He was strongly committed to the success of the union of states and consistently warned against immediate revision or reconstruction of the Articles of Confederation proposed by its severe critics. Lee feared that granting more power to the central government would put liberties of the people at risk. In this letter to Samuel Adams, the great revolutionary leader of Massachusetts, Lee defended the status quo.

Why did Lee oppose fundamental revision of the Articles of Confederation? Compare his views in this letter to those of George Washington in Document 27. How and why does he differ from Washington on the issue of revising the Articles of Confederation?

The selfishness and corruption of Europe I have no doubt about, and therefore wish most sincerely that our free Republics may not suffer themselves to be changed and wrongly wrought upon by the corrupt maxims of policy that pervade European Councils—where artful and refined plausibility is forever called in to aid the most pernicious designs. It would seem as if there were a general jealousy beyond the water, of the powerful effects to be derived from Republican virtue here, and so we hear a constant cry from thence, echoed & reechoed here by all Expectants from the Treasury of the United States—That Congress must have more power—That we cannot be secure & happy until Congress command implicitly both purse & sword. So that our confederation must be perpetually changing to answer sinister views in the greater part, until every fence is thrown down that was designed to protect & cover the rights of Mankind. It is a melancholy consideration that many wise & good men have, some how or other, fallen in with these ruinous opinions. I think Sir that the first maxim of a man who loves liberty should be, never to grant to Rulers an atom of power that is not most clearly & indispensably necessary for the safety and well being of Society. To say that these Rulers are revocable, and holding their places during pleasure may not be supposed to design evil for self-aggrandizement, is affirming what I cannot easily admit. Look to history and see how often the liberties of mankind have been opressed & ruined by the same delusive hopes & falacious reasoning. The fact is, that power poisons the mind of its possessor and aids him to remove the shackles that restrain itself. To be sure, all things human must partake of human infirmity, and therefore the Confederation should not be presumptuously called an infallible system for all times and all situations—but tho' this is true, yet as it is a great and fundamental system of Union & Security, no change should be admitted until proved to be necessary by the fairest fullest & most mature experience. . . . But happily for us, our political disease admits of simple remedies for its cure, if rightly judged of, and wisely practised upon. Let it be therefore the effort of every Patriot to encourage a punctual payment of each State's quota of the foederal demand, and let the money be found in ways most agreable to the circumstances of every State. This is the plan of the Confederation, and this I own will be mine, until more satisfactory experience has proved its inefficacy.

Source: James Curtis Ballagh, ed., *The Letters of Richard Henry Lee,* Vol. 2 (New York: Macmillan, 1911), pp. 343–45.

DOCUMENT 29: Letter to George Washington (John Jay, June 27, 1786)

John Jay of New York had served in the Continental Congress and was convinced of its fundamental flaws, which, if not corrected, would destroy the United States. His concerns were heightened by outbreaks of political unrest in the states. Jay expressed his concerns to George Washington of Virginia, the great hero and general of the American War of Independence. Jay wanted a federal government strong enough to maintain order and secure the rights of individuals to property and liberty. According to Jay, what were the potentially fatal flaws of the Articles of Confederation? What should be done to correct them?

To OPPOSE POPULAR PREJUDICES, to censure the proceedings, and expose the improprieties of states is an unpleasant task, but it must be done. Our affairs seem to lead to some crisis, some revolution—something that I cannot foresee or conjecture. I am uneasy and apprehensive; more so than during the war. Then we had a fixed object, and though the means and time of obtaining it were often problematical, yet I did firmly believe we should ultimately succeed, because I was convinced that justice was with us. The case is now altered; we are going and doing wrong, and therefore I look forward to evils and calamities, but without being able to guess at the instrument, nature, or measure of them.

That we shall again recover and things again go well, I have no doubt. Such a variety of circumstances would not, almost miraculously, have combined to liberate and make us a nation for transient and unimportant purposes. I therefore believe that we are yet to become a great and respectable people; but when or how, the spirit of prophecy can only discern.

There doubtless is much reason to think and to say that we are woefully and, in many instances, wickedly misled. Private rage for property suppresses public considerations, and personal rather than national interests have become the great objects of attention. Representative bodies will ever be faithful copies of their originals, and generally exhibit a checkered assemblage of virtue and vice, of abilities and weakness.

The mass of men are neither wise nor good, and the virtue like the other resources of a country can only be drawn to a point and exerted by strong circumstances ably managed, or a strong government ably administered. New governments have not the aid of habit and hereditary respect, and being generally the result of preceding tumult and confusion, do not immediately acquire stability or strength. Besides, in times of commotion, some men will gain confidence and importance, who merit neither, and who, like political mountebanks, are less solicitous about the health of the credulous crowd than about making the most of their nostrums and prescriptions.

New York was rendered less federal by the opinions of the late president of Congress. This is a singular though not unaccountable fact—indeed, human actions are seldom inexplicable.

What I most fear is that the better kind of people, by which I mean the people who are orderly and industrious, who are content with their situations and not uneasy in their circumstances, will be led by the insecurity of property, the loss of confidence in their rulers, and the want of public faith and rectitude to consider the charms of liberty as imaginary and delusive. A state of fluctuation and uncertainty must disgust and alarm such men, and prepare their minds for almost any change that may promise them quiet and security.

Source: Henry P. Johnston, ed., *The Correspondence and Public Papers of John Jay,* Vol. 3 (New York: G. P. Putnam's Sons, 1890), pp. 203–5.

DOCUMENT 30: Letter to John Jay (George Washington, August 1, 1786)

George Washington responded to John Jay's letter (see Document 29) from his home at Mount Vernon in Virginia. Washington agreed with Jay. He, too, feared the imminent possibility of disunion and disorder, unless effective powers were granted to a central government that could enforce social order and secure personal liberty. What reasons did he provide in support of his views? Compare Washington's views with those of Lee (see Document 28). To what extent did he agree or disagree with Lee's views?

... Your sentiments, that our affairs are drawing rapidly to a crisis, accord with my own. What the event will be is also beyond the reach of my foresight. We have errors to correct. We have probably had too good an opinion of human nature in forming our confederation. Experience has taught us that men will not adopt and carry into execution measures the best calculated for their own good without the intervention of a coercive power. I do not conceive we can exist long as a nation without having lodged somewhere a power which will pervade the whole Union in as energetic a manner as the authority of the state governments extends over the several states.

To be fearful of investing Congress, constituted as that body is, with ample authorities for national purposes appears to me the very climax of popular absurdity and madness. Could Congress exert them for the detriment of the public without injuring themselves in an equal or greater proportion? Are not their interests inseparably connected with those of their constituents? By the rotation of appointment, must they not mingle frequently with the mass of citizens? Is it not rather to be apprehended, if they were possessed of the powers before described, that the individual members would be induced to use them, on many occasions, very timidly and inefficaciously for fear of losing their popularity and future election? We must take human nature as we find it. Perfection falls not to the share of mortals.

Many are of opinion that Congress have too frequently made use of the suppliant, humble tone of requisition in applications to the states, when they had a right to assert their imperial dignity and command obedience. Be that as it may, requisitions are a perfect nullity where thirteen sovereign, independent, disunited states are in the habit of discussing and refusing compliance with them at their option. Requisitions are actually little better than a jest and a by-word throughout the land. If you tell the legislatures they have violated the treaty of peace and invaded the prerogatives of the confederacy, they will laugh in your face. What then is to be done? Things cannot go on in the same train forever. It is much to be feared, as you observe, that the better kind of people, being disgusted with the circumstances, will have their minds prepared for any revolution whatever. We are apt to run from one extreme into another. To anticipate and prevent disastrous contingencies would be the part of wisdom and patriotism.

What astonishing changes a few years are capable of producing. I am told that even respectable characters speak of a monarchical form of government without horror. From thinking proceeds speaking; thence to acting is often but a single step. But how irrevocable and tremendous! What a triumph for our enemies to verify their predictions! What a triumph for the advocates of despotism to find that we are incapable of governing ourselves, and that systems founded on the basis of equal liberty are merely ideal and fallacious! Would to God that wise measures may be taken in time to avert the consequences we have but too much reason to apprehend.

Retired as I am from the world, I frankly acknowledge I cannot feel myself an unconcerned spectator. Yet, having happily assisted in bringing the ship into port, and having been fairly discharged, it is not my business to embark again on a sea of troubles. Nor could it be expected that my sentiments and opinions would have much weight on the minds of my countrymen. They have been neglected, though given as a last legacy in the most solemn manner. I had then perhaps some claims to public attention. I consider myself as having none at present.

Source: Jared Sparks, ed., *The Writings of George Washington,* Vol. 9 (Boston: American Stationers' Co., 1837), pp. 187 89.

DOCUMENT 31: Proceedings of the State Commissioners at Annapolis, Maryland (September 11–14, 1786)

James Madison, a representative to Congress from Virginia, persuaded his state legislature to call for a convention of the thirteen states to discuss common problems of interstate commerce and revisions of the Articles of Confederation to overcome these problems and others related to them. However, only five states sent delegates to attend this meeting: New York, New Jersey, Pennsylvania, Delaware, and Virginia. Disappointed at the turnout, Madison and others at this Annapolis Convention decided to issue a report on the need to improve the government of the United States. This report, drafted by Alexander Hamilton of New York, proposed that another convention of the states should be held for the purpose of revising the Articles of Confederation. Congress approved this proposal and called for a convention of the states at Philadelphia in May 1787.

In this report, Hamilton expressed strong concerns about weaknesses in government affecting the United States. What other criticisms of the Articles of Confederation did Hamilton express in this report? Compare the criticisms of the Articles in this document with those presented by Washington in Document 27. What were the similarities or differences of the criticisms discussed in these two documents?

Annapolis in the State of Maryland September 11th. 1786.
At a meeting of Commissioners from the States of New York, New Jersey Pennsylvania, Delaware and Virginia— . . .

Mr. Dickinson was unanimously elected Chairman.

The Commissioners produced their Credentials from their respective States: which were read.

After a full communication of Sentiments, and deliberate consideration of what would be proper to be done by the Commissioners now assembled it was unanimously agreed, that a Committee be appointed to prepare a draft of a Report to be made to the States having Commissioners— attending at this meeting— . . .

That the express terms of the powers to your Commissioners supposing a deputation from all the States, and having for object the Trade and commerce of the United States, Your Commissioners did not conceive it advisable to proceed on the business of their mission, under the Circumstance of so partial and defective a representation.

Deeply impressed however with the magnitude and importance of the object confided to them on this occasion, Your Commissioners cannot forbear to indulge an expression of their earnest and unanimous wish. that speedy measures may be taken, to effect a general meeting, of the States, in a future Convention, for the same, and such other purposes, as the situation of public affairs, may be found to require.

If in expressing this wish or in intimating any other sentiment, Your Commissioners should seem to exceed the strict bounds of their appointment, they entertain a full confidence, that a conduct, dictated by an anxiety for the welfare, of the United States, will not fail to receive an indulgent construction.

In this persuasion, Your Commissioners submit an opinion, that the Idea of extending the powers of their Deputies, to other objects than those of Commerce which has been adopted by the State of New Jersey, was an improvement on the original plan, and will deserve to be incorporated into that of a future Convention, they are the more naturally led to this conclusion, as in the course of their reflections on the subject, they have been induced to think, that the power of regulating trade is of such comprehensive extent, and will enter so far into the general System of the foederal government, that to give it efficacy, and to obviate questions and doubts concerning its precise nature and limits may require a correspondent adjustment of other parts of the Foederal System.

That there are important defects in the system of the Foederal Government is acknowledged by the Acts of all those States, which have concurred in the present Meeting; That the defects, upon a closer examination, may be found greater and more numerous, than even these acts imply, is at least so far probable, from the embarrassments which characterise the present State of our national affairs—foreign and domestic, as may reasonably be supposed to merit a deliberate and candid discussion, in some mode, which will unite the Sentiments and Councils of all the States. In the choice of the mode your Commissioners are of opinion,—that a Convention of Deputies from the different States, for the special and sole purpose of entering into this investigation and digesting a plan for supplying such defects as may be discovered to exist, will be entitled to a preference from considerations which will occur, without being particularised.

Your Commissioners decline an enumeration of those national circumstances on which their opinion respecting the propriety of a future Convention with more enlarged powers, is founded; as it would be an useless intrusion of facts and observations, most of which have been frequently the subject of public discussion, and none of which can have escaped the penetration of those to whom they would in this instance be addressed. They are however of a nature so serious, as, in the view of your Commissioners to render the situation of the United States delicate and critical, calling for an exertion of the united virtue and wisdom of all the members of the Confederacy.

Under this impression, Your Commissioners, with the most respectful deference, beg leave to suggest their unanimous conviction, that it may essentially tend to advance the interests of the union, if the States, by whom they have been respectively delegated, would themselves concur, and use their endeavours to procure the concurrence of the other States, in the appointment of Commissioners, to meet at Philadelphia on the second Monday in May next, to take into consideration the situation of the United States, to devise such further provisions as shall appear to them necessary to render the constitution of the Foederal Government adequate to the exigencies of the Union; and to report such an Act for that purpose to the United States in Congress Assembled, as when agreed to, by them, and afterwards confirmed by the Legislatures of every State will effectually provide for the same.

Though your Commissioners could not with propriety—address these observations and sentiments to any but the states they have the honor to Represent, they have nevertheless concluded from motives of respect, to transmit Copies of this report to the United States in Congress assembled, and to the executives of the other States.

By order of the Commissioners

Dated at Annapolis
September 14th, 1786

Source: Jonathan Elliot, ed., *The Debates in the Several State Conventions on the Adoption of the Federal Constitution*, Vol. 1 (Philadelphia: J. B. Lippincott, 1881), pp. 116–19.

DOCUMENT 32: Letter to Edward Carrington (Thomas Jefferson, January 16, 1787)

Thomas Jefferson was in Paris, representing the United States to the government of France, when he heard about Shays's Rebellion in Massachusetts (see Introduction to Part IV). Unlike John Jay and George Washington (see Documents 29 and 30), Jefferson was not particularly alarmed about popular unrest in the states. He presented his views about the people and government in this letter to a friend in Virginia. What did Jefferson think is more important, public order or the right of the people to protest, even in error? What did Jefferson say about the freedom of the press and the right of people to freely read newspapers? To what extent do you agree with Jefferson's views?

... The Tumults in America I expected would have produced in Europe an unfavorable opinion of our political state. But it has not. On the contrary, the small effect of these tumults seems to have given more confidence in the firmness of our governments. The interposition of the people themselves on the side of government has had a great effect on the opinion here. I am persuaded myself that the good sense of the people will always be found to be the best army. They may be led astray for a moment, but will soon correct themselves.

The people are the only censors of their governors; and even their errors will tend to keep these to the true principles of their institution. To punish these errors too severely would be to suppress the only safeguard of the public liberty. The way to prevent these irregular interpositions of the people is to give them full information of their affairs through the channel of the public papers, and to contrive that those papers should penetrate the whole mass of the people. The basis of our governments being the opinion of the people, the very first object should be to keep that right; and were it left to me to decide whether we should have a government without newspapers, or newspapers without a government, I should not hesitate a moment to prefer the latter. But I should mean that every man should receive those papers, and be capable of reading them.

I am convinced that those societies (as the Indians) which live without government enjoy in their general mass an infinitely greater degree of happiness than those who live under the European governments. Among the former, public opinion is in the place of law, and restrains morals as powerfully as laws ever did anywhere. Among the latter, under pretense of governing, they have divided their nations into two classes, wolves and sheep. I do not exaggerate.

This is a true picture of Europe. Cherish, therefore, the spirit of our people, and keep alive their intention. Do not be too severe upon their errors, but reclaim them by enlightening them. If once they become inattentive to the public affairs, you and I, and Congress and assemblies, judges and governors shall all become wolves. It seems to be the law of our general nature, in spite of individual exceptions; and experience declares that man is the only animal which devours his own kind; for I can apply no milder term to the governments of Europe, and to the general prey of the rich on the poor.

Source: Paul L. Ford, ed., *The Writings of Thomas Jefferson,* Vol. 4 (New York: G. P. Putnam's Sons, 1894), pp. 357–58.

DOCUMENT 33: Letter to James Madison (Thomas Jefferson, January 30, 1787)

Shortly after writing from Paris to Edward Carrington, Jefferson sent a letter to his friend and neighbor in Virginia, James Madison. He offered his views of Shays's Rebellion (see Introduction to Part IV), and rebellion in general, to Madison. Jefferson believed in participation by the people in the affairs of their government as the best means to check abuses of power by governors. He supported public protests as a way to prevent abuses of power and to protect liberty. Thus, popular uprisings, such as Shays's Rebellion, did not appear to disturb him, as it vexed some American leaders.

What good did Jefferson see coming out of rebellion? How does his response to political disorder and rebellion differ from the views of Jay and Washington (see Documents 29 and 30)? To what extent do you agree with Jefferson's views on rebellion?

. . . I am impatient to learn your sentiments on the late troubles in the Eastern states. So far as I have yet seen, they do not appear to threaten serious consequences. Those states have suffered by the stoppage of the channels of their commerce, which have not yet found other issues. This must render money scarce, and make the people uneasy. This uneasiness has produced acts absolutely unjustifiable: but I hope they will provoke no severities from their governments. A consciousness of those in power that their administration of the public affairs has been honest, may perhaps produce too great a degree of indignation: and those characters wherein fear predominates over hope may apprehend too much from these instances of irregularity. They may conclude too hastily that nature has formed man insusceptible of any other government but that of force, a conclusion not founded in truth, nor experience. Societies exist under three forms sufficiently distinguishable. 1. Without government, as among our Indians. 2. Under governments wherein the will of every one has a just influence, as is the case in England in a slight degree, and in our states in a great one. 3. Under governments of force: as is the case in all other monarchies and in most of the other republics. To have an idea of the curse of existence under these last, they must be seen. It is a government of wolves over sheep. It is a problem, not clear in my mind, that the 1st. condition is not the best. But I believe it to be inconsistent with any great degree of population. The second state has a great deal of good in it. The mass of mankind under that enjoys a precious degree of liberty and happiness. It has it's evils too: the principal of which is the turbulence to which it is subject. But weigh this against the oppressions of monarchy, and it becomes nothing. *Malo periculosam, libertatem quam quietam servitutem.* Even this evil is productive of good. It prevents the degeneracy of government, and nourishes a general attention to the public affairs. I hold it that a little rebellion now and then is a good thing, and as necessary in the political world as storms in the physical. Unsuccessful rebellions indeed generally establish the incroachments on the rights of the people which have produced them. An observation of this truth should render honest republican governors so mild in their punishment of rebellions, as not to discourage them too much. It is a medecine necessary for the sound health of government. . . .

Source: Paul L. Ford, ed., *The Writings of Thomas Jefferson,* Vol. 4 (New York: G. P. Putnam's Sons, 1894), pp. 361–62.

DOCUMENT 34: Northwest Ordinance (July 13, 1787)

The last achievement of government under the Articles of Confederation was enactment of the Northwest Ordinance, a plan for government in the territory north and west of the Ohio River. It stipulated that no less than three and no more than five states would be created out of the Northwest Territory.

The Ordinance of 1787 provided a three-stage procedure by which a territory could become a state on equal terms with all other states of the federal union. During stage one, a governor, secretary, and three judges—all appointed by the Congress—would govern the territory. During stage two, when the population surpassed 5,000 adult males, eligible voters (male owners of at least fifty acres of land) would elect representatives to the lower house of the territorial legislature. Main power of the territorial government, during stage two, would be exercised by the executive officials and the upper house of the legislature, a five-member body appointed by the Congress. A territory would enter stage three when its population exceeded 60,000 inhabitants. At this point, the territory could write a state constitution and petition Congress for statehood.

In six Articles of Compact, the Northwest Ordinance guaranteed certain natural rights of individuals, such as free exercise of religion, trial by jury, due process in legal proceedings, and sanctity of contracts. Slavery was prohibited in the territories north and west of the Ohio River. What other rights were guaranteed to individuals by the Northwest Ordinance? Compare the rights guaranteed by the Six Articles of Compact of the Northwest Ordinance with the declarations of rights of such states as Virginia, Pennsylvania, and Massachusetts (see Documents 10, 12, and 14). How are the guarantees of rights in the Northwest Ordinance similar to or different from the declarations of rights of the original thirteen states?

An Ordinance for the government of the
territory of the United States northwest of the river Ohio

Section 1. *Be it ordained by the United States in Congress assembled,* That the said Territory, for the purpose of temporary government, be one district, subject, however, to be divided into two districts, as future circumstances may, in the opinion of Congress, make it expedient.

Sec. 2. *Be it ordained by the authority aforesaid,* That the estates both of resident and non-resident proprietors in the said territory, dying intestate, shall descend to, and be distributed among, their children and the descendants of a deceased child in equal parts....

SEC. 3. *Be it ordained by the authority aforesaid,* That there shall be appointed, from time to time, by Congress, a governor, whose commission shall continue in force for the term of three years, unless sooner revoked by Congress; he shall reside in the district, and have a freehold estate therein, in one thousand acres of land, while in the exercise of his office.

SEC. 4. There shall be appointed from time to time, by Congress, a secretary, whose commission shall continue in force for four years, unless sooner revoked; he shall reside in the district, and have a freehold estate therein, in five hundred acres of land, while in the exercise of his office. It shall be his duty to keep and preserve the acts and laws passed by the legislature, and the public records of the district, and the proceedings of the governor in his executive department, and transmit authentic copies of such acts and proceedings every six months to the Secretary of Congress. There shall also be appointed a court, to consist of three judges, any two of whom to form a court, who shall have a common-law jurisdiction and reside in the district, and have each therein a freehold estate, in five hundred acres of land, while in the exercise of their offices; and their commissions shall continue in force during good behavior.

SEC. 5. The governor and judges, or a majority of them, shall adopt and publish in the district such laws of the original States, criminal and civil, as may be necessary, and best suited to the circumstances of the district, and report them to Congress from time to time, which laws shall be in force in the district until the organization of the general assembly therein, unless disapproved of by Congress; but afterwards the legislature shall have authority to alter them as they shall think fit.

SEC. 6. The governor, for the time being, shall be commander-in-chief of the militia, appoint and commission all officers in the same below the rank of general officers; all general officers shall be appointed and commissioned by Congress.

SEC. 7. Previous to the organization of the general assembly the governor shall appoint such magistrates, and other civil officers, in each county or township, as he shall find necessary for the preservation of the peace and good order in the same. After the general assembly shall be organized the powers and duties of magistrates and other civil officers shall be regulated and defined by the said assembly; but all magistrates and other civil officers, not herein otherwise directed, shall, during the continuance of this temporary government, be appointed by the governor.

SEC. 8. For the prevention of crimes, and injuries, the laws to be adopted or made shall have force in all parts of the district, and for the execution of process, criminal and civil, the governor shall make proper divisions thereof; and he shall proceed, from time to time, as circumstances may require, to lay out the parts of the district in which the Indian titles shall have been extinguished, into counties and townships, subject, however, to such alterations as may thereafter be made by the legislature.

SEC. 9. So soon as there shall be five thousand free male inhabitants, of full age, in the district, upon giving proof thereof to the governor, they shall receive authority, with time and place, to elect representatives from their counties or townships, to represent them in the general assembly: *Provided*, That for every five hundred free male inhabitants there shall be one representative, and so on, progressively, with the number of free male inhabitants, shall the right of representation increase, until the number of representatives shall amount to twenty-five; after which the number and proportion of representatives shall be regulated by the legislature: *Provided*, That no person be eligible or qualified to act as a representative, unless he shall have been a citizen of one of the United States three years, and be a resident in the district, or unless he shall have resided in the district three years; and, in either case, shall likewise hold in his own right, in fee-simple, two hundred acres of land within the same: *Provided also*, That a free-hold in fifty acres of land in the district, having been a citizen of one of the States, and being resident in the district, or the like freehold and two years' residence in the district, shall be necessary to qualify a man as an elector of a representative.

SEC. 10. The representatives thus elected shall serve for the term of two years; and in case of the death of a representative, or removal from office, the governor shall issue a writ to the county or township, for which he was a member, to elect another in his stead, to serve for the residue of the term.

SEC. 11. The general assembly, or legislature, shall consist of the governor, legislative council, and a house of representatives. The legislative council shall consist of five members, to continue in office five years, unless sooner removed by Congress; any three of whom to be a quorum; and the members of the council shall be nominated and appointed in the following manner, to wit: As soon as representatives shall be elected the governor shall appoint a time and place for them to meet together, and when met they shall nominate ten persons, resident in the district, and each possessed of a freehold in five hundred acres of land, and return their names to Congress, five of whom Congress shall appoint and commission to serve as aforesaid; and whenever a vacancy shall happen in the Council, by death or removal from office, the house of representatives shall nominate two persons, qualified as aforesaid, for each vacancy, and return their names to Congress, one of whom Congress shall appoint and commission for the residue of the term; and every five years, four months at least before the expiration of the time of service of the members of the council, the said house shall nominate ten persons, qualified as aforesaid, and return their names to Congress, five of whom Congress shall appoint and commission to serve as members of the council five years, unless sooner removed. And the governor, legislative council, and house of representatives shall have authority to make laws in all cases for the good government of the district, not repugnant to the principles and articles in this ordinance established and declared. And all bills, having passed by a majority in the house, and by a majority in the council, shall be referred to the governor for his assent; but no bill, or legislative act whatever, shall be of any force without his assent. The governor shall have power to convene, prorogue, and dissolve the general assembly when, in his opinion, it shall be expedient.

SEC. 12. The governor, judges, legislative council, secretary, and such other officers as Congress shall appoint in the district, shall take an oath or affirmation of fidelity, and of office; the governor before the President of Congress, and all other officers before the governor. As soon as a legislature shall be formed in the district, the council and house assembled, in one room, shall have authority, by joint ballot, to elect a delegate to Congress, who shall have a seat in Congress, with a right of debating, but not of voting, during this temporary government.

SEC. 13. And for extending the fundamental principles of civil and religious liberty, which form the basis whereon these republics, their laws and constitutions, are erected; to fix and establish those principles as the basis of all laws, constitutions, and governments, which forever hereafter shall be formed in the said territory; to provide, also, for the establishment of States, and permanent government therein, and for their admission to a share in the Federal councils on an equal footing with the original States, at as early periods as may be consistent with the general interest:

SEC. 14. It is hereby ordained and declared, by the authority aforesaid, that the following articles shall be considered as articles of compact, between the original States and the people and States in the said territory, and forever remain unalterable, unless by common consent, to wit:

Article I

No person, demeaning himself in a peaceable and orderly manner, shall ever be molested on account of his mode of worship, or religious sentiments, in the said territory.

Article II

The inhabitants of the said territory shall always be entitled to the benefits of the writs of *habeas corpus,* and of the trial by jury; of a proportionate representation of the people in the legislature, and of judicial proceedings according to the course of the common law. All persons shall be bailable, unless for capital offences, where the proof shall be evident, or the presumption great. All fines shall be moderate; and no cruel or unusual punishment shall be inflicted. No man shall be deprived of his liberty or property, but by the judgment of his peers, or the law of the land, and should the public exigencies make it necessary, for the common preservation, to take any person's property, or to demand his particular services, full compensation shall be made for the same. And, in the just preservation of rights and property, it is understood and declared, that no law ought ever to be made or have force in the said territory, that shall, in any manner whatever, interfere with or affect private contracts, or engagements, *bona fide,* and without fraud previously formed.

Article III

Religion, morality, and knowledge being necessary to good government and the happiness of mankind, schools and the means of education shall forever be encouraged. The utmost good faith shall always be observed towards the Indians; their lands and property shall never be taken from them without their consent; and in their property, rights, and liberty they never shall be invaded or disturbed unless in just and lawful wars authorized by Congress; but laws founded in justice and humanity shall, from time to time, be made, for preventing wrongs being done to them, and for preserving peace and friendship with them.

Article IV

The said territory, and the States which may be formed therein, shall forever remain a part of this confederacy of the United States of America, subject to the articles of Confederation, and to such alterations therein as shall be constitutionally made; and to all the acts and ordinances of the United States in Congress assembled, conformable thereto. The inhabitants and settlers in the said territory shall be subject to pay a part of the Federal debts, contracted, or to be contracted, and a proportional part of the expenses of government to be apportioned on them by Congress, according to the same common rule and measure by which apportionments thereof shall be made on the other States; and the taxes for paying their proportion shall be laid and levied by the authority and direction of the legislatures of the district, or districts, or new States, as in the original States, within the time agreed upon by the United States in Congress assembled. The legislatures of those districts, or new States, shall never interfere with the primary disposal of the soil by the United

States in Congress assembled, nor with any regulations Congress may find necessary for securing the title in such soil to the *bona-fide* purchasers. No tax shall be imposed on lands the property of the United States; and in no case shall non-resident proprietors be taxed higher than residents. The navigable waters leading into the Mississippi and Saint Lawrence, and the carrying places between the same, shall be common highways, and forever free, as well to the inhabitants of the said territory as to the citizens of the United States, and those of any other States that may be admitted into the confederacy, without any tax, impost, or duty therefor.

Article V

There shall be formed in the said territory not less than three nor more than five States. . . . And whenever any of the said States shall have sixty thousand free inhabitants therein, such State shall be admitted by its delegates, into the Congress of the United States, on an equal footing with the original States, in all respects whatever; and shall be at liberty to form a permanent constitution and State government: *Provided,* The constitution and government, so to be formed, shall be republican, and in conformity to the principles contained in these articles, and, so far as it can be consistent with the general interest of the confederacy, such admission shall be allowed at an earlier period, and when there may be a less number of free inhabitants in the State than sixty thousand.

Article VI

There shall be neither slavery nor involuntary servitude in the said territory, otherwise than in the punishment of crimes, whereof the party shall have been duly convicted: *Provided always,* That any person escaping into the same, from whom labor or service is lawfully claimed in any one of the original States, such fugitive may be lawfully reclaimed, and conveyed to the person claiming his or her labor or service as aforesaid.

Be it ordained by the authority aforesaid, That the resolutions of the 23rd of April, 1784, relative to the subject of this ordinance, be, and the same are hereby, repealed, and declared null and void.

Done by the United States, in Congress assembled, the 13th day of July, in the year of our Lord 1787, and of their sovereignty and independence the twelfth.

Source: Worthington C. Ford, ed., *Journals of the Continental Congress, 1774–1789,* Vol. 32 (Washington, D.C.: U.S. Government Printing Office, 1910), pp. 334–43.

FURTHER READING

Burnett, Edmund Cody. *The Continental Congress, 1774–1789*. New York: W. W. Norton and Company, 1964.

Cunningham, Noble E., Jr. *In Pursuit of Reason: The Life of Thomas Jefferson*. Baton Rouge: Louisiana State University Press, 1987.

Jensen, Merrill. *The New Nation: A History of the United States During the Confederation, 1781–1789*. New York: Alfred A. Knopf, 1950.

Morris, Richard B. *The Forging of the Union, 1781–1789*. New York: Harper and Row, 1987.

Morris, Richard B. *The Peacemakers: The Great Powers and American Independence*. New York: Harper and Row, 1983.

Onuf, Peter S., *Statehood and Union: A History of the Northwest Ordinance*. Bloomington: Indiana University Press, 1987.

Rakove, Jack N. *James Madison and the Creation of the American Republic*. Glenview, Ill.: Scott, Foresman/Little, Brown, 1990.

Szatmary, David. *Shays's Rebellion: The Making of an Agrian Insurrection*. Amherst: University of Massachusetts Press, 1980.

Taylor, Robert M., Jr. *The Northwest Ordinance, 1787: A Bicentennial Handbook*. Indianapolis: Indiana Historical Society, 1987.

Part V

The Federal Convention and the Constitution, 1787

On February 21, 1787, the Continental Congress resolved that there would be a convention "on the second Monday of May next" at Philadelphia, composed of representatives from the "several states . . . for the sole and express purpose of revising the Articles of Confederation [in order to] render the federal constitution adequate to the exigencies of Government & the preservation of the Union."[1] Aggressive advocates of constitutional change, such as Alexander Hamilton and James Madison, had achieved the objective of their report to Congress from the Annapolis Convention of September 11–14, 1786 (see Document 31). Now, they had their chance to fix the flaws of the Confederation. But they had to act within the broad American consensus on certain essential principles, such as republican government, federalism, constitutionalism, popular sovereignty, and unalienable rights of individuals. If not, the people surely would reject their work as a violation of Anglo-American political traditions nurtured during the long colonial period and defended, refined, and improved by the American Revolution.

More than the others bound for Philadelphia, James Madison of Virginia read and thought deeply about how to construct a republican, federal, and constitutional government that could preserve both the union of American states and the liberties of the people. He had decided long before the Federal Convention that a mere revision of the Articles of Confederation would be an inadequate response. Rather, Madison wanted a totally new constitution, which, if constructed properly, could treat the perennial problem of achieving liberty with order—how to establish government strong enough to maintain order and safety and limited enough to prevent tyranny.

Madison clearly revealed his plans for fundamental constitutional change in a letter to George Washington (Document 35), written during April 1787. Instead of new provisions for the Articles of Confederation, he intended a "new system," which would greatly expand the powers of the central government in relationship to the state governments to bring order and stability as foundations for freedom.

James Madison came to Philadelphia on May 5, 1787. He was the first delegate to arrive at the Federal Convention, which did not begin until May 25, upon achievement of a quorum of seven state delegations. He was one of fifty-five delegates from twelve states who eventually came to the Convention, but usually fewer than forty delegates participated in any of the meetings. Rhode Island was not represented, and New Hampshire's delegates did not appear until late July.

During eleven days before the Federal Convention began, James Madison and others of the Virginia delegation met daily to develop their Virginia Plan (Document 36), which Edmund Randolph presented to the Convention on May 29. James Madison, however, was the principal source of the Virginia Plan's fifteen resolutions, which proposed a new national government with power to bypass the states and act directly on the people to collect taxes and enforce laws.

The next day (May 30), the Convention agreed "that a national Government ought to be established consisting of a supreme Legislative, Executive & Judiciary."[2] Thus, the delegates moved from the Continental Congress's instructions about "revising the Articles of Confederation" to the construction of an entirely new frame of government. Supporters of the Virginia Plan argued that the delegates could legitimately go beyond mere revision of the Articles because the Convention had been instructed by the Continental Congress "to render the federal constitution adequate to the exigencies of Government & the preservation of the Union." Madison argued that mere revision of the Articles would not save the Union, and the majority of the Convention agreed with him.

Madison and his allies had set the agenda and terms of discussion for the Convention. From May 30 to June 13, the delegates discussed and refined the Virginia Plan. They agreed that the new Congress should be bicameral (composed of two houses), not unicameral as it was under the Articles of Confederation. Further, the bicameral legislature should be countered and balanced by separate executive and judicial branches of government.

The delegates argued, however, about representation in the new two-house Congress. How should the representatives in Congress be elected? To what extent should they represent the people or the states of the Union? An example of the contending views on these questions was provided by Madison's notes on the Convention's debate, June 6 (see Document 37).

Some delegates, such as Roger Sherman (Connecticut), Charles Pinckney (South Carolina), and Elbridge Gerry (Massachusetts) were opposed to popular election of representatives to Congress, not even to the so-called people's branch, the House of Representatives. They wanted both houses of the Congress to be selected by the state legislatures. By contrast, James Wilson (Pennsylvania) and George Mason (Virginia) persuasively argued for broad popular representation. They were joined by James Madison, who held that members of the House of Representatives, at least, should be elected directly by the people of each state, whom they would represent. John Dickinson (Delaware) concurred with Madison's position on direct popular election of the House of Representatives and proposed, in modification of Madison's Virginia Plan, that members of the upper house or Senate should be chosen by the legislatures of each state of the Union.

Madison's June 6 speech on representation in a federal republic was notable for his articulation of a threat to liberty peculiar to republican government, the tyranny of the majority against the rights of unpopular individuals or minorities. Madison's careful studies of ancient and modern republics, and his observations of excessive legislative supremacy in most American state governments, had convinced him of the reality of majoritarian tyranny, exercised by the democratically elected representatives of the people against individuals they opposed.

Virtually all Americans agreed with Madison about the worth and desirability of majority rule. They also agreed that an unrestrained monarchy or oligarchy would lead to tyranny of one or a few over the many. There was hot debate, however, about Madison's view that in a republic, with government by elected representatives of the people, the great threat to liberty would come from unrestrained majority rule.

Throughout the debate on the American Constitution, from 1787 to 1789, Madison proposed republican remedies to the peculiar problem of insufficiently restrained republican government, the problem of majoritarian tyranny. He advanced these views in his June 6 speech at the Convention (Document 37). And he presented them most fully and persuasively in *Federalist Papers* 10 and 51 (see Documents 48 and 51).

In brief, Madison argued for a republican government of national scope, an extended federal republic of the United States, which would be conducive to election of worthy representatives and prevention of oppression by a monolithic and unyielding majority faction. Why? Because by extending the scope of the people's government from the limited territories of the several states to the expansive territory of the whole nation, the diversity of people, groups, and interests would be greatly increased. This vast diversity of groups and interests would make it difficult for one of them to dominate the others continuously and tyrannically. Rather, various groups and individuals would have to compromise and collaborate to make decisions by majority vote, thereby affording greater protection for the rights of all persons, who might at various times find themselves temporarily in the minority in response to public issues. This was Madison's ultimate argument for shifting power from the small republican governments of the states to the large federal and republican government of the United States.

The Convention's debates on representation and other facets of the Virginia Plan led to the Report of the Committee of the Whole on June 13. This report (Document 38), which consisted of 19 resolutions, was the Convention's summary of agreements on modification of the Virginia Plan. It sparked the first crisis of the Convention, which emerged after introduction on June 15 of nine resolutions by William Paterson of New Jersey (see Document 39).

Paterson's New Jersey Plan endorsed the Articles of Confederation and called for their revision, not their suppression. This plan affirmed the existing unicameral Congress, with its equal representation of the states, not the people. However, it proposed separate executive and judicial departments, expanded the expressly delegated powers of the central government, and asserted the supremacy of the central government, within its limited range of powers.

Vigorous debate followed introduction of the New Jersey Plan (see Document 40). Then the Convention voted against it, seven states to three (New York, New Jersey, and Delaware). The Maryland delegation was split, thereby neutering its vote.

The Convention moved ahead with the Virginia Plan, as modified by the June 13 Report of the Committee of the Whole. But New Jersey Plan supporters plus Maryland and Connecticut became so upset that the Convention was in jeopardy. The primary conflict concerned representation in Congress, with the small states favoring equal representation and voting power in Congress. Their large-state opponents continued to support proportional representation and voting power based on variations in population, as provided by the Virginia Plan.

The Connecticut delegation arranged a Great Compromise that saved the Convention. It provided that the Senate would be organized according to the old confederal principle of the New Jersey Plan—two senators (and two votes) for each state, whether large or small in population, with the legislature of each state selecting the two senators from that state. The House of Representatives would be organized according to the new nationalist principles of the Virginia Plan—the number of Representatives (and the number of votes) for each state would vary according to population size (larger states would have more representatives and votes). Eligible voters in each state would elect their representatives. The provisions of this Great Compromise were included in Article I, Sections 2 and 3 of the United States Constitution (see Document 43).

James Madison reported in his notes on the Convention the views of Oliver Ellsworth of Connecticut, one of the designers of the Great Compromise: "The proportional representation in the first branch was conformable to the national principle and would secure the large states against the small. An equality of voices in the second branch was conformable to the federal principle and was necessary to secure the small states against the large. He trusted that on this middle ground a compromise would take place."[3] Another change that accommodated concerns of the New Jersey Plan supporters was dropping the word "national" from the document, as in "National Legislature" or "National Executive."

During the conflict between large and small states, resolved finally by the Great Compromise, James Madison noted another imminent controversy at the Convention, which would be treated by constitutional compromise, but not really resolved at Philadelphia. On June 30, Madison wrote that "the states were divided into different interests not by their difference of size, but by other circumstances; the most material of which resulted partly from climate, but principally from the effects of their having or not having slaves. These two causes concurred in forming the great division of interests in the United States. It did not lie between the large & small States: it lay between the Northern & Southern."[4]

Three issues over slavery bitterly divided the Convention. They pertained to (1) representation, (2) the external slave trade, and (3) recovery of fugitives from slavery. These issues were resolved by compromises that no one has called "great," but that virtually everyone has recognized as the costly price of union in 1787.

The debates on slavery were fervent and divisive (see Document 41). Delegates from South Carolina and Georgia threatened to leave the Convention and reject the Constitution unless certain concessions were made to slavery. In response, there were denunciations of slavery by a few delegates, including George Mason, a Virginia slaveholder. The strongest denunciation of slavery came from Gouverneur Morris of Pennsylvania (August 8) who said, according to Madison's notes, "He would never concur in upholding domestic slavery. It was the curse of heaven on the States where it prevailed."[5] Morris blasted the concept of the eventual "three-fifths" compromise on representation in Congress. He said "Upon what principle is it that slaves shall be counted in the representation [counting them either as one person or three-fifths of a person]. The admission of slaves into the Representation [in any way at all] comes to this: that the inhabitant of Georgia and South Carolina who goes to the coast of Africa and in defiance of the most sacred laws of humanity tears away his fellow creatures from their dearest connections and damns them to the most cruel bondage, shall have more votes in a Government instituted for protection of the rights of mankind, than the citizen of Pennsylvania or New Jersey who views with a laudable horror, so nefarious a practice."[6]

Despite a few moving protests, such as Morris's, the Convention made four explicit concessions to slavery in the Constitution of 1787 (see Document 43). First was the three-fifths rule for counting slaves as a basis for representation in Congress, which enabled slave-holding states to thereby increase their representation and voting power (Article I, Section 2). Opponents of slavery argued that slaves should not be counted at all, because they were not permitted to vote or otherwise participate in goverment. The slave owners wanted each slave to be counted as one person. Both sides of this controversy accepted the three-fifths compromise as the best deal they could manage at this time. Second was the provision for importing slaves from abroad, which could not be prohibited until 1808 (Article I, Section 9). Third was the provision for returning interstate fugitives from slavery to their owners (Article IV, Section 2). Fourth was the ban on any constitutional amendment on the external slave trade before 1808, when Congress could enact legislation to prohibit it (Article V).

Most delegates at the Convention were sufficiently distressed by their bargains on human bondage that they contrived to keep the words "slave" and "slavery" out of the Constitution. The clauses on slaves euphemistically included such terms as "other persons" or "such persons." And the external slave trade was described as "Migration or Importation." Further, there is no explicit mention of race, neither white nor black, in the Constitution. Finally, if the Convention did not immediately ban the foreign slave trade, it provided for its prohibition after 1808. The fact remains, however, that the Constitution of 1787 permitted slavery in the states that wanted this awful institution and included concessions to those who practiced it.

Near the end of the Convention, on September 12, George Mason proposed inclusion of a bill of rights in the Constitution. He offered the 1776 Virginia Declaration of Rights, written mainly by him, as a model (see Document 10). Elbridge Gerry of Massachusetts readily agreed. But not one state delegation voted for Mason's proposal, and it was dropped. This omission provided a rallying cry of protest for opponents of the Constitution during the subsequent ratification debates (see Documents 46 and 47).

On September 17, the framers of the Constitution gathered for the last meeting of the Convention. Benjamin Franklin of Pennsylvania, at 81 the oldest delegate, had prepared a final speech pleading with all members present to sign the final draft of the Constitution, even if they did not agree with it completely (see Document 42). Only three refused to sign: Edmund Randolph and George Mason of Virginia and Elbridge Gerry of Massachusetts. However, the majority of members present from each delegation of the twelve participating states signed the document. This gave an appearance of unanimous approval by the states, if not by all the delegates. The Convention was ended, and the product of its work, the Constitution, was sent to the Continental Congress in New York City.

The Federal Convention, through reflection, deliberation, debate, and compromise, had created an unprecedented framework for a republican, federal, and constitutional government. Documents 35–43 exemplify the orderly, if contentious, development of this Constitution, from the Continental Congress's approval of the Federal Convention to the submission of the Convention's product back to the Congress that originated the process. Thomas Jefferson, observing events in America from France, proudly noted, "The example of changing a constitution by assembling the wise men of the State, instead of assembling armies, will be worth as much to the world as the former examples we had given them."[7] He predicted that this example provided by the framers of the Constitution would forever be a model worthy of emulation by people throughout the world.

NOTES

1. Charles C. Tansill, ed., *Documents Illustrative of the Formation of the Union of the American States* (Washington, D.C.: U.S. Government Printing Office, 1927), p. 44.

2. Gaillard Hunt and James Brown Scott, eds., *The Debates in the Federal Convention of 1787 which Framed the Constitution of the United States of America, Reported by James Madison* (New York: Oxford University Press, 1920), p. 27.

3. Ibid., p. 189.

4. Ibid., pp. 194–95.

5. Ibid., p. 360.

6. Ibid.

7. Dumas Malone, *Jefferson and the Rights of Man* (Boston: Little, Brown, 1951), pp. 177–78.

DOCUMENT 35: Letter to George Washington (James Madison, April 16, 1787)

In preparation for the Philadelphia Convention, James Madison wrote letters to colleagues expressing core ideas on changes in government needed to solve problems of government under the Articles of Confederation. Thus, Madison hoped to win support for these ideas among important political leaders. His letter to George Washington included several provisions that later appeared in the Virginia Plan (Document 36) introduced at the beginning of the Federal Convention in Philadelphia.

Madison stressed that the power of the state governments should be diminished relative to the power of the U.S. government. In particular, he wanted the central government to have power to veto "legislative acts of the states," a provision also included in the Virginia Plan. Further, Madison wanted to add separate and effective executive and judicial branches to the structure of the central government. Finally, he recommended that more populous states should have more representatives and more voting power in the Congress than less populous states. What other major ideas on good constitutional government were presented in this letter to Washington? In particular, what did Madison say in this letter about representation in government, more power for the central government, and less power for state governments?

DEAR SIR,—I have been honored with your letter of the 31 March, and find, with much pleasure, that your views of the reform which ought to be pursued by the Convention give a sanction to those which I have entertained. Temporising applications will dishonor the Councils which propose them, and may foment the internal malignity of the disease, at the same time they produce an ostensible palliation of it. Radical attempts although unsuccessful will at least justify the authors of them.

Having been lately led to revolve the subject which is to undergo the discussion of the Convention, and formed *some* outlines of a new system, I take the liberty of submitting them without apology to your eye.

Conceiving that an individual independence of the States is utterly irreconcileable with their aggregate sovereignty, and that a consolidation of the whole into one simple republic would be as inexpedient as it is unattainable, I have sought for some middle ground, which may at once support a due supremacy of the national authority, and not exclude the local authorities wherever they can be subordinately useful.

I would propose as the groundwork that a change be made in the principle of representation. According to the present form of the Union, in which the intervention of the States is in all great cases necessary to effectuate the measures of Congress, an equality of suffrage, does not destroy the inequality of importance in the several members. No one deny that Virginia and Massachusetts have more weight and influence, both within and without Congress, than Delaware or Rhode Island. Under a system which would operate in many essential points without the intervention of the State legislatures, the case would be materially altered. A vote in the national Councils from Delaware, would then have the same effect and value as one from the largest State in the Union. I am ready to believe that such a change would not be attended with much difficulty. A majority of the States, and those of greatest influence, will regard it as favorable to them. To the northern States it will be recommended by their present populousness; to the Southern, by their expected advantage in this respect. The lesser States must in every event yield to the predominant will. But the consideration which particularly urges a change in the representation is that it will obviate the principle objections of the larger States to the necessary concessions of power.

I would propose next that in addition to the present federal powers, the national Government should be armed with positive and compleat authority in all cases which require uniformity; such as the regulation of trade, including the right of taxing both exports and imports, the fixing the terms and forms of naturalization, &c., &c.

Over and above this positive power, a negative *in all cases whatsoever* on the legislative acts of the States, as heretofore exercised by the Kingly prerogative, appears to me to be absolutely necessary, and to be the least possible encroachment on the State jurisdictions. Without this defensive power, every positive power that can be given on paper will be evaded and defeated. The States will continue to invade the National jurisdiction, to violate treaties and the law of nations and to harass each other with rival and spiteful measures dictated by mistaken views of interest. Another happy effect of this prerogative would be its controul on the internal vicissitudes of State policy, and the aggressions of interested majorities on the rights of minorities and of individuals. The great desideratum, which has not yet been found for Republican Governments seems to be some disinterested and dispassionate umpire in disputes between different passions and interests in the State. The majority who alone have the right of decision, have frequently an interest, real or supposed in abusing it. In Monarchies the Sovereign is more neutral to the interests and views of different parties; but, unfortunately he too often forms interests of his own repugnant to those of the whole. Might not the national prerogative here suggested be found sufficiently disinterested for the decision of local questions of policy, whilst it would itself be sufficiently restrained from the pursuit of interests adverse to those of the whole Society? There has not been any moment since the peace at which the representatives of the Union would have given an assent to paper money or any other measure of a kindred nature.

The national supremacy ought also to be extended, as I conceive, to the Judiciary departments. If those who are to expound and apply the laws are connected by their interests and their oaths with the particular States wholly, and not with the Union, the participation of the Union in the making of the laws may be possibly rendered unavailing. It seems at least necessary that the oaths of the Judges should include a fidelity to the general as well as local constitution, and that an appeal should lie to some National tribunal in all cases to which foreigners or inhabitants of other States may be parties. The admiralty jurisdiction seems to fall entirely within the purview of the national Government.

The National supremacy in the Executive departments is liable to some difficulty, unless the officers administering them could be made appointable by the supreme Government. The Militia ought certainly to be placed in some form or other under the authority which is entrusted with the general protection and defence.

A Government composed of such extensive powers should be well organized and balanced. The legislative department might be divided into two branches; one of them chosen every ——— years by the people at large, or by the Legislatures; the other to consist of fewer members, to hold their places for a longer term, and go out in such a rotation as always to leave in office a large majority of old members. Perhaps the negative on the laws might be most conveniently exercised by this branch. As a further check, a council of revision including the great ministerial officers might be superadded.

A National Executive must also be provided. I have scarcely ventured as yet to form my own opinion either of the manner in which it ought to be constituted or of the authorities with which it ought to be cloathed.

An article should be inserted expressly guarantying the tranquillity of the States against internal as well as external dangers.

In like manner the right of coercion should be expressly declared. With the resources of Commerce in hand, the National administration might always find means of exerting it either by sea or land. But the difficulty and awkwardness of operating by force on the collective will of a State render it particularly desirable that the necessity of it might be precluded. Perhaps the negative on the laws might create such a mutuality of dependence between the General and particular authorities, as to answer this purpose or, perhaps, some defined objects of taxation might be submitted along with commerce, to the general authority.

To give a new System its proper validity and energy, a ratification must be obtained from the people, and not merely from the ordinary authority of the Legislatures. This will be the more essential as inroads on the *existing Constitutions* of the States will be unavoidable. . . .

Source: Gaillard Hunt, ed., *The Writings of James Madison,* Vol. 2. (New York: G. P. Putnam's Sons, 1900), pp. 344–49.

DOCUMENT 36: Virginia Plan (Reported by James Madison, May 29, 1787)

At the Convention, Governor Edmund Randolph presented the Virginia Plan, which called for a new national constitution, not merely a revision of the Articles of Confederation. Thus, it set the Convention on a new course at variance with the explicit instructions of the Continental Congress, which had called for revision of the Articles of Confederation. Note the similarity of the Virginia Plan to ideas in Madison's letter to George Washington (Document 35), which provides evidence that James Madison, not Edmund Randolph, was the primary source of ideas on the Virginia Plan. Madison recorded Randolph's presentation of the Virginia Plan in his notes on the proceedings of the Convention.

Randolph's speech began with a summary of commonly recognized defects of the Articles of Confederation, such as the central government's weaknesses that prevented it from providing security against foreign enemies or domestic disorder. Then, Randolph presented fifteen resolutions on how to remedy the defects of government under the Articles of Confederation. These resolutions provided for a national government with sufficient power to make and enforce laws and regulate relations among the states of the union. Representation of states in the national legislature would vary according to population and wealth (see resolution 2). The national executive and judicial departments would have power to check with veto power the actions of the national and state legislatures (see resolution 8). What other major provisions for constructing a national government were presented by Randolph? How did the Virginia Plan propose to shift the locus of power from the state governments to the government of the United States?

MR. RANDOLPH then opened the main business.

. . .

He expressed his regret, that it should fall to him, rather than those, who were of longer standing in life and political experience, to open the great subject of their mission. But, as the convention had originated from Virginia, and his colleagues supposed that some proposition was expected from them, they had imposed this task on him.

He then commented on the difficulty of the crisis, and the necessity of preventing the fulfilment of the prophecies of the American downfal. . . .

He then proceeded to enumerate the defects: 1. that the confederation produced no security against foreign invasion; congress not being permitted to prevent a war nor to support it by their own authority—Of this he cited many examples; most of which tended to shew, that they could not cause infractions of treaties or of the law of nations, to be punished: that particular states might by their conduct provoke war without controul; and that neither militia nor draughts being fit for defence on such occasions, inlistments only could be successful, and these could not be executed without money.

2. that the fœderal government could not check the quarrels between states, nor a rebellion in any, not having constitutional power nor means to interpose according to the exigency:

3. that there were many advantages, which the U.S. might acquire, which were not attainable under the confederation—such as a productive impost—counteraction of the commercial regulations of other nations—pushing of commerce ad libitum—etc. etc.

4. that the fœderal government could not defend itself against the incroachments from the states.

5. that it was not even paramount to the state constitutions, ratified, as it was in ma[n]y of the states. . . .

He then proceeded to the remedy; the basis of which he said must be the republican principle. . . .

1. Resolved that the Articles of Confederation ought to be so corrected & enlarged as to accomplish the objects proposed by their institution; namely, "common defence, security of liberty, and general welfare."

2. Resolved therefore that the rights of suffrage in the National Legislature ought to be proportioned to the Quotas of contribution, or to the number of free inhabitants, as the one or the other rule may seem best in different cases.

3. Resolved that the National Legislature ought to consist of two branches.

4. Resolved that the members of the first branch of the National Legislature ought to be elected by the people of the several States every   for the term of   ; to be of the age of   years at least, to receive liberal stipends by which they may be compensated for the devotion of their time to public service; to be ineligible to any office established by a particular State, or under the authority of the United States, except those peculiarly belonging to the functions of the first branch, during the term of service, and for the space of   after its expiration; to be incapable of reelection for the space of   after the expiration of their term of service, and to be subject to recall.

5. Resolved that the members of the second branch of the National Legislature ought to be elected by those of the first, out of a proper number of persons nominated by the individual Legislatures, to be of the age of   years at least; to hold their offices for a term sufficient to ensure their independency; to receive liberal stipends, by which they

may be compensated for the devotion of their time to public service; and to be ineligible to any office established by a particular State, or under the authority of the United States, except those peculiarly belonging to the functions of the second branch, during the term of service, and for the space of   after the expiration thereof.

6. Resolved that each branch ought to possess the right of originating Acts; that the National Legislature ought to be impowered to enjoy the Legislative Rights vested in Congress by the Confederation & moreover to legislate in all cases to which the separate States are incompetent, or in which the harmony of the United States may be interrupted by the exercise of individual Legislation; to negative all laws passed by the several States, contravening in the opinion of the National Legislature the articles of Union; and to call forth the force of the Union against any member of the Union failing to fulfill its duty under the articles thereof.

7. Resolved that a National Executive be instituted; to be chosen by the National Legislature for the term of   years, to receive punctually at stated times, a fixed compensation for the services rendered, in which no increase or diminution shall be made so as to affect the Magistracy, existing at the time of increase or diminution, and to be ineligible a second time; and that besides a general authority to execute the National laws, it ought to enjoy the Executive rights vested in Congress by the Confederation.

8. Resolved that the Executive and a convenient number of the National Judiciary, ought to compose a Council of revision with authority to examine every act of the National Legislature before it shall operate, & every act of a particular Legislature before a Negative thereon shall be final; and that the dissent of the said Council shall amount to a rejection, unless the Act of the National Legislature be again passed, or that of a particular Legislature be again negatived by   of the members of each branch.

9. Resolved that a National Judiciary be established to consist of one or more supreme tribunals, and of inferior tribunals to be chosen by the National Legislature, to hold their offices during good behaviour; and to receive punctually at stated times fixed compensation for their services, in which no increase or diminution shall be made so as to affect the persons actually in office at the time of such increase or diminution; that the jurisdiction of the inferior tribunals shall be to hear & determine in the first instance, and of the supreme tribunal to hear and determine in the dernier resort, all piracies & felonies on the high seas, captures from an enemy, cases in which foreigners or citizens of other States applying to such jurisdictions may be interested, or which respect the collection of the National revenue; impeachments of any National officers, and questions which may involve the national peace and harmony.

10. Resolved that provision ought to be made for the admission of

States lawfully arising within the limits of the United States, whether from a voluntary junction of Government & Territory or otherwise, with the consent of a number of voices in the National legislature less than the whole.

11. Resolved that a Republican Government & the territory of each State, except in the instance of a voluntary junction of Government & territory, ought to be guarantied by the United States to each State

12. Resolved that provision ought to be made for the continuance of Congress and their authorities and privileges, until a given day after the reform of the articles of Union shall be adopted, and for the completion of all their engagements.

13. Resolved that provision ought to be made for the amendment of the Articles of Union whensoever it shall seem necessary, and that the assent of the National Legislature ought not to be required thereto.

14. Resolved that the Legislative Executive & Judiciary powers within the several States ought to be bound by oath to support the articles of Union.

15. Resolved that the amendments which shall be offered to the Confederation, by the Convention ought at a proper time, or times, after the approbation of Congress to be submitted to an assembly or assemblies of Representatives, recommended by the several Legislatures to be expressly chosen by the people, to consider & decide thereon.

He concluded with an exhortation, not to suffer the present opportunity of establishing general peace, harmony, happiness and liberty in the U.S. to pass away unimproved.

Source: Gaillard Hunt and James Brown Scott, eds., *The Debates in the Federal Convention of 1787 which Framed the Constitution of the United States of America, Reported by James Madison* (New York: Oxford University Press, 1920), pp. 22–26.

DOCUMENT 37: Debate on the Virginia Plan (June 6, 1787)

The Convention organized itself into a Committee of the Whole to debate the Virginia Plan. This debate began May 30 and continued daily to June 13. An especially controversial part of the Virginia Plan was the proposal to divide Congress into two houses, the first to be elected by the people and the second by members of the first house. So, the state governments would have no part in the election of any part of the national legislature.

In his notes on the Convention, James Madison recorded the debate of June 6 on the issue of representation in the government, especially the means of electing representatives to the national legislature. Some participants wanted representatives of at least one branch of the national legislature to be elected by the state legislatures, not directly by the people (see the statements of Pinckney, Sherman, and Dickinson). Others, such as James Wilson, disagreed and stressed direct election of representatives by the people.

During this debate James Madison, in his first great speech of the Convention, agreed with Wilson. Further, he discussed his novel idea of an extended federal republic, with a diversity of groups and interests, as the best means of protecting individual rights against the threat of majoritarian tyranny. What arguments does Madison present in favor of the Virginia Plan's scheme of representation? Compare the arguments of Madison and Wilson with those of Pinckney, Sherman, and Dickinson. (Note Madison's incorrect spelling of Pinckney's name.)

Mr. PINKNEY . . . moved "that the first branch of the national Legislature be elected by the State Legislatures, and not by the people." contending that the people were less fit Judges in such a case, and that the Legislatures would be less likely to promote the adoption of the new Government, if they were to be excluded from all share in it.

Mr. RUTLIDGE seconded the motion. . . .

Mr. WILSON. He wished for vigor in the Government, but he wished that vigorous authority to flow immediately from the legitimate source of all authority. The Government ought to possess not only first the *force,* but secondly the *mind* or *sense* of the people at large. The Legislature ought to be the most exact transcript of the whole Society. Representation is made necessary only because it is impossible for the people to act collectively. The opposition was to be expected he said from the *Governments,* not from the Citizens of the States. The latter had parted as was observed (by Mr. King) with all the necessary powers; and it was immaterial to them, by whom they were exercised, if well exercised. The State officers were to be the losers of power. The people he supposed would be rather more attached to the national Government than to the State Governments as being more important in itself, and more flattering to their pride. There is no danger of improper elections if made by *large* districts. Bad elections proceed from the smallness of the districts which give an opportunity to bad men to intrigue themselves into office.

Mr. SHERMAN. If it were in view to abolish the State Governments the elections ought to be by the people. If the State Governments are to be continued, it is necessary in order to preserve harmony between the National & State Governments that the elections to the former should be made by the latter. The right of participating in the National Government would be sufficiently secured to the people by their election of the State Legislatures. . . .

Mr. MADISON considered an election of one branch at least of the Legislature by the people immediately, as a clear principle of free Government and that this mode under proper regulations had the additional advantage of securing better representatives, as well as of avoiding too great an agency of the State Governments in the General one.—He differed from the member from Connecticut [Mr. Sherman] in thinking the objects mentioned to be all the principal ones that required a National Government. Those were certainly important and necessary objects; but he combined with them the necessity of providing more effectually for the security of private rights, and the steady dispensation of Justice. Interferences with these were evils which had more perhaps than any thing else, produced this convention. Was it to be supposed that republican liberty could long exist under the abuses of it practised in some of the States. The gentleman [Mr. Sherman] had admitted that in a very small State, faction & oppression would prevail. It was to be inferred then that wherever these prevailed the State was too small. Had they not prevailed in the largest as well as the smallest tho' less than in the smallest; and were we not thence admonished to enlarge the sphere as far as the nature of the Government would admit. This was the only defence against the inconveniencies of democracy consistent with the democratic form of Government. All civilized Societies would be divided into different Sects, Factions, & interests, as they happened to consist of rich & poor, debtors & creditors, the landed, the manufacturing, the commercial interests, the inhabitants of this district or that district, the followers of this political leader or that political leader, the disciples of this religious Sect or that religious Sect. In all cases where a majority are united by a common interest or passion, the rights of the minority are in danger. What motives are to restrain them? A prudent regard to the maxim that honesty is the best policy is found by experience to be as little regarded by bodies of men as by individuals. Respect for character is always diminished in proportion to the number among whom the blame or praise is to be divided. Conscience, the only remaining tie, is known to be inadequate in individuals: In large numbers, little is to be expected from it. Besides, Religion itself may become a motive to persecution & oppression.— These observations are verified by the Histories of every Country antient & modern. In Greece & Rome the rich & poor, the creditors & debtors, as well as the patricians & plebians alternately oppressed each other with equal unmercifulness. What a source of oppression was the relation between the parent cities of Rome, Athens & Carthage, & their respective provinces: the former possessing the power, & the latter being sufficiently distinguished to be separate objects of it? Why was America so justly apprehensive of Parliamentary injustice? Because Great Britain had a separate interest real or supposed, & if her authority had been admitted, could have pursued that interest at our expence. We have seen the mere distinction of colour made in the most enlightened period of time, a ground of the most oppressive dominion ever exercised by man over man. What has been the source of those unjust laws complained of among ourselves? Has it not been the real or supposed interest of the major number? Debtors have defrauded their creditors. The landed interest has borne hard on the mercantile interest. The Holders of one species of property have thrown a disproportion of taxes on the holders of another species. The lesson we are to draw from the whole is that where a majority are united by a common sentiment, and have an opportunity, the rights of the minor party become insecure. In a Republican Government the Majority if united have always an opportunity. The only remedy is to enlarge the sphere, & thereby divide the community into so great a number of interests & parties, that in the first place a majority will not be likely at the same moment to have a common interest separate from that of the whole or of the minority; and in the second place, that in case they should have such an interest, they may not be apt to unite in the pursuit of it. It was incumbent on us then to try this remedy, and with that view to frame a republican system on such a scale and in such form as will controul all the evils which have been experienced.

Mr. DICKENSON considered it as essential that one branch of the Legislature should be drawn immediately from the people; and as expedient that the other should be chosen by the Legislatures of the States. This combination of the State Governments with the national Government was as politic as it was unavoidable. In the formation of the Senate we ought to carry it through such a refining process as will assimilate it as near as may be to the House of Lords in England. He repeated his warm eulogiums on the British Constitution. He was for a strong National Government but for leaving the States a considerable agency in the System. . . .

Source: Gaillard Hunt and James Brown Scott, eds., *The Debates in the Federal Convention of 1787 which Framed the Constitution of the United States of America, Reported by James Madison* (New York: Oxford University Press, 1920), pp. 62–69.

DOCUMENT 38: Report of the Committee of the Whole (June 13, 1787)

The first round of debates on the Virginia Plan concluded on June 13, with the presentation of nineteen resolutions. These statements were a summary of the Constitutional Convention's decisions about support for certain provisions of the Virginia Plan and revisions or deletions of other parts of it. The Convention agreed on separation of powers among three independent branches of the national government: legislative, executive, and judicial. There would be a bicameral legislature, the members of the first branch to be elected by the people and the members of the second branch to be elected by the state legislatures. The national executive would be able to check the legislative power with a "negative" or veto, which could be overturned by a two-thirds vote of both branches of the legislature. Further, the national government would have power to check state government actions that violated "the articles of Union" (see resolution 6). What other key proposals for the national government were included in this report?

Compare this nineteen-resolution report with the original Virginia Plan (Document 36). What provisions of the Virginia Plan were dropped? What additions were made to the Virginia Plan?

1. RESOLVED, That it is the opinion of this Committee, that a national government ought to be established, consisting of a Supreme Legislative, Judiciary, and Executive.

2. Resolved, That the National Legislature ought to consist of Two Branches.

3. Resolved, That the members of the first branch of the national Legislature ought to be elected by the People of the several States, for the term of Three years; to receive fixed stipends, by which they may be compensated for the devotion of their time to public service, to be paid out of the National Treasury; to be ineligible to any Office established by a particular State, or under the authority of the United States (except those peculiarly belonging to the functions of the first branch) during the term of service, and under the national government for the space of one year after its expiration.

4. Resolved, That the Members of the second Branch of the national Legislature ought to be chosen by the individual Legislatures; to be of the age of thirty years at least; to hold their offices for a term sufficient to ensure their independency, namely, seven years; to receive fixed sti-

pends, by which they may be compensated for the devotion of their time to public service, to be paid out of the National Treasury; to be ineligible to any Office established by a particular State, or under the authority of the United States (except those peculiarly belonging to the functions of the second branch) during the term of service, and under the national government, for the space of one Year after its expiration.

5. Resolved, That each branch ought to possess the right of originating acts.

6. Resolved, That the national Legislature ought to be empowered to enjoy the legislative rights vested in Congress by the confederation; and moreover to legislate in all cases to which the separate States are incompetent, or in which the harmony of the United States may be interrupted by the exercise of individual legislation; to negative all laws passed by the several States contravening, in the opinion of the national legislature, the articles of union, or any treaties subsisting under the authority of the union.

7. Resolved, That the right of suffrage in the first branch of the national Legislature ought not to be according to the rule established in the articles of confederation, but according to some equitable ratio of representation; namely, in proportion to the whole number of white and other free citizens and inhabitants, of every age, sex, and condition, including those bound to servitude for a term of years, and three fifths of all other persons not comprehended in the foregoing description, except Indians not paying taxes in each State.

8. Resolved, That the right of suffrage in the second branch of the national Legislature ought to be according to the rule established for the first.

9. Resolved, That a national Executive be instituted to consist of a Single Person; to be chosen by the National Legislature, for the term of Seven years; with power to carry into execution the National Laws; to appoint to Offices in cases not otherwise provided for; to be ineligible the second time; and to be removable on impeachment and conviction of malpractice, or neglect of duty; to receive a fixed stipend, by which he may be compensated for the devotion of his time to public service, to be paid out of the national Treasury.

10. Resolved, That the national executive shall have a right to negative any legislative act, which shall not be afterwards passed unless by two third parts of each branch of the national Legislature.

11. Resolved, That a national Judiciary be established to consist of One supreme Tribunal; the Judges of which to be appointed by the second Branch of the National Legislature; to hold their offices during good behaviour; to receive punctually, at stated times, a fixed compensation for their services, in which no encrease or diminution shall be made, so

as to affect the persons actually in office at the time of such encrease or diminution.

12. Resolved, That the national Legislature be empowered to appoint inferior Tribunals.

13. Resolved, That the jurisdiction of the national Judiciary shall extend to cases which respect the collection of the national revenue; impeachments of any National officers; and questions which involve the national peace and harmony.

14. Resolved, That provision ought to be made for the admission of States, lawfully arising within the limits of the United States, whether from a voluntary junction of government and territory, or otherwise, with the consent of a number of voices in the National legislature less than the whole.

15. Resolved, That provision ought to be made for the continuance of Congress and their authorities until a given day after the reform of the articles of Union shall be adopted; and for the completion of all their engagements.

16. Resolved, That a republican Constitution, and its existing laws, ought to be guaranteed to each State by the United States.

17. Resolved, That provision ought to be made for the amendment of the articles of Union, whensoever it shall seem necessary.

18. Resolved, That the Legislative, Executive, and Judiciary powers within the several States ought to be bound by oath to support the articles of Union.

19. Resolved, That the amendments which shall be offered to the confederation by the Convention, ought at a proper time or times, after the approbation of Congress, to be submitted to an assembly or assemblies of representatives, recommended by the several Legislatures, to be submitted to an assembly or assemblies of representatives, recommended by the several Legislatures, to be expressly chosen by the People to consider and decide thereon.

Source: Gaillard Hunt and James Brown Scott, eds., *The Debates in the Federal Convention of 1787 which Framed the Constitution of the United States of America, Reported by James Madison* (New York: Oxford University Press, 1920), pp. 99–101.

DOCUMENT 39: New Jersey Plan (June 15, 1787)

Delegates from five states opposed the nationalistic tone of the Virginia Plan. In particular, they rejected the proposed scheme of representation in the two-house national legislature, which deprived the state governments of direct and equal representation. So, William Paterson of New Jersey proposed an alternate to the Virginia Plan. Paterson's New Jersey Plan was a series of nine propositions to amend the Articles of Confederation, not to replace this document with a new frame of government. It provided equal representation and voting power for the states in a unicameral Congress. But in Resolution 6, this plan paradoxically included a national supremacy clause, the antithesis of the state-based powers and rights of the Articles of Confederation, which eventually became part of Article VI of the U.S. Constitution (see Document 43). Compare the New Jersey Plan with the summary and revision of the Virginia Plan in Document 38. What are the major differences in the two plans for constitutional government?

Mr. PATTERSON, laid before the Convention the plan which he said several of the deputations wished to be substituted in place of that proposed by Mr. Randolph. . . .

The propositions from N. Jersey moved by Mr. Patterson were in the words following.

1. Resolved that the articles of Confederation ought to be so revised, corrected & enlarged, as to render the federal Constitution adequate to the exigencies of Government, & the preservation of the Union.

2. Resolved that in addition to the powers vested in the United States in Congress, by the present existing articles of Confederation, they be authorized to pass acts for raising a revenue, by levying a duty or duties on all goods or merchandizes of foreign growth or manufacture, imported into any part of the United States, by Stamps on paper, vellum or parchment, and by a postage on all letters or packages passing through the general post-office, to be applied to such federal purposes as they shall deem proper & expedient; to make rules & regulations for the collection thereof; and the same from time to time, to alter & amend in such manner as they shall think proper: to pass Acts for the regulation of trade & commerce as well with foreign nations as with each other: provided that all punishments, fines, forfeitures & penalties to be incurred for contravening such acts rules and regulations shall be adjudged

by the Common law Judiciaries of the State in which any offence contrary to the true intent & meaning of such Acts rules & regulations shall
have been committed or perpetrated, with liberty of commencing in the
first instance all suits & prosecutions for that purpose in the superior
common law Judiciary in such State, subject nevertheless, for the correc-
tion of all errors, both in law & fact in rendering Judgment, to an appeal
to the Judiciary of the United States.

3. Resolved that whenever requisitions shall be necessary, instead of
the rule for making requisitions mentioned in the articles of Confederation, the United States in Congress be authorized to make such requisitions in proportion to the whole number of white & other free citizens
& inhabitants of every age sex and condition including those bound to
servitude for a term of years & three fifths of all other persons not comprehended in the foregoing description, except Indians not paying taxes;
that if such requisitions be not complied with, in the time specified
therein, to direct the collection thereof in the non complying States & for
that purpose to devise and pass acts directing & authorizing the same;
provided that none of the powers hereby vested in the United States in
Congress shall be exercised without the consent of at least   States, and
in that proportion if the number of Confederated States should hereafter
be increased or diminished.

4. Resolved that the United States in Congress be authorized to elect
a federal Executive to consist of   persons, to continue in office for the
term of   years, to receive punctually at stated times a fixed compensation for their services, in which no increase or diminution shall be
made so as to affect the persons composing the Executive at the time of
such increase or diminution, to be paid out of the federal treasury; to be
incapable of holding any other office or appointment during their time
of service and for   years thereafter; to be ineligible a second time, &
removeable by Congress on application by a majority of the Executives
of the several States; that the Executives besides their general authority
to execute the federal acts ought to appoint all federal officers not otherwise provided for, & to direct all military operations; provided that
none of the persons composing the federal Executive shall on any occasion take command of any troops, so as personally to conduct any
enterprise as General or in other capacity.

5. Resolved that a federal Judiciary be established to consist of a supreme Tribunal the Judges of which to be appointed by the Executive,
& to hold their offices during good behaviour, to receive punctually at
stated times a fixed compensation for their services in which no increase
or diminution shall be made, so as to affect the persons actually in office
at the time of such increase or diminution; that the Judiciary so established shall have authority to hear & determine in the first instance on
all impeachments of federal officers, & by way of appeal in the dernier

resort in all cases touching the rights of Ambassadors, in all cases of captures from an enemy, in all cases of piracies & felonies on the high Seas, in all cases in which foreigners may be interested, in the construction of any treaty or treaties, or which may arise on any of the Acts for regulation of trade, or the collection of the federal Revenue: that none of the Judiciary shall during the time they remain in office be capable of receiving or holding any other office or appointment during their time of service, or for   thereafter.

6. Resolved that all Acts of the United States in Congress made by virtue & in pursuance of the powers hereby & by the articles of Confederation vested in them, and all Treaties made & ratified under the authority of the United States shall be the supreme law of the respective States so far forth as those Acts or Treaties shall relate to the said States or their Citizens, and that the Judiciary of the several States shall be bound thereby in their decisions, any thing in the respective laws of the Individual States to the contrary notwithstanding; and that if any State, or any body of men in any State shall oppose or prevent the carrying into execution such acts or treaties, the federal Executive shall be authorized to call forth the power of the Confederated States, or so much thereof as may be necessary to enforce and compel an obedience to such Acts, or an observance of such Treaties.

7. Resolved that provision be made for the admission of new States into the Union.

8. Resolved the rule for naturalization ought to be the same in every State.

9. Resolved that a Citizen of one State committing an offense in another State of the Union, shall be deemed guilty of the same offense as if it had been committed by a Citizen of the State in which the offense was committed.

Source: Gaillard Hunt and James Brown Scott, eds., *The Debates in the Federal Convention of 1787 which Framed the Constitution of the United States of America, Reported by James Madison* (New York: Oxford University Press, 1920), pp. 102–4.

DOCUMENT 40: Debate on the New Jersey and Virginia Plans (June 16, 1787)

The Convention debated the worth of the two plans presented by Paterson and Randolph. Delegates from five states originally backed Paterson's New Jersey Plan: Connecticut, New York, New Jersey, Delaware, and Maryland. With the exception of New York, these were the "small states." New Hampshire was not yet represented at the Convention, and Rhode Island never sent representatives. Delegates from the other six states, the so-called "large states"—in fact or in ambition—rejected Paterson's proposals and supported the revised Virginia Plan (see Document 38). The vote on this issue rejected the New Jersey Plan.

Supporters of the Paterson or New Jersey Plan favored retention of the confederation, with modifications to give more authority to the unicameral Congress of the United States. By contrast, backers of the Randolph or Virginia Plan favored a three-branch national government, with a bicameral legislature, which would diminish the powers enjoyed by the states under the Articles of Confederation. The conflict between advocates of the Virginia and New Jersey plans was settled by the Great Compromise, which provided for a two-house Congress with different principles of organization. The House of Representatives would be based on the national principle, as its members would be elected directly by the people of each state with variation by population in the size of state delegations; that is, larger states would have more representatives and votes than smaller states. By contrast, the Senate would be based on the federal principle, as its members would be selected by the state legislatures and each state would be represented equally by two members.

What were main arguments for the New Jersey Plan by William Paterson and John Lansing of New York? What were the competing arguments by James Wilson of Pennsylvania and Edmund Randolph? What facets of the New Jersey Plan eventually were included in the U.S. Constitution? (See Document 43, Article I, Section 3; Article I, Section 8; Article III, Section 1; and Article VI.)

Mr. LANSING called for the reading of the first resolution of each plan, which he considered as involving principles directly in contrast; that of Mr. Patterson says he sustains the sovereignty of the respective States, that of Mr. Randolph distroys it: the latter requires a negative on all the laws of the particular States; the former, only certain general powers for the general good. The plan of Mr. Randolph in short absorbs all power except what may be exercised in the little local matters of the States which are not objects worthy of the supreme cognizance. He grounded his preference of Mr. Patterson's plan, chiefly on two objections against that of Mr. Randolph. 1. want of power in the Convention to discuss & propose it. 2. the improbability of its being adopted. . . .

Mr. PATTERSON, said as he had on a former occasion given his sentiments on the plan proposed by Mr. Randolph he would now avoiding repetition as much as possible give his reasons in favor of that proposed by himself. He preferred it because it accorded 1. with the powers of the Convention, 2. with the sentiments of the people. If the confederacy was radically wrong, let us return to our States, and obtain larger powers, not assume them of ourselves. . . . If the sovereignty of the States is to be maintained, the Representatives must be drawn immediately from the States, not from the people: and we have no power to vary the idea of equal sovereignty. . . . A distinct executive & Judiciary also were equally provided by his plan. It is urged that two branches in the Legislature are necessary. Why? for the purpose of a check. But the reason of the precaution is not applicable to this case. Within a particular State, where party heats prevail, such a check may be necessary. In such a body as Congress it is less necessary, and besides, the delegations of the different States are checks on each other. Do the people at large complain of Congress? No, what they wish is that Congress may have more power. If the power now proposed be not enough, the people hereafter will make additions to it. With proper powers Congress will act with more energy & wisdom than the proposed National Legislature. . . .

Mr. WILSON entered into a contrast of the principal points of the two plans so far he said as there had been time to examine the one last proposed. These points were 1. in the Virginia plan there are two & in some degree three branches in the Legislature: in the plan from N.J. there is to be a *single* legislature only—2. Representation of the people at large is the basis of the one:—the State Legislatures, the pillars of the other—3. proportional representation prevails in one:—equality of suffrage in the other—4. A single Executive Magistrate is at the head of the one:—a plurality is held out in the other.—5. in the one the majority of the people of the U.S. must prevail:—in the other a minority may prevail. 6. the National Legislature is to make laws in all cases to which the separate States are incompetent &—:—in place of this Congress are to have additional power in a few cases only—7. A negative on the laws of the States:—in place of this coertion to be substituted—8. The Executive to be removeable on impeachment & conviction;—in one plan: in the other to be removeable at the instance of majority of the Executives of the States—9. Revision of the laws provided for in one:—no such check in the other—10. inferior national tribunals in one:—none such in the other. 11. In the one jurisdiction of National tribunals to extend &c—; an appellate jurisdiction only allowed in the other. 12. Here the jurisdiction is to extend to all cases affecting the National peace & harmony: there, a few cases only are marked out. 13. finally the ratification is in this to be by the people themselves:—in that by the legislative authorities according to the thirteenth article of Confederation. . . .

Proceeding now to the first point on which he had contrasted the two plans, he observed that anxious as he was for some augmentation of the federal powers, it would be with extreme reluctance indeed that he could ever consent to give powers to Congress he had two reasons either of which was sufficient. 1. Congress as a Legislative body does not stand on the people. 2. it is a *single* body. 1. He would not repeat the remarks he had formerly made on the principles of Representation. he would only say that an inequality in it, has ever been a poison contaminating every branch of Government . . . 2. *Congress is a single Legislature.* Despotism comes on Mankind in different Shapes, sometimes in an Executive, sometimes in a Military, one. Is there no danger of a Legislative despotism? Theory & practice both proclaim it. If the Legislative authority be not restrained, there can be neither liberty nor stability; and it can only be restrained by dividing it within itself, into distinct and independent branches. In a single House there is no check, but the inadequate one, of the virtue & good sense of those who compose it.

On another great point, the contrast was equally favorable to the plan reported by the Committee of the whole. It vested the Executive powers in a single Magistrate. The plan of New Jersey, vested them in a plurality. In order to controul the Legislative authority, you must divide it. In order to controul the Executive you must unite it. One man will be more responsible than three. . . .

Mr. RANDOLPH, was not scrupulous on the point of power. When the salvation of the Republic was at stake, it would be treason to our trust, not to propose what we found necessary. He painted in strong colours, the imbecility of the existing Confederacy, & the danger of delaying a substantial reform. . . .

The true question is whether we shall adhere to the federal plan, or introduce the national plan. The insufficiency of the former has been fully displayed by the trial already made. . . . We must resort therefor to a National *Legislation over individuals,* for which Congress are unfit. To vest such power in them, would be blending the Legislative with the Executive, contrary to the recognized maxim on this subject: If the Union of these powers heretofore in Congress has been safe, it has been owing to the general impotency of that body. Congress are moreover not elected by the people, but by the Legislatures who retain even a power of recall. They have therefore no will of their own, they are a mere diplomatic body, and are always obsequious to the views of the States, who are always encroaching on the authority of the United States. A provision for harmony among the States, as in trade, naturalization, etc.—for crushing rebellion whenever it may rear its crest—and for certain other general benefits, must be made. The powers for these purposes, can never be given to a body, inadequate as Congress are in point of representation, elected in the mode in which they are, and possessing no more confidence than they do; for notwithstanding what has been said to the contrary, his own experience satisfied him that a rooted distrust of Congress pretty generally prevailed. A National Government alone, properly constituted, will answer the purpose; and he begged it to be considered that the present is the last moment for establishing one. After this select experiment, the people will yield to despair.

Source: Gaillard Hunt and Jane Brown Scott, eds., *The Debates in the Federal Convention of 1787 which Framed the Constitution of the United States of America, Reported by James Madison* (New York: Oxford University Press, 1920), pp. 104–11.

DOCUMENT 41: Debate on Slavery (August 21–22, 1787)

Slavery and the slave trade were mentioned and discussed with intensity at the Convention, but these odious words did not appear in the Constitution, even though the framers of this document made compromises and concessions on the practices of human bondage. (See the Constitution of the United States, Document 43, Article 1, Section 2; Article 1, Section 9; Article IV, Section 2; and Article V.) The debate on the slave trade at the Convention was recorded by James Madison.

Notice the opposition to slavery and the slave trade expressed by Luther Martin of Maryland, George Mason of Virginia, and John Dickinson of Delaware. Mason, ironically, owned a big plantation with many slaves, yet he spoke strongly against slavery. He pointed out that Virginia and Maryland had already prohibited the importation of slaves, and argued that the Constitution should also prohibit it. Defenders of the slave trade, such as General Pinckney of South Carolina and Oliver Ellsworth of Connecticut, argued that Virginia, with a large surplus of U.S.-born slaves for sale within the United States, would gain financially from a constitutional ban of the foreign slave trade.

Delegates from North Carolina (Williamson) and South Carolina (Pinckney and Rutledge) argued for certain concessions on slavery and the slave trade. They wanted the importation of slaves to be a choice of each state, and argued against any constitutional provision to end it. Further, they threatened to oppose the new Constitution and withdraw from the United States if their views on the slave trade were rejected.

Notice that delegates from northern states, such as Connecticut (Sherman and Ellsworth) and Massachusetts (Gerry), while not arguing for slavery, appeared willing to compromise and make certain concessions about it. They represented states with merchants and shippers active in the overseas slave trade. Further, they agreed with others at the Convention that toleration of the slave trade in some states was necessary to achieve ratification of the Constitution and maintenance of the Union. They noted that slavery was dying in the northern states, and they seemed to believe it would soon pass away in the South too.

What specific arguments were presented against slavery or the slave trade by Martin, Mason, and Dickinson? By contrast, what did Pinckney and Rutledge say in favor of the importation of slaves and against a constitutional provision against it? What were the arguments of Sherman, Ellsworth, and Gerry against a constitutional ban against the slave trade? Note the incorrect spellings by the author of this document (James Madison) of the names of Ellsworth, Pinckney, and Rutledge.

Mr. L. MARTIN, proposed to . . . allow a prohibition or tax on the importation of slaves. As five slaves are to be counted as three free men in the apportionment of Representatives; such a clause would leave an encouragement to this traffic. Slaves weakened one part of the Union which the other parts were bound to protect, the privelege of importing them was therefore unreasonable. It was inconsistent with the principles of the revolution and dishonorable to the American character to have such a feature in the Constitution.

Mr. RUTLIDGE . . . was not apprehensive of insurrections and would readily exempt the other states from the obligation to protect the Southern against them. . . . The true question at present is whether the Southern States shall or shall not be parties to the Union. If the Northern States consult their interest, they will not oppose the increase of Slaves which will increase the commodities of which they will become carriers.

Mr. ELSWORTH . . . Let every State import what it pleases. The morality or wisdom of slavery are considerations belonging to the States themselves. What enriches a part enriches the whole, and the States are the best judges of their particular interest. . . .

Mr. PINKNEY . . . South Carolina can never receive the plan if it prohibits the slave trade. In every proposed extension of the powers of Congress, that State has expressly & watchfully excepted that of meddling with the importation of negroes. . . .

Mr. SHERMAN . . . disapproved of the slave trade; yet as the States were now possessed of the right to import slaves, as the public good did not require it to be taken from them, & as it was expedient to have as few objections as possible to the proposed scheme of Government, he thought it best to leave the matter as we find it. He observed that the abolition of Slavery seemed to be going on in the U.S. & that the good sense of the several States would probably by degrees compleat it. He urged the Convention the necessity of dispatching its business.

Col. MASON . . . The present question concerns not the importing States alone but the whole Union. . . . Maryland & Virginia he said had already prohibited the importation of slaves expressly. N. Carolina had done the same in substance. All this would be in vain if S. Carolina & Georgia be at liberty to import. The Western people are already calling out for slaves for their new lands, and will fill that Country with slaves if they can be got through S. Carolina & Georgia. Slavery discourages arts & manufactures. The poor despise labor when performed by slaves. They prevent the immigration of Whites, who really enrich & strengthen a Country. They produce the most pernicious effect on manners. Every master of slaves is a petty tyrant. They bring the judgment of heaven on a Country.

As nations cannot be rewarded or punished in the next world they must be in this. By an inevitable chain of causes & effects providence punishes national sins by national calamities. He lamented that some of our Eastern brethren had from a lust of gain embarked in this nefarious traffic. As to the States being in possession of the Right to import, this was the case with many other rights, now to be properly given up. He held it essential in every point of view that the General Government should have powere to prevent the increase of slavery.

Mr. ELSWORTH. As he had never owned a slave could not judge of the effects of slavery on character. He said however that if it was to be considered in a moral light we ought to go farther and free those already in the Country. As slaves also multiply so fast in Virginia & Maryland that it is cheaper to raise than import them, whilst in the sickly rice swamps [of South Carolina and Georgia] foreign supplies are necessary. If we go no farther than is urged, we shall be unjust towards S. Carolina & Georgia. Let us not intermeddle. As population increases poor laboreres will be so plenty as to render slaves useless. Slavery in time will not be a speck in our Country. Provision is already made in Connecticut for abolishing it. And the abolition has already taken place in Massachusetts. . . .

General PINKNEY . . . S. Carolina & Georgia cannot do without slaves. As to Virginia she will gain by stopping the importations. Her slaves will rise in value, & she has more than she wants. It would be unequal to require S. Carolina & Georgia to confederate on such unequal terms. . . .

Mr. GERRY thought we had nothing to do with the conduct of the States as to Slaves, but ought to be careful not to give any sanction to it.

Mr. DICKENSON considered it as inadmissible on every principle of honor & safety that the importation of slaves should be authorised to the States by the Constitution. The true question was whether the national happiness would be promoted or impeded by the importation, and this question ought to be left to the National Government not to the States particularly interested. . . .

Mr. WILLIAMSON stated the law of N. Carolina on the subject, to wit that it did not directly prohibit the importation of slaves. It imposed a duty . . . on each slave imported. . . . He thought the Southern States could not be members of the Union if the [importation of slaves] should be rejected, and that it was wrong to force anything down, not absolutely necessary which any State must disagree to. . . .

Mr. RUTLIDGE. If the Convention thinks that N. Carolina, S. Carolina & Georgia will ever agree to the plan, unless their right to import slaves be untouched, the expectation is vain. The people of these States will never be such fools as to give up so important an interest.

Source: Gaillard Hunt and James Brown Scott, eds., *The Debates in the Federal Convention of 1787 which Framed the Constitution of the United States of America, Reported by James Madison* (New York: Oxford University Press, 1920), pp. 442–46.

DOCUMENT 42: Signing the Constitution and Concluding the Convention (September 17, 1787)

On the last day of the Convention, the old and infirm Benjamin Franklin presented a speech, read for him by James Wilson, in favor of the final draft of the Constitution. He urged all delegates there to sign the document, even if they still had objections to some parts of it. Franklin recognized imperfections and accommodations to expediency in the document. He also believed that it was the best frame of government that could be achieved at this time. Further, he feared that the United States would fall apart without it.

Three delegates refused to go along with Franklin's plea: Edmund Randolph and George Mason of Virginia and Elbridge Gerry of Massachusetts. Mason and Gerry objected to omission of a formal bill of rights. Mason and Randolph also feared that certain interests of Virginia and other states were not sufficiently protected against abuse by the federal government proposed by the new Constitution. Documents 46 and 47 reveal several specific objections of Gerry and Mason to the Constitution produced by the Federal Convention at Philadelphia.

What reasons did Benjamin Franklin present in favor of unanimous approval of the Constitution produced by the Federal Convention? What view of the future was expressed by Franklin at the end of the Federal Convention?

. . . I confess that there are several parts of this constitution which I do not at present approve, but I am not sure I shall never approve them. For having lived long, I have experienced many instances of being obliged by better information, or fuller consideration, to change opinions even on important subjects, which I once thought right, but found to be otherwise. . . .

In these sentiments, Sir, I agree to this Constitution with all its faults, if they are such; because I think a general Government necessary for us, and there is no form of Government but what may be a blessing to the people if well administered, and believe farther that this is likely to be well administered for a course of years, and can only end in Despotism, as other forms have done before it, when the people shall become so corrupted as to need despotic Government, being incapable of any other. I doubt too whether any other Convention we can obtain, may be able to make a better Constitution. For when you assemble a number of men to have the advantage of their joint wisdom, you inevitably assemble with those men, all their prejudices, their passions, their errors of opinion, their local interests, and their selfish views. From such an assembly can a perfect production be expected? It therefore astonishes me, Sir, to find this system approaching so near to perfection as it does; and I think it will astonish our enemies, who are waiting with confidence to hear that our councils are confounded like those of the Builders of Babel; and that our States are on the point of separation, only to meet hereafter for the purpose of cutting one another's throats. Thus I consent, Sir, to this Constitution because I expect no better, and because I am not sure, that it is not the best. The opinions I have had of its errors, I sacrifice to the public good. I have never whispered a syllable of them abroad. Within these walls they were born, and here they shall die. If every one of us in returning to our Constituents were to report the objections he has had to it, and endeavor to gain partizans in support of them, we might prevent its being generally received, and thereby lose all the salutary effects and great advantages resulting naturally in our favor among foreign Nations as well as among ourselves, from our real or apparent unanimity. Much of the strength and efficiency of any Government in procuring and securing happiness to the people, depends, on opinion, on the general opinion of the goodness of the Government, as well as of the wisdom and integrity of its Governors. I hope therefore that for our own sakes as a part of the people, and for the sake of posterity, we shall act heartily and unanimously in recommending this constitution (if approved by Congress and confirmed by the Conventions) wherever our influence may extend, and turn our future thoughts and endeavors to the means of having it well administered.

On the whole, Sir, I can not help expressing a wish that every member of the convention who may still have objections to it, would with me, on this occasion doubt a little of his own infallibility, and to make manifest our unanimity, put his name to this instrument. . . .

The members then proceeded to sign the instruments.

Whilst the last members were signing it DR. FRANKLIN looking towards the President's Chair, at the back of which a rising sun happened to be painted, observed to a few members near him, that Painters had found it difficult to distinguish in their art a rising from a setting sun. I have said he, often and often in the course of the Session, and the vicisitudes of my hopes and fears as to its issue, looked at that behind the President without being able to tell whether it was rising or setting: But now at length I have the happiness to know that it is a rising and not a setting Sun.

The Constitution being signed by all the members except Mr. Randolph, Mr. Mason, and Mr. Gerry who declined giving it the sanction of their names, the Convention dissolved itself by an Adjournment sine die—

Source: Gaillard Hunt and James Brown Scott, eds., *The Debates in the Federal Convention of 1787 which Framed the Constitution of the United States of America, Reported by James Madison* (New York: Oxford University Press, 1920), pp. 577–83.

DOCUMENT 43: The Constitution of the United States of America, Signed by Thirty-Nine Delegates to the Federal Convention (September 17, 1787)

The Federal Constitutional Convention voted to approve the Constitution on September 15, 1787, signed it on September 17, and submitted it to the Continental Congress, still operating under the Articles of Confederation. This Constitution of 1787 included seven Articles, which listed powers granted in the name of the people to the U.S. government, and by implication, powers reserved to the state governments. Limitations on the powers of both the U.S. government and the state governments were expressed. According to Article VI, the U.S. Constitution, plus laws and treaties enacted in conformity with it, would be the supreme law of the country, which the states would be obligated to uphold. Thus, without mentioning the word *federalism* in their document, the framers of this Constitution provided for a division of powers between the U.S. government and the state governments, which constituted the framers' unprecedented concept of a federal system of U.S. government. What examples of the framers' principle of federalism can you find in Articles I, IV, and VI of the U.S. Constitution?

The 1787 U.S. Constitution described the powers and duties of three distinct branches of government: legislative (Article I), executive (Article II), and judicial (Article III). Thus, without mentioning the phrase *separation of powers* in their document, the framers of this Constitution effectively included this principle of government emphasized strongly by John Adams in his *Thoughts on Government* (Document 9) and the Massachusetts Declaration of Rights of 1780 (Document 15). What examples of the framers' concept of separation of powers can you find in Articles I, II, and III? The 1787 Constitution included a system of checks and balances among the three branches of government. What examples of this system can you find in Articles I, II, and III?

The 1787 Constitution, according to its framers, exemplified the twin principles of republican government and popular sovereignty. James Madison argued during and after the Convention for an unprecedented concept of an extended republic (see Documents 37 and 48). And Americans of the founding era were committed to the idea of popular sovereignty, that is, government by consent of the governed. What examples of republican government and popular sovereignty can you find in this document? (See Articles I, IV, and VII.)

The 1787 Constitution was supposed to be a limited government for the ultimate purpose of protecting the unalienable rights of individuals. The framers believed they were acting in conformity with the criteria for good government proclaimed in the Declaration of Independence: Governments are instituted among "Men" to secure their "unalienable" rights to life, liberty and the pursuit of happiness, which are equally the possessions of all persons (see Document 7). What arguments and examples can be presented in support of the view that this Constitution was designed "to secure these Rights"? What arguments and examples can be presented to indicate shortcomings or deficiencies in the 1787 Constitution in regard to the Declaration of Independence's criteria for good government?

THE CONSTITUTION OF THE UNITED STATES

We the People of the United States, in Order to form a more perfect Union, establish Justice, insure domestic Tranquility, provide for the common defence, promote the general Welfare, and secure the Blessings of Liberty to ourselves and our Posterity, do ordain and establish this Constitution for the United States of America.

Article. I.

Section. 1. All legislative Powers herein granted shall be vested in a Congress of the United States, which shall consist of a Senate and House of Representatives.

Section. 2. The House of Representatives shall be composed of Members chosen every second Year by the People of the several States, and the Electors in each State shall have the Qualifications requisite for Electors of the most numerous Branch of the State Legislature.

No Person shall be a Representative who shall not have attained to the Age of twenty five Years, and been seven Years a Citizen of the United States, and who shall not, when elected, be an Inhabitant of that State in which he shall be chosen.

Representatives and direct Taxes shall be apportioned among the several States which may be included within this Union, according to their respective Numbers, which shall be determined by adding to the whole Number of free Persons, including those bound to Service for a Term of Years, and excluding Indians not taxed, three fifths of all other Persons. The actual Enumeration shall be made within three Years after the first Meeting of the Congress of the United States, and within every subsequent Term of ten Years, in such Manner as they shall by Law direct. The Number of Representatives shall not exceed one for every thirty Thousand, but each State shall have at Least one Representative; and until such enumeration shall be made, the State of New Hampshire shall be entitled to chuse three, Massachusetts eight, Rhode-Island and Providence Plantations one, Connecticut five, New-York six, New Jersey four, Pennsylvania eight, Delaware one, Maryland six, Virginia ten, North Carolina five, South Carolina five, and Georgia three.

When vacancies happen in the Representation from any State, the Executive Authority thereof shall issue Writs of Election to fill such Vacancies.

The House of Representatives shall chuse their Speaker and other Officers; and shall have the sole Power of Impeachment.

Section. 3. The Senate of the United States shall be composed of two Senators from each State, chosen by the Legislature thereof, for six Years; and each Senator shall have one Vote.

Immediately after they shall be assembled in Consequence of the first Election, they shall be divided as equally as may be into three Classes. The Seats of the Senators of the first Class shall be vacated at the Expiration of the second Year, of the second Class at the Expiration of the fourth Year, and of the third Class at the Expiration of the sixth Year, so that one third may be chosen every second Year; and if Vacancies happen by Resignation, or otherwise, during the Recess of the Legislature of any State, the Executive thereof may make temporary Appointments until the next Meeting of the Legislature, which shall then fill such Vacancies.

No Person shall be a Senator who shall not have attained to the Age of thirty Years, and been nine Years a Citizen of the United States, and who shall not, when elected, be an Inhabitant of that State for which he shall be chosen.

The Vice President of the United States shall be President of the Senate, but shall have no Vote, unless they be equally divided.

The Senate shall chuse their other Officers, and also a President pro tempore, in the Absence of the Vice President, or when he shall exercise the Office of President of the United States.

The Senate shall have the sole Power to try all Impeachments. When sitting for that Purpose, they shall be on Oath or Affirmation. When the President of the United States is tried, the Chief Justice shall preside: And no Person shall be convicted without the Concurrence of two thirds of the Members present.

Judgment in Cases of Impeachment shall not extend further than to removal from Office, and disqualification to hold and enjoy any Office of honor, Trust or Profit under the United States: but the Party convicted shall nevertheless be liable and subject to Indictment, Trial, Judgment and Punishment, according to Law.

Section. 4. The Times, Places and Manner of holding Elections for Senators and Representatives, shall be prescribed in each State by the Legislature thereof; but the Congress may at any time by Law make or alter such Regulations, except as to the Places of chusing Senators.

The Congress shall assemble at least once in every Year, and such Meeting shall be on the first Monday in December, unless they shall by Law appoint a different Day.

Section. 5. Each House shall be the Judge of the Elections, Returns and Qualifications of its own Members, and a Majority of each shall constitute a Quorum to do Business; but a smaller Number may adjourn from day to day, and may be authorized to compel the Attendance of absent Members, in such Manner, and under such Penalties as each House may provide.

Each House may determine the Rules of its Proceedings, punish its Members for disorderly Behaviour, and, with the Concurrence of two thirds, expel a Member.

Each House shall keep a Journal of its Proceedings, and from time to time publish the same, excepting such Parts as may in their Judgment require Secrecy; and the Yeas and Nays of the Members of either House on any question shall, at the Desire of one fifth of those Present, be entered on the Journal.

Neither House, during the Session of Congress, shall, without the Consent of the other, adjourn for more than three days, nor to any other Place than that in which the two Houses shall be sitting.

Section. 6. The Senators and Representatives shall receive a Compensation for their Services, to be ascertained by Law, and paid out of the Treasury of the United States. They shall in all Cases, except Treason, Felony and Breach of the Peace, be privileged from Arrest during their Attendance at the Session of their respective Houses, and in going to and returning from the same; and for any Speech or Debate in either House, they shall not be questioned in any other Place.

No Senator or Representative shall, during the Time for which he was elected, be appointed to any civil Office under the Authority of the United States, which shall have been created, or the Emoluments whereof shall have been encreased during such time; and no Person holding any Office under the United States, shall be a Member of either House during his Continuance in Office.

Section. 7. All Bills for raising Revenue shall originate in the House of Representatives; but the Senate may propose or concur with Amendments as on other Bills.

Every Bill which shall have passed the House of Representatives and the Senate, shall, before it become a Law, be presented to the President of the United States; If he approve he shall sign it, but if not he shall return it, with his Objections to that House in which it shall have originated, who shall enter the Objections at large on their Journal, and proceed to reconsider it. If after such Reconsideration two thirds of that House shall agree to pass the Bill, it shall be sent, together with the Objections, to the other House, by which it shall likewise be reconsidered, and if approved by two thirds of that House, it shall become a Law. But in all such Cases the Votes of both Houses shall be determined by yeas and Nays, and the Names of the Persons voting for and against the Bill shall be entered on the Journal of each House respectively. If any Bill shall not be returned by the President within ten Days (Sundays excepted) after it shall have been presented to him, the Same shall be a Law, in like Manner as if he had signed it, unless the Congress by their Adjournment prevent its Return in which Case it shall not be a Law.

Every Order, Resolution, or Vote to which the Concurrence of the Senate and House of Representatives may be necessary (except on a question of Adjournment) shall be presented to the President of the United States; and before the Same shall take Effect, shall be approved by him, or being disapproved by him, shall be repassed by two thirds of the Senate and House of Representatives, according to the Rules and Limitations prescribed in the Case of a Bill.

Section. 8. The Congress shall have Power To lay and collect Taxes, Duties, Imposts and Excises, to pay the Debts and provide for the common Defence and general Welfare of the United States; but all Duties, Imposts and Excises shall be uniform throughout the United States;

To borrow Money on the credit of the United States;

To regulate Commerce with foreign Nations, and among the several States, and with the Indian Tribes;

To establish an uniform Rule of Naturalization, and uniform Laws on the subject of Bankruptcies throughout the United States;

To coin Money, regulate the Value thereof, and of foreign Coin, and fix the Standard of Weights and Measures;

To provide for the Punishment of counterfeiting the Securities and current Coin of the United States;

To establish Post Offices and post Roads;

To promote the Progress of Science and useful Arts, by securing for limited Times to Authors and Inventors the exclusive Right to their respective Writings and Discoveries;

To constitute Tribunals inferior to the supreme Court;

To define and punish Piracies and Felonies committed on the high Seas, and Offences against the Law of Nations;

To declare War, grant Letters of Marque and Reprisal, and make Rules concerning Captures on Land and Water;

To raise and support Armies, but no Appropriation of Money to that Use shall be for a longer Term than two Years;

To provide and maintain a Navy;

To make Rules for the Government and Regulation of the land and naval Forces;

To provide for calling forth the Militia to execute the Laws of the Union, suppress Insurrections and repel Invasions;

To provide for organizing, arming, and disciplining, the Militia, and for governing such Part of them as may be employed in the Service of the United States, reserving to the States respectively, the Appointment of the Officers, and the Authority of training the Militia according to the discipline prescribed by Congress;

To exercise exclusive Legislation in all Cases whatsoever, over such District (not exceeding ten Miles square) as may, by Cession of particular States, and the Acceptance of Congress, become the Seat of the Government of the United States, and to exercise like Authority over all Places purchased by the Consent of the Legislature of the State in which the Same shall be, for the Erection of Forts, Magazines, Arsenals, dock-Yards, and other needful Buildings;—And

To make all Laws which shall be necessary and proper for carrying into Execution the foregoing Powers, and all other Powers vested by this Constitution in the Government of the United States, or in any Department or Officer thereof.

Section. 9. The Migration or Importation of such Persons as any of the States now existing shall think proper to admit, shall not be prohibited by the Congress prior to the Year one thousand eight hundred and eight, but a Tax or duty may be imposed on such Importation, not exceeding ten dollars for each Person.

The Privilege of the Writ of Habeas Corpus shall not be suspended, unless when in Cases of Rebellion or Invasion the public Safety may require it.

No Bill of Attainder or ex post facto Law shall be passed.

No Capitation, or other direct, Tax shall be laid, unless in Proportion to the Census or Enumeration herein before directed to be taken.

No Tax or Duty shall be laid on Articles exported from any State.

No Preference shall be given by any Regulation of Commerce or Revenue to the Ports of one State over those of another: nor shall Vessels bound to, or from, one State, be obliged to enter, clear, or pay Duties in another.

No Money shall be drawn from the Treasury, but in Consequence of Appropriations made by Law; and a regular Statement and Account of the Receipts and Expenditures of all public Money shall be published from time to time.

No Title of Nobility shall be granted by the United States: And no Person holding any Office of Profit or Trust under them, shall, without the Consent of the Congress, accept of any present, Emolument, Office, or Title, of any kind whatever, from any King, Prince, or foreign State.

Section. 10. No State shall enter into any Treaty, Alliance, or Confederation; grant Letters of Marque and Reprisal; coin Money; emit Bills of Credit; make any Thing but gold and silver Coin a Tender in Payment of Debts; pass any Bill of Attainder, ex post facto Law, or Law impairing the Obligation of Contracts, or grant any Title of Nobility.

No State shall, without the Consent of the Congress, lay any Imposts or Duties on Imports or Exports, except what may be absolutely necessary for executing it's inspection Laws: and the net Produce of all Duties and Imposts, laid by any State on Imports or Exports, shall be for the Use of the Treasury of the United States; and all such Laws shall be subject to the Revision and Controul of the Congress.

No State shall, without the Consent of Congress, lay any Duty of Tonnage, keep Troops, or Ships of War in time of Peace, enter into any Agreement or Compact with another State, or with a foreign Power, or engage in War, unless actually invaded, or in such imminent Danger as will not admit of delay.

Article. II.

Section. 1. The executive Power shall be vested in a President of the United States of America. He shall hold his Office during the Term of four Years, and, together with the Vice President, chosen for the same Term, be elected as follows

Each State shall appoint, in such Manner as the Legislature thereof may direct, a Number of Electors, equal to the whole Number of Senators and Representatives to which the State may be entitled in the Congress: but no Senator or Representative, or Person holding an Office of Trust or Profit under the United States, shall be appointed an Elector.

The Electors shall meet in their respective States, and vote by Ballot for two Persons, of whom one at least shall not be an Inhabitant of the same State with themselves. And they shall make a List of all the Persons voted for, and of the Number of Votes for each; which List they shall sign and certify, and transmit sealed to the Seat of the Government of the United States, directed to the President of the Senate. The President of the Senate shall, in the Presence of the Senate and House of Representatives, open all the Certificates, and the Votes shall then be counted. The Person having the greatest Number of Votes shall be the President, if such Number be a Majority of the whole Number of Electors appointed; and if there be more than one who have such Majority, and have an equal Number of Votes, then the House of Representatives shall immediately chuse by Ballot one of them for President; and if no Person have a Majority, then from the five highest on the List the said House shall in like Manner chuse the President. But in chusing the President, the Votes shall be taken by States, the Representation from each State having one Vote; A quorum for this Purpose shall consist of a Member or Members from two thirds of the States, and a Majority of all the States shall be necessary to a Choice. In every Case, after the Choice of the

President, the Person having the greatest Number of Votes of the Electors shall be the Vice President. But if there should remain two or more who have equal Votes, the Senate shall chuse from them by Ballot the Vice President.

The Congress may determine the Time of chusing the Electors, and the Day on which they shall give their Votes; which Day shall be the same throughout the United States.

No Person except a natural born Citizen, or a Citizen of the United States, at the time of the Adoption of this Constitution, shall be eligible to the Office of President; neither shall any Person be eligible to that Office who shall not have attained to the Age of thirty five Years, and been fourteen Years a Resident within the United States.

In Case of the Removal of the President from Office, or of his Death, Resignation, or Inability to discharge the Powers and Duties of the said Office, the Same shall devolve on the Vice President, and the Congress may by Law provide for the Case of Removal, Death, Resignation or Inability, both of the President and Vice President, declaring what Officer shall then act as President, and such Officer shall act accordingly, until the Disability be removed, or a President shall be elected.

The President shall, at stated Times, receive for his Services, a Compensation, which shall neither be encreased nor diminished during the Period for which he shall have been elected, and he shall not receive within that Period any other Emolument from the United States, or any of them.

Before he enter on the Execution of his Office, he shall take the following Oath or Affirmation:—"I do solemnly swear (or affirm) that I will faithfully execute the Office of President of the United States, and will to the best of my Ability, preserve, protect and defend the Constitution of the United States."

Section. 2. The President shall be Commander in Chief of the Army and Navy of the United States, and of the Militia of the several States, when called into the actual Service of the United States; he may require the Opinion, in writing, of the principal Officer in each of the executive Departments, upon any Subject relating to the Duties of their respective Offices, and he shall have Power to grant Reprieves and Pardons for Offences against the United States, except in Cases of Impeachment.

He shall have Power, by and with the Advice and Consent of the Senate, to make Treaties, provided two thirds of the Senators present concur; and he shall nominate, and by and with the Advice and Consent of the Senate, shall appoint Ambassadors, other public Ministers and Consuls, Judges of the supreme Court, and all other Officers of the United States, whose Appointments are not herein otherwise provided for, and which shall be established by Law: but the Congress may by Law vest the Appointment of such inferior Officers, as they think proper, in the President alone, in the Courts of Law, or in the Heads of Departments.

The President shall have Power to fill up all Vacancies that may happen during the Recess of the Senate, by granting Commissions which shall expire at the End of their next Session.

Section. 3. He shall from time to time give to the Congress Information of the State of the Union, and recommend to their Consideration such Measures as he shall judge necessary and expedient; he may, on extraordinary Occasions, convene both Houses, or either of them, and in Case of Disagreement between them, with Respect to the Time of Adjournment, he may adjourn them to such Time as he shall think proper; he shall receive Ambassadors and other public Ministers; he shall take Care that the Laws be faithfully executed, and shall Commission all the Officers of the United States.

Section. 4. The President, Vice President and all civil Officers of the United States, shall be removed from Office on Impeachment for, and Conviction of, Treason, Bribery, or other high Crimes and Misdemeanors.

Article. III.

Section. 1. The judicial Power of the United States, shall be vested in one supreme Court, and in such inferior Courts as the Congress may from time to time ordain and establish. The Judges, both of the supreme and inferior Courts, shall hold their Offices during good Behaviour, and shall, at stated Times, receive for their Services, a Compensation, which shall not be diminished during their Continuance in Office.

Section. 2. The judicial Power shall extend to all Cases, in Law and Equity, arising under this Constitution, the Laws of the United States, and Treaties made, or which shall be made, under their Authority;—to all Cases affecting Ambassadors, other public Ministers and Consuls;—to all Cases of admiralty and maritime Jurisdiction;—to Controversies to which the United States shall be a Party;—to Controversies between two or more States;—between a State and Citizens of another State;—between Citizens of different States,—between Citizens of the same State claiming Lands under Grants of different States, and between a State, or the Citizens thereof, and foreign States, Citizens or Subjects.

In all Cases affecting Ambassadors, other public Ministers and Consuls, and those in which a State shall be Party, the supreme Court shall have original Jurisdiction. In all the other Cases before mentioned, the supreme Court shall have appellate Jurisdiction, both as to Law and Fact, with such Exceptions, and under such Regulations as the Congress shall make.

The Trial of all Crimes, except in Cases of Impeachment, shall be by

Jury; and such Trial shall be held in the State where the said Crimes shall have been committed; but when not committed within any State, the Trial shall be at such Place or Places as the Congress may by Law have directed.

Section. 3. Treason against the United States, shall consist only in levying War against them, or in adhering to their Enemies, giving them Aid and Comfort. No Person shall be convicted of Treason unless on the Testimony of two Witnesses to the same overt Act, or on Confession in open Court.

The Congress shall have Power to declare the Punishment of Treason, but no Attainder of Treason shall work Corruption of Blood, or Forfeiture except during the Life of the Person attainted.

Article. IV.

Section. 1. Full Faith and Credit shall be given in each State to the public Acts, Records, and judicial Proceedings of every other State. And the Congress may by general Laws prescribe the Manner in which such Acts, Records and Proceedings shall be proved, and the Effect thereof.

Section. 2. The Citizens of each State shall be entitled to all Privileges and Immunities of Citizens in the several States.

A Person charged in any State with Treason, Felony, or other Crime, who shall flee from Justice, and be found in another State, shall on Demand of the executive Authority of the State from which he fled, be delivered up, to be removed to the State having Jurisdiction of the Crime.

No Person held to Service or Labour in one State, under the Laws thereof, escaping into another, shall, in Consequence of any Law or Regulation therein, be discharged from such Service or Labour, but shall be delivered up on Claim of the Party to whom such Service or Labour may be due.

Section. 3. New States may be admitted by the Congress into this Union; but no new State shall be formed or erected within the Jurisdiction of any other State; nor any State be formed by the Junction of two or more States, or Parts of States, without the Consent of the Legislatures of the States concerned as well as of the Congress.

The Congress shall have Power to dispose of and make all needful Rules and Regulations respecting the Territory or other Property belonging to the United States; and nothing in this Constitution shall be so construed as to Prejudice any Claims of the United States, or of any particular State.

Section. 4. The United States shall guarantee to every State in this Union a Republican Form of Government, and shall protect each of them against Invasion; and on Application of the Legislature, or of the Executive (when the Legislature cannot be convened) against domestic Violence.

Article. V.

The Congress, whenever two thirds of both Houses shall deem it necessary, shall propose Amendments to this Constitution, or, on the Application of the Legislatures of two thirds of the several States, shall call a Convention for proposing Amendments, which, in either Case, shall be valid to all Intents and Purposes, as Part of this Constitution, when ratified by the Legislatures of three fourths of the several States, or by Conventions in three fourths thereof, as the one or the other Mode of Ratification may be proposed by the Congress; Provided that no Amendment which may be made prior to the Year One thousand eight hundred and eight shall in any Manner affect the first and fourth Clauses in the Ninth Section of the first Article; and that no State, without its Consent, shall be deprived of it's equal Suffrage in the Senate.

Article. VI.

All Debts contracted and Engagements entered into, before the Adoption of this Constitution, shall be as valid against the United States under this Constitution, as under the Confederation.

This Constitution, and the Laws of the United States which shall be made in Pursuance thereof; and all Treaties made, or which shall be made, under the Authority of the United States, shall be the supreme Law of the Land; and the Judges in every State shall be bound thereby, any Thing in the Constitution or Laws of any State to the Contrary notwithstanding.

The Senators and Representatives before mentioned, and the Members of the several State Legislatures, and all executive and judicial Officers, both of the United States and of the several States, shall be bound by Oath or Affirmation, to support this Constitution; but no religious Test shall ever be required as a Qualification to any Office or public Trust under the United States.

Article. VII.

The Ratification of the Conventions of nine States, shall be sufficient for the Establishment of this Constitution between the States so ratifying the Same.

The Word, "the," being interlined between the seventh and eighth Lines of the first Page, The Word "Thirty" being partly written on an Erazure in the fifteenth Line of the first Page, The Words "is tried" being interlined between the thirty second and thirty third Lines of the first Page and the Word "the" being interlined between the forty third and forty fourth Lines of the second Page.

Attest WILLIAM JACKSON Secretary done in Convention by the Unanimous Consent of the States present the Seventeenth Day of September in the Year of our Lord one thousand seven hundred and Eighty seven and of the Independence of the United States of America the Twelfth In witness whereof We have hereunto subscribed our Names,

G⁰ WASHINGTON—Presidᵗ
and deputy from Virginia

New Hampshire	{ JOHN LANGDON NICHOLAS GILMAN
Massachusetts	{ NATHANIEL GORHAM RUFUS KING
Connecticut	{ Wᴹ Samˡ JOHNSON ROGER SHERMAN
New York . .	ALEXANDER HAMILTON
New Jersey	{ WIL: LIVINGSTON DAVID BREARLEY. Wᴹ PATERSON. JONA: DAYTON
Pennsylvania	{ B FRANKLIN THOMAS MIFFLIN ROBᵀ MORRIS GEO. CLYMER THOˢ FITZSIMONS JARED INGERSOLL JAMES WILSON GOUV MORRIS
Delaware	{ GEO: READ GUNNING BEDFORD jun JOHN DICKINSON RICHARD BASSETT JACO: BROOM
Maryland	{ JAMES MᶜHENRY DAN OF Sᵀ THOˢ JENIFER DANˡ CARROLL
Virginia	{ JOHN BLAIR— JAMES MADISON Jr.

North Carolina $\left\{\begin{array}{l} \text{W}^{\text{M}} \text{ BLOUNT} \\ \text{RICH}^{\text{D}} \text{ DOBBS SPAIGHT.} \\ \text{HU WILLIAMSON} \end{array}\right.$

South Carolina $\left\{\begin{array}{l} \text{J. RUTLEDGE} \\ \text{CHARLES COTESWORTH PINCKNEY} \\ \text{CHARLES PINCKNEY} \\ \text{PIERCE BUTLER.} \end{array}\right.$

Georgia $\left\{\begin{array}{l} \text{WILLIAM FEW} \\ \text{ABR BALDWIN} \end{array}\right.$

Source: Gaillard Hunt and James Brown Scott, eds., *The Debates in the Federal Convention of 1787 which Framed the Constitution of the United States of America, Reported by James Madison* (New York: Oxford University Press, 1920), pp. 627–38.

FURTHER READING

Anastaplo, George. *The Constitution of 1787: A Commentary.* Baltimore: The Johns Hopkins University Press, 1989.

Bowen, Catherine Drinker. *Miracle at Philadelphia: The Story of the Constitutional Convention, May to September 1787.* Boston: Little, Brown, 1966.

Kaminski, John P. *A Necessary Evil: Slavery and the Debate over the Constitution.* Madison, Wis.: Madison House, 1995.

Ketcham, Ralph. *Framed for Posterity: The Enduring Philosophy of the Constitution.* Lawrence: University Press of Kansas, 1993.

Levy, Leonard W., and Dennis J. Mahoney, eds. *The Framing and Ratification of the Constitution.* New York: Macmillan, 1987.

McDonald, Forrest. *Novus Ordo Seclorum: The Intellectual Origins of the Constitution.* Lawrence: University Press of Kansas, 1985.

Miller, William Lee. *The Business of May Next: James Madison and the Founding.* Charlottesville: University Press of Virginia, 1992.

Morgan, Robert J. *James Madison on the Constitution and the Bill of Rights.* Westport, Conn.: Greenwood Press, 1988.

Peters, William. *A More Perfect Union: The Making of the United States Constitution.* New York: Crown Publishers, 1987.

Rossiter, Clinton. *1787: The Grand Convention.* New York: W. W. Norton and Company, 1966.

Rutland, Robert A. *James Madison: The Founding Father.* New York: Macmillan, 1987.

Part VI

Debate on the Constitution: Federalists Versus Anti-Federalists, 1787–1788

On September 28, 1787, the Continental Congress, acting under the Articles of Confederation, discussed the Constitution of the United States proposed by "the Convention lately assembled in Philadelphia." The Congress voted unanimously to send it to the legislature of each of the thirteen states "in Order to be submitted to a convention of Delegates chosen in each state by the people thereof."[1] Congress requested each state to convene a special ratifying convention to approve or reject the Constitution of 1787. If nine states' ratifying conventions would approve it, this Constitution would become the supreme law of the United States.

Arguments on the new Constitution flared throughout the country in taverns, clubrooms, street corners, and newspapers. Alexander Hamilton wrote to George Washington, "The Constitution proposed has in this state [New York] warm friends and warm enemies."[2] Scathing attacks, for example, were printed in the *New York Journal* (see Document 44) and other newspapers, which upset and alarmed supporters of the Constitution.

Alexander Hamilton planned a series of newspaper articles to refute the "warm enemies" of the Constitution and persuaded James Madison and John Jay to join him. They became authors of eighty-five papers in support of the Constitution, a collection called *The Federalist*. Each paper was signed with a pseudonym, Publius, after Publius Valerius Publicola, a great defender of the ancient Roman Republic. Most of Publius's papers were printed originally in New York City newspapers. In 1788, they were published collectively as a two-volume work, *The Federalist*. Hamilton, major author of *The Federalist,* wrote fifty-one of the eighty-five papers: 1, 6–9, 11–13, 15–17, 21–36, 59–61, and 65–85 (see Documents 45 and 53, examples of *Federalist* papers by Hamilton). Madison wrote twenty-nine papers: 10, 14, 18–20, 37–58, and 62–63 (see Documents 48, 50 and 51, examples of *Federalist* papers by Madison). Illness forced John Jay to withdraw from the project, and he wrote only five essays: 2–5 and 64.

With the name *The Federalist,* they scored a public relations victory against their opponents, who accepted by default the label *Anti-Federalist,* which suggested only negative views, with no positive plans to improve the government. There was irony in these names, because the opponents of Hamilton, Madison, and Jay considered themselves the "true" federalists—supporters of strong state powers in a federal system created by sovereign state governments. The so-called Anti-Federalists viewed Hamilton and his allies as "consolidationists"—na-tionalists who would subordinate state powers to an overbearing central government.

Hundreds of essays, letters, and speeches were written and published on both sides of this extended debate. The eighty-five papers of *The Federalist,* for example, were a small fraction of the total number of pieces written by supporters of the Constitution of 1787. And hundreds of Anti-Federalist papers were written on the other side of this great debate.

Throughout their controversy, however, the Federalists and Anti-Federalists agreed on the fundamental principles of good government. Both, for example, were ardent constitutionalists, supporters of consti-tutional limitations on government to provide the rule of law. They equally preferred republican government and popular sovereignty, with the people as the sole foundation for representative public insti-tutions and officials. Both sides to the great debate wanted some type of federalism, that is, division of governmental powers between a cen-tral government and several state governments that constituted a fed-eration. Finally, both Federalists and Anti-Federalists were committed to the idea of free government, that is, government designed and ded-icated to guarantee or secure the natural rights of individuals.

There was broad consensus on the desirability of constitutionalism, republican government, popular sovereignty, federalism, and security for individual rights. But there was sharp debate on how to design and establish a government that could adequately exemplify and imple-ment these core ideas of the American founding era. The Federalists argued that the Constitution of 1787 provided for constitutional gov-ernment that would be satisfactorily republican, federal, and free. Anti-Federalists did not believe that the Constitution of 1787 could be an instrument for the satisfactory practice of good government.

Anti-Federalist views are exemplified by Documents 44, 46, 47, 49, and 52. Brutus (pseudonym), a New York Anti-Federalist, warned the people "that a consolidation of this extensive continent under one government . . . cannot succeed without a sacrifice of your liberties." He argued that the Constitution of 1787 gave the central government too much power at the expense of state governments of the federal union (see Document 44).

Brutus and other Anti-Federalists argued that the Constitution of 1787 violated or contradicted the true and traditional conception of federalism, the only one that had ever been recorded in world history. According to the Anti-Federalists, a traditional and true federal system or confederation is created by sovereign states for certain limited purposes, such as conduct of foreign affairs and defense against external enemies. The central government of the confederation is directly accountable to the sovereign states that created it. And each state of the confederation is directly accountable to its people. The central government of the confederation does not act directly on the persons of the states; only the state governments can do this with regard to their own inhabitants. Further, the powers of the central government are limited to those few expressly delegated to it by sovereign states. All other powers of government are reserved to the states.

The Anti-Federalist conception of federalism fit the Articles of Confederation, but not the Constitution of 1787. Anti-Federalists claimed this Constitution would lead to a consolidated national government, which would usurp the powers of state governments and render insecure the natural rights of the people. Anti-Federalists wanted a confederation of small republics (states) with a very limited central or federal government and stronger state governments. They saw the individual states as the true republics. They pointed to the writings of great political philosophers, such as the celebrated Frenchman, Montesquieu, who wrote in *The Spirit of the Laws* (1748) that "it is natural for a republic to have only a small territory; otherwise it can scarcely continue to exist. . . . [By contrast] a large empire presupposes a despotic authority in the one who governs."[3] They argued that a national government of the United States could not be a true republic because the nation was too large and the population too diverse. Throughout world history, republican government had existed only in small territories with rather homogeneous populations.

The key to liberty, according to Anti-Federalists, is direct and substantial representation of the people in their government, which is close to them. They rejected the conception of an extended federal republic, such as the U.S. government would be under the Constitution of 1787. This new national government would be too far removed from the people and too little accountable to them.

In addition to their charges that the proposed Constitution violated the true conceptions of federalism and republicanism, the Anti-Federalists made the following criticisms:

- It had no declaration of rights of the people

- The power of the central government to tax, command militia of the states, and maintain an army in peacetime was excessive and objectionable

- The power of Congress to pass any law "necessary and proper" to carry out its enumerated powers would mean it could too easily and greatly expand its powers and threaten rights of the people

- The President and Senate had too much power relative to the House of Representatives, the branch of government closest to the people

- The judicial branch in the Constitution of 1787 would threaten liberty, because it was too removed from accountability to the people and could overrule acts of state governments

The Federalists rejected these criticisms. They offered distinctive, new conceptions of federalism and republican government, which are exemplified by Documents 45, 48, 50, 51, and 53.

Hamilton and Madison, as Publius, argued that the U.S. government had to be strong enough, by constitutional design, to enforce order and provide safety for the people and their property. But its power had to be limited enough, by constitutional design, to prevent tyranny and abuses of individual rights. Publius (Madison) aptly expressed this timeless problem of constitutional design for ordered liberty: "You must first enable the government to controul the governed; and in the next place oblige it to controul itself" (see *Federalist* 51, Document 51).

According to Publius, the 1787 Constitution provided to the U.S. government every power needed to carry out duties the people would expect of it, such as protection against foreign invasions and internal disorder that could threaten the safety, security, and liberty of individuals. In *Federalist* 1 (Document 45), Publius (Hamilton) warned that "the vigour of government is essential to the security of liberty." And in *Federalist* 23, Publius (Hamilton) stressed "The necessity of a Constitution [with sufficient power] to the preservation of the Union."[4]

The Constitution of 1787 provided for new conceptions of federalism and republican government that would enable the U.S. government to act directly on the people to collect taxes, maintain military and police forces, regulate interstate commerce, and otherwise enforce federal laws. The federal government would be supreme over state governments within limitations set by the 1787 Constitution.

Publius tried to allay fears about dangers to free government and natural rights raised by Anti-Federalist critics. He stressed in *Federalist* 10 (Document 48) that a "well-constructed Union" can secure natural rights and protect the people against tyranny—especially the tyranny of majorities against unpopular individuals or minorities, a flaw of traditional republican governments in small territories. He argued that the essential elements of a "well-constructed Union" and constitutional system were (1) federalism in a large republic and (2) separation of powers, with checks and balances in the federal government.

Publius held that federalism in a large republic would check tyranny by dividing powers between a central government of the United States and the several state governments, so that the two levels of government could check and control one another. Further, he maintained that the social diversity of a large federal republic, such as the vast territory of the United States under the 1787 Constitution, would be conducive to security for the natural rights of individuals against majoritarian tyranny, which was a great threat to liberty in a government by majority rule of the people's elected representatives and had been a bane of small republics of the past. Publius wrote that the vast number of different groups and interests in a large federal republic of national scope would be an enormous barrier to the formation of a permanent and overbearing majority faction that could dominate others oppressively. Various groups and interests would have to compromise and collaborate to make decisions by majority rule (see *Federalist* 10, 39, and 51, Documents 48, 50, and 51).

The primary constitutional instrument for limiting government to protect individual rights, according to Publius, would be separation of powers among three branches of government. Publius wrote (*Federalist* 47): "The accumulation of all powers, legislative, executive, and judiciary, in the same hands . . . may justly be pronounced the very definition of tyranny."[5] The Constitution of 1787 was designed to prevent accumulation of too much power by any group or person, because each separate branch of the government would have constitutional power to check the others. Further, each branch would be accountable to the others, and all branches would be accountable to the people (see Document 51).

The Federalists prevailed over the Anti-Federalists in the debate on the Constitution, which was ratified by the requisite nine states in 1788. In September 1788, the Continental Congress, formed under the Articles of Confederation, recognized the legitimacy of the new Constitution. It fixed the dates of elections of representatives to the new federal government and the first meeting of the new federal Congress. Then, the Continental Congress dissolved at the end of 1788 to make way for the new federal government to be instituted in 1789.

The intense contest over ratification of the 1787 Constitution was an extraordinary example of public deliberation and choice in the formation of government, whereby the people determined through their public forums how they would be constituted and ruled. Nothing quite like it had ever happened before anywhere in the world.

The Federalists' victory was achieved through accommodation to certain Anti-Federalist concerns. They publicly pledged that the first Congress would receive and act upon amendments to the new Constitution proposed by Anti-Federalists to secure the rights of the states and the people within the new federal system. (The consequences of this Federalist pledge to the Anti-Federalists are discussed in Part VII.) The terms of the debate on good government between Federalists and Anti-Federalists are exemplified by Documents 44–53 of Part VI. Ideas in these documents have remained relevant to Americans, who have continued to discuss the perennial issues about good government raised during the founding era and framed by the Federalists and their Anti-Federalist opponents.

NOTES

1. Merril Jensen, ed., *The Documentary History of the Ratification of the Constitution,* Vol. 1 (Madison, Wis.: State Historical Society of Wisconsin, 1976), p. 327.

2. Henry C. Lodge, ed., *The Works of Alexander Hamilton,* Vol. 9 (New York: G.P. Putnam's Sons, 1904), p. 425.

3. Anne Cohler, Basia Miller, and Harold Stone, eds., *Montesquieu, The Spirit of the Laws* (Cambridge: Cambridge University Press, 1989), pp. 124, 126.

4. Garry Wills, ed., *The Federalist Papers by Alexander Hamilton, James Madison and John Jay* (New York: Bantam Books, 1982), p. 111.

5. Ibid., p. 244.

DOCUMENT 44: Essay I (Brutus, October 18, 1787)

Brutus, the pseudonym of an adept Anti-Federalist, wrote sixteen essays opposing the Constitution of 1787, which were printed in the *New York Journal* from October 18, 1787 to April 10, 1788. These essays have been attributed to a New York Anti-Federalist, Robert Yates, but no one has solid evidence of Brutus's identity. There is no doubt, however, about the formidable ability of Brutus, whose essays have been judged among the best expressions of the Anti-Federalist position.

In his first essay, Brutus discussed his arguments against the 1787 Constitution, which he elaborated upon in fifteen subsequent essays. He feared that the Constitution provided a national government that would subordinate the states, destroy true federalism, and erode the republican governments of the states and the rights of their citizens. He argued that the Constitution gave too much power to the U.S. government and placed too few restrictions on it. Further, the people would not be adequately represented in this new constitutional government. Thus, liberty would be lost.

What did Brutus say about the dangers of a consolidated or national government? According to Brutus, why was the Constitution of 1787 likely to bring about a consolidated government? Why, according to Brutus, was the Constitution of 1787 deficient in its provision for representation of the people in government? Why did Brutus believe that the Constitution of 1787 was based on flawed conceptions of federalism and republicanism? Why did Brutus believe that the Constitution of 1787, if instituted, would threaten the rights to liberty of the people? What is your evaluation of Brutus's concepts of federalism and republican government?

To the CITIZENS *of the* STATE *of* NEW-YORK.

When the public is called to investigate and decide upon a question in which not only the present members of the community are deeply interested, but upon which the happiness and misery of generations yet unborn is in great measure suspended, the benevolent mind cannot help feeling itself peculiarly interested in the result. . . .

The first question that presents itself on the subject is, whether a confederated government be the best for the United States or not? Or in other words, whether the thirteen United States should be reduced to one great republic, governed by one legislature, and under the direction of one executive and judicial; or whether they should continue thirteen confederated republics, under the direction and controul of a supreme federal head for certain defined national purposes only?

This enquiry is important, because, although the government reported by the convention does not go to a perfect and entire consolidation, yet it approaches so near to it, that it must, if executed, certainly and infallibly terminate in it. . . .

It is here taken for granted, that all agree in this, that whatever government we adopt, it ought to be a free one; that it should be so framed as to secure the liberty of the citizens of America, and such an one as to admit of a full, fair, and equal representation of the people. The question then will be, whether a government thus constituted, and founded on such principles, is practicable, and can be exercised over the whole United States, reduced into one state? . . .

History furnishes no example of a free republic, any thing like the extent of the United States. The Grecian republics were of small extent; so also was that of the Romans. Both of these, it is true, in process of time, extended their conquests over large territories of country; and the consequence was, that their governments were changed from that of free governments to those of the most tyrannical that ever existed in the world.

Not only the opinion of the greatest men, and the experience of mankind, are against the idea of an extensive republic, but a variety of reasons may be drawn from the reason and nature of things, against it. In every government, the will of the sovereign is the law. In despotic governments, the supreme authority being lodged in one, his will is law, and can be as easily expressed to a large extensive territory as to a small one. In a pure democracy the people are the sovereign, and their will is declared by themselves; for this purpose they must all come together to deliberate, and decide. This kind of government cannot be exercised, therefore, over a country of any considerable extent; it must be confined to a single city, or at least limited to such bounds as that the people can conveniently assemble, be able to debate, understand the subject submitted to them, and declare their opinion concerning it.

In a free republic, although all laws are derived from the consent of the people, yet the people do not declare their consent by themselves in person, but by representatives, chosen by them, who are supposed to know the minds of their constituents, and to be possessed of integrity to declare this mind.

In every free government, the people must give their assent to the laws by which they are governed. This is the true criterion between a free government and an arbitrary one. The former are ruled by the will of the whole, expressed in any manner they may agree upon; the latter by the will of one, or a few. If the people are to give their assent to the laws, by persons chosen and appointed by them, the manner of the choice and the number chosen, must be such, as to possess, be disposed, and consequently qualified to declare the sentiments of the people; for if they do not know, or are not disposed to speak the sentiments of the people, the people do not govern, but the sovereignty is in a few. Now, in a large extended country, it is impossible to have a representation, possessing the sentiments, and of integrity, to declare the minds of the people, without having it so numerous and unwieldly, as to be subject in great measure to the inconveniency of a democratic government.

The territory of the United States is of vast extent; it now contains near three millions of souls, and is capable of containing much more than ten times that number. Is it practicable for a country, so large and so numerous as they will soon become, to elect a representation, that will speak their sentiments, without their becoming so numerous as to be incapable of transacting public business? It certainly is not.

In a republic, the manners, sentiments, and interests of the people should be similar. If this be not the case, there will be a constant clashing of opinions; and the representatives of one part will be continually striving against those of the other. This will retard the operations of government, and prevent such conclusions as will promote the public good. If we apply this remark to the condition of the United States, we shall be convinced that it forbids that we should be one government. The United States includes a variety of climates. The productions of the different parts of the union are very variant, and their interests, of consequence, diverse. Their manners and habits differ as much as their climates and productions; and their sentiments are by no means coincident. The laws and customs of the several states are, in many respects, very diverse, and in some opposite; each would be in favor of its own interests and customs, and, of consequence, a legislature, formed of representatives from the respective parts, would not only be too numerous to act with any care or decision, but would be composed of such heterogenous and discordant principles, as would constantly be contending with each other. . . .

In a republic of such vast extent as the United-States, the legislature cannot attend to the various concerns and wants of its different parts. It cannot be sufficiently numerous to be acquainted with the local condition and wants of the different districts, and if it could, it is impossible it should have sufficient time to attend to and provide for all the variety of cases of this nature, that would be continually arising.

In so extensive a republic, the great officers of government would soon become above the controul of the people, and abuse their power to the purpose of aggrandizing themselves, and oppressing them. The trust committed to the executive offices, in a country of the extent of the United-States, must be various and of magnitude. The command of all the troops and navy of the republic, the appointment of officers, the power of pardoning offences, the collecting of all the public revenues, and the power of expending them, with a number of other powers, must be lodged and exercised in every state, in the hands of a few. When these are attended with great honor and emolument, as they always will be in large states, so as greatly to interest men to pursue them, and to be proper objects for ambitious and designing men, such men will be ever restless in their pursuit after them. They will use the power, when they have acquired it, to the purposes of gratifying their own interest and ambition, and it is scarcely possible, in a very large republic, to call them to account for their misconduct, or to prevent their abuse of power.

These are some of the reasons by which it appears, that a free republic cannot long subsist over a country of the great extent of these states. If then this new constitution is calculated to consolidate the thirteen states into one, as it evidently is, it ought not to be adopted. . . .

Source: The Journal (New York, October 18, 1787). Collections of important Anti-Federalist papers have been published in various sources during the nineteenth and twentieth centuries. Two excellent, accessible collections are Bernard Bailyn, ed., *The Debate on the Constitution*, 2 vol. (New York: Library of America, 1993) and Herbert Storing, ed., *The Anti-Federalist* (Chicago: University of Chicago Press, 1981).

DOCUMENT 45: *The Federalist* 1 (Publius [Alexander Hamilton], October 27, 1787)

Alexander Hamilton, stung by sharp Anti-Federalist essays against the 1787 Constitution, responded in the first of eighty-five *Federalist* papers, written mostly by him and James Madison and published originally in New York City newspapers. In *Federalist* 1, Publius discussed the overriding purposes of his proposed series of papers. He would explain how the proposed Constitution could be used to remedy the deficiencies of government under the Articles of Confederation. Further, he would demonstrate that the new Constitution was designed in conformity with the principles of republican government and liberty. Finally, Publius asserted that the American people faced a great national crisis that demanded careful consideration of their choices to produce wise decisions for national union and personal liberty. According to Publius, what was the crisis faced by the American people? How could they respond successfully to this crisis?

To the People of the State of New-York.

After an unequivocal experience of the inefficacy of the subsisting Fœderal Government, you are called upon to deliberate on a new Constitution for the United States of America. The subject speaks its own importance; comprehending in its consequences, nothing less than the existence of the UNION, the safety and welfare of the parts of which it is composed, the fate of an empire, in many respects, the most interesting in the world. It has been frequently remarked, that it seems to have been reserved to the people of this country, by their conduct and example, to decide the important question, whether societies of men are really capable or not, of establishing good government from reflection and choice, or whether they are forever destined to depend, for their political constitutions, on accident and force. If there be any truth in the remark, the crisis, at which we are arrived, may with propriety be regarded as the era in which that decision is to be made; and a wrong election of the part we shall act, may, in this view, deserve to be considered as the general misfortune of mankind.

This idea will add the inducements of philanthropy to those of patriotism to heighten the sollicitude, which all considerate and good men must feel for the event. Happy will it be if our choice should be decided by a judicious estimate of our true interests, unperplexed and unbiassed by considerations not connected with the public good. But this is a thing more ardently to be wished, than seriously to be expected. The plan offered to our deliberations, affects too many particular interests, innovates upon too many local institutions, not to involve in its discussion a variety of objects foreign to its merits, and of views, passions and prejudices little favourable to the discovery of truth. . . .

A torrent of angry and malignant passions will be let loose. To judge from the conduct of the opposite parties, we shall be led to conclude, that they will mutually hope to evince the justness of their opinions, and to increase the number of their converts by the loudness of their declamations, and by the bitterness of their invectives. An enlightened zeal for the energy and efficiency of government will be stigmatised, as the off-spring of a temper fond of despotic power and hostile to the principles of liberty. An overscrupulous jealousy of danger to the rights of the people, which is more commonly the fault of the head than of the heart, will be represented as mere pretence and artifice; the bait for popularity at the expence of public good. It will be forgotten, on the one hand, that jealousy is the usual concomitant of violent love, and that the noble enthusiasm of liberty is too apt to be infected with a spirit of narrow and illiberal distrust. On the other hand, it will be equally forgotten, that the vigour of government is essential to the security of liberty; that, in the contemplation of a sound and well informed judgment, their interest can never be separated; and that a dangerous ambition more often lurks behind the specious mask of zeal for the rights of the people, than under the forbidding appearance of zeal for the firmness and efficiency of government. History will teach us, that the former has been found a much more certain road to the introduction of despotism, than the latter, and that of those men who have overturned the liberties of republics the greatest number have begun their career, by paying an obsequious court to the people, commencing Demagogues and ending Tyrants.

In the course of the preceeding observations I have had an eye, my Fellow Citizens, to putting you upon your guard against all attempts, from whatever quarter, to influence your decision in a matter of the utmost moment to your welfare by any impressions other than those which may result from the evidence of truth. You will, no doubt, at the same time, have collected from the general scope of them that they proceed from a source not unfriendly to the new Constitution. Yes, my Countrymen, I own to you, that, after having given it an attentive consideration, I am clearly of opinion, it is your interest to adopt it. I am convinced, that this is the safest course for your liberty, your dignity, and your happiness. I affect not reserves, which I do not feel. I will not amuse you with an appearance of deliberation, when I have decided. I frankly acknowledge to you my convictions, and I will freely lay before you the reasons on which they are founded. The consciousness of good intentions disdains ambiguity. I shall not however multiply professions on this head. My motives must remain in the depositary of my own breast: My arguments will be open to all, and may be judged of by all. They shall at least be offered in a spirit, which will not disgrace the cause of truth.

I propose in a series of papers to discuss the following interesting particulars—*The utility of the* UNION *to your political prosperity—The insufficiency of the present Confederation to preserve that Union—The necessity of a government at least equally energetic with the one proposed to the attainment of this object—The conformity of the proposed Constitution to the true principles of republican government—Its analogy to your own state constitution—*and lastly, *The additional security, which its adoption will afford to the preservation of that species of government, to liberty and to property.*

In the progress of this discussion I shall endeavour to give a satisfactory answer to all the objections which shall have made their appearance that may seem to have any claim to your attention. . . .

Source: Independent Journal (New York, October 27, 1787). Collections of the *Federalist* papers have been published in many different editions during the nineteenth and twentieth centuries. Two excellent, accessible collections are Bernard Bailyn, ed., *The Debate on the Constitution,* 2 vol. (New York: Library of America, 1993) and Jacob E. Cooke, ed., *The Federalist* (Middletown, Conn.: Wesleyan University Press, 1961).

DOCUMENT 46: Letter to the General Court of Massachusetts (Elbridge Gerry, November 3, 1787)

Elbridge Gerry represented Massachusetts at the Federal Convention, which produced the Constitution. But he refused to sign the finished document. Gerry felt obligated to explain his criticism of the Constitution of 1787 to the Massachusetts legislature, the General Court, which he did in a letter drafted October 18, 1787 and published later in a Boston newspaper. Gerry's main objections to the Constitution of 1787 were that it provided a national rather than a federal government, violated the right of the people to be represented adequately in their government, gave too much power to the executive and judicial branches of government, and threatened the people's liberties. What other objections did Gerry express?

Compare Gerry's objections to the criticisms of Brutus (Document 44). Did Gerry and Brutus have similar views on the flaws of the 1787 Constitution?

GENTLEMEN, I have the honour to inclose, pursuant to my commission, the constitution proposed by the federal Convention.

To this system I gave my dissent, and shall submit my objections to the honourable Legislature.

It was painful for me, on a subject of such national importance, to differ from the respectable members who signed the constitution: But conceiving as I did, that the liberties of America were not secured by the system, it was my duty to oppose it.—

My principal objections to the plan, are, that there is no adequate provision for a representation of the people—that they have no security for the right of election—that some of the powers of the Legislature are ambiguous, and others indefinite and dangerous—that the Executive is blended with and will have an undue influence over the Legislature— that the judicial department will be oppressive—that treaties of the highest importance may be formed by the President with the advice of two thirds of a *quorum* of the Senate—and that the system is without the security of a bill of rights. These are objections which are not local, but apply equally to all the States.

As the Convention was called for "the *sole* and *express* purpose of revising the Articles of Confederation, and reporting to Congress and the several Legislatures such alterations and provisions as shall render the Federal Constitution adequate to the exigencies of government and the preservation of the union," I did not conceive that these powers extended to the formation of the plan proposed, but the Convention being of a different *opinion,* I acquiesced in *it,* being fully convinced that to preserve the union, an efficient government was indispensibly necessary; and that it would be difficult to make proper amendments to the articles of Confederation.

The Constitution proposed has few, if any *federal* features, but is rather a system of *national* government: Nevertheless, in many respects I think it has great merit, and by proper amendments, may be adapted to the "exigencies of government," and preservation of liberty.

The question on this plan involves others of the highest importance— 1st. Whether there shall be a dissolution of the *federal* government? 2dly. Whether the several State Governments shall be so altered, as in effect to be dissolved? and 3dly. Whether in lieu of the *federal* and *State* Governments, the *national* Constitution now proposed shall be substituted without amendment? Never perhaps were a people called on to decide a question of greater magnitude—Should the citizens of America adopt the plan as it now stands, their liberties may be lost: Or should they reject it altogether Anarchy may ensue. It is evident therefore, that they should not be precipitate in their decisions; that the subject should be well understood, lest they should refuse to *support* the government, after having *hastily* accepted it.

If those who are in favour of the Constitution, as well as those who are against it, should preserve moderation, their discussions may afford much information and finally direct to an happy issue.

It may be urged by some, that an *implicit* confidence should be placed in the Convention: But, however respectable the members may be who signed the Constitution, it must be admitted, that a free people are the proper guardians of their rights and liberties—that the greatest men may err—and that their errours are sometimes, of the greatest magnitude.

Others may suppose, that the Constitution may be safely adopted, because therein provision is made to *amend* it: But cannot *this object* be better attained before a ratification, than after it? And should a *free* people adopt a form of Government, under conviction that it wants amendment?

And some may conceive, that if the plan is not accepted by the people, they will not unite in another: But surely whilst they have the power to amend, they are not under the necessity of rejecting it.

I have been detained here longer than I expected, but shall leave this place in a day or two for Massachusetts, and on my arrival shall submit the reasons (if required by the Legislature) on which my objections are grounded.

I shall only add, that as the welfare of the union requires a better Constitution than the Confederation, I shall think it my duty as a citizen of Massachusetts, to support that which shall be finally adopted, sincerely hoping it will secure the liberty and happiness of America.

I have the honour to be, Gentlemen, with the highest respect for the honourable Legislature and yourselves, your most obedient, and very humble servant, E. GERRY.

Source: Massachusetts Centinel (Boston, November 3, 1787).

DOCUMENT 47: Objections to the Constitution (George Mason, November 22, 1787)

George Mason, a Virginia delegate to the Federal Convention, was a leading advocate for a Bill of Rights in the Constitution of 1787. In Mason's opinion, the federal government proposed by the Constitution of 1787 was strong enough to threaten the liberties of the people, unless strict limits were placed on its supreme powers. At the end of the Convention, Mason refused to sign the Constitution and drafted a paper explaining his objections to it, which was informally circulated in October 1787 and published in November. Mason said the omission from the Constitution of a declaration of rights was a fatal error. He also feared that the people would not be properly represented in the national legislature. Further, he argued that the Senate, the presidency, and the judiciary had too many powers that could threaten the rights of the states and their citizens. What other objections to the Constitution of 1787 did Mason discuss as reasons for rejecting it?

There is no declaration of rights; and the laws of the general government being paramount to the laws and constitutions of the several States, the declarations of rights in the separate States are no security. Nor are the people secured even in the enjoyment of the benefits of the common law, which stands here upon no other foundation than its having been adopted by the respective acts forming the constitutions of the several States.

In the House of Representatives there is not the substance, but the shadow only of representation; which can never produce proper information in the Legislature, or inspire confidence in the people; the laws will therefore be generally made by men little concerned in, and unacquainted with their effects and consequences.

The Senate have the power of altering all money-bills, and of originating appropriations of money, and the salaries of the officers of their own appointment in conjunction with the President of the United States; although they are not the representatives of the people, or amenable to them.

These with their other great powers (viz. their power in the appointment of ambassadors and other public officers, in making treaties, and in trying all impeachments) their influence upon and connection with the supreme executive from these causes, their duration of office, and their being a constant existing body almost continually sitting, joined with their being one complete branch of the Legislature, will destroy any balance in the government, and enable them to accomplish what usurpations they please upon the rights and liberties of the people.

The judiciary of the United States is so constructed and extended as to absorb and destroy the judiciaries of the several States; thereby rendering law as tedious, intricate and expensive, and justice as unattainable by a great part of the community, as in England, and enabling the rich to oppress and ruin the poor.

The President of the United States has no constitutional council (a thing unknown in any safe and regular government) he will therefore be unsupported by proper information and advice; and will be generally directed by minions and favorites—or he will become a tool to the Senate—or a Council of State will grow out of the principal officers of the great departments; the worst and most dangerous of all ingredients for such a council in a free country; for they may be induced to join in any dangerous or oppressive measures, to shelter themselves, and prevent an inquiry into their own misconduct in office; whereas had a constitutional council been formed (as was proposed) of six members, viz. two from the eastern, two from the middle, and two from the southern States, to be appointed by vote of the States in the House of Representatives, with the same duration and rotation in office as the Senate, the Executive would always have had safe and proper information and advice, the President of such a council might have acted as Vice-President of the United States, pro tempore, upon any vacancy or disability of the chief Magistrate; and long continued sessions of the Senate would in a great measure have been prevented.

From this fatal defect of a constitutional council has arisen the improper power of the Senate, in the appointment of public officers, and the alarming dependance and connection between that branch of the Legislature and the supreme Executive.

Hence also sprung that unnecessary and dangerous officer the Vice-President; who for want of other employment is made President of the Senate; thereby dangerously blending the executive and legislative powers; besides always giving to some one of the States an unnecessary and unjust pre-eminence over the others.

The President of the United States has the unrestrained power of granting pardons for treason; which may be sometimes exercised to screen from punishment those whom he had secretly instigated to commit the crime, and thereby prevent a discovery of his own guilt.

By declaring all treaties supreme laws of the land, the Executive and the Senate have, in many cases, an exclusive power of legislation; which might have been avoided by proper distinctions with respect to treaties, and requiring the assent of the House of Representatives, where it could be done with safety.

By requiring only a majority to make all commercial and navigation laws, the five southern States (whose produce and circumstances are totally different from that of the eight northern and eastern States) will be ruined; for such rigid and premature regulations may be made, as will enable the merchants of the northern and eastern States not only to demand an exorbitant freight, but to monopolize the purchase of the commodities at their own price, for many years: To the great injury of the landed interest, and impoverishment of the people: And the danger is the greater, as the gain on one side will be in proportion to the loss on the other. Whereas requiring two-thirds of the members present in both houses would have produced mutual moderation, promoted the general interest and removed an insuperable objection to the adoption of the government.

Under their own construction of the general clause at the end of the enumerated powers, the Congress may grant monopolies in trade and commerce, constitute new crimes, inflict unusual and severe punishments, and extend their power as far as they shall think proper; so that the State Legislatures have no security for the powers now presumed to remain to them; or the people for their rights.

There is no declaration of any kind for preserving the liberty of the press, the trial by jury in civil causes; nor against the danger of standing armies in time of peace.

The State Legislatures are restrained from laying export duties on their own produce.

The general Legislature is restrained from prohibiting the further importation of slaves for twenty odd years; though such importations render the United States weaker, and more vulnerable, and less capable of defence.

Both the general Legislature and the State Legislatures are expressly prohibited making ex post facto laws; though there never was nor can be a Legislature but must and will make such laws, when necessity and the public safety require them, which will hereafter be a breach of all the constitutions in the Union, and afford precedents for other innovations.

This government will commence in a moderate aristocracy; it is at present impossible to foresee whether it will, in its operation, produce a monarchy, or a corrupt oppressive aristocracy; it will most probably vibrate some years between the two, and then terminate between the one and the other.

Source: Virginia Journal (Alexandria, November 22, 1787).

DOCUMENT 48: *The Federalist* 10 (Publius [James Madison], November 22, 1787)

The tenth *Federalist* paper was James Madison's first effort as Publius. In this paper, he discussed his novel conception of an extended republic, which the U.S. government would become under the Constitution of 1787. (See Documents 37 and 51 to examine other discussions by Madison of the extended republic.)

The creation of an extended republican government of the United States was Madison's remedy to a malady of the traditional republican government in a small territory, oppression of minorities by an overbearing majority faction. To explain this point, Madison emphasized the differences between two types of popular government, a pure democracy and a republic. In a pure democracy, the people rule directly. In a republic, by contrast, the people rule indirectly through their elected representatives. In a direct democracy, the size of the realm and population must be small to enable all citizens to participate directly in their government. In a republic, it is possible to increase the size of the realm and the population over which the representatives in government rule.

According to Madison, the larger the size and population of the republic, the smaller the likelihood of tyranny through majority rule by a faction of like-minded citizens. Why? Because in a larger republic, there will usually be a great diversity of groups with different political interests. The greater the diversity of interests in a society, the lesser the likelihood that a permanent majority will form around a single interest and use its power persistently and tyrannically against the minority. Rather, in larger diverse societies, majority rule usually results from compromises among different contending groups. A monolithic majority faction, which could violate the rights of unpopular minorities or individuals, is not likely to exist, and if it does form, it is not likely to endure. Thus, the extended republic, consisting of diverse groups and interests, includes countervailing pressures and shifting majority coalitions, which precludes or minimizes the formation of an overbearing majority faction and the threat of its tyranny against others.

How does the extended republic proposed by Madison in *Federalist* 10 overcome weaknesses of direct or pure democracy? How would the peculiar republican problem of majoritarian tyranny be resolved by the extended republic proposed in *Federalist* 10? How does Madison's conception of government in an extended republic incorporate both majority rule and minority rights? Is Madison's concept of republican government compatible with our contemporary idea of representative democracy?

To the People of the State of New-York.

Among the numerous advantages promised by a well constructed Union, none deserves to be more accurately developed than its tendency to break and control the violence of faction. The friend of popular governments, never finds himself so much alarmed for their character and fate, as when he contemplates their propensity to this dangerous vice. He will not fail therefore to set a due value on any plan which, without violating the principles to which he is attached, provides a proper cure for it. . . .

By a faction I understand a number of citizens, whether amounting to a majority or minority of the whole, who are united and actuated by some common impulse of passion, or of interest, adverse to the rights of other citizens, or to the permanent and aggregate interests of the community.

There are two methods of curing the mischiefs of faction: the one, by removing its causes; the other, by controling its effects.

There are again two methods of removing the causes of faction: the one by destroying the liberty which is essential to its existence; the other, by giving to every citizen the same opinions, the same passions, and the same interests.

It could never be more truly said than of the first remedy, that it is worse than the disease. Liberty is to faction, what air is to fire, an aliment without which it instantly expires. But it could not be a less folly to abolish liberty, which is essential to political life, because it nourishes faction, than it would be to wish the annihilation of air, which is essential to animal life, because it imparts to fire its destructive agency.

The second expedient is as impracticable, as the first would be unwise. As long as the reason of man continues fallible, and he is at liberty to exercise it, different opinions will be formed. As long as the connection subsists between his reason and his self-love, his opinions and his passions will have a reciprocal influence on each other; and the former will be objects to which the latter will attach themselves. The diversity in the faculties of men from which the rights of property originate, is not less an insuperable obstacle to a uniformity of interests. The protection of these faculties is the first object of Government. From the protection of different and unequal faculties of acquiring property, the possession of different degrees and kinds of property immediately results: and from the influence of these on the sentiments and views of the respective proprietors, ensues a division of the society into different interests and parties.

The latent causes of faction are thus sown in the nature of man; and we see them every where brought into different degrees of activity, according to the different circumstances of civil society. A zeal for different opinions concerning religion, concerning Government, and many other points, as well of speculation as of practice; an attachment to different leaders ambitiously contending for pre-eminence and power; or to persons of other descriptions whose fortunes have been interesting to the human passions, have in turn divided mankind into parties, inflamed them with mutual animosity, and rendered them much more disposed to vex and oppress each other, than to co-operate for their common good. So strong is this propensity of mankind to fall into mutual animosities, that where no substantial occasion presents itself, the most frivolous and fanciful distinctions have been sufficient to kindle their unfriendly passions, and excite their most violent conflicts. But the most common and durable source of factions, has been the various and unequal distribution of property. Those who hold, and those who are without property, have ever formed distinct interests in society. Those who are creditors, and those who are debtors, fall under a like discrimination. A landed interest, a manufacturing interest, a mercantile interest, a monied interest, with many lesser interests, grow up of necessity in civilized nations, and divide them into different classes, actuated by different sentiments and views. The regulation of these various and interfering interests forms the principal task of modern Legislation, and involves the spirit of party and faction in the necessary and ordinary operations of Government.

No man is allowed to be a judge in his own cause; because his interest would certainly bias his judgment, and, not improbably, corrupt his integrity. With equal, nay with greater reason, a body of men, are unfit to be both judges and parties, at the same time; yet, what are many of the most important acts of legislation, but so many judicial determinations, not indeed concerning the rights of single persons, but concerning the rights of large bodies of citizens; and what are the different classes of legislators, but advocates and parties to the causes which they determine? Is a law proposed concerning private debts? It is a question to which the creditors are parties on one side, and the debtors on the other. Justice ought to hold the balance between them. Yet the parties are and must be themselves the judges; and the most numerous party, or, in other words, the most powerful faction must be expected to prevail. . . .

The inference to which we are brought, is, that the *causes* of faction cannot be removed; and that relief is only to be sought in the means of controling its *effects*.

If a faction consists of less than a majority, relief is supplied by the republican principle, which enables the majority to defeat its sinister views by regular vote: It may clog the administration, it may convulse the society; but it will be unable to execute and mask its violence under the forms of the Constitution. When a majority is included in a faction, the form of popular government on the other hand enables it to sacrifice to its ruling passion or interest, both the public good and the rights of other citizens. To secure the public good, and private rights, against the danger of such a faction, and at the same time to preserve the spirit and the form of popular government, is then the great object to which our enquiries are directed: Let me add that it is the great desideratum, by which alone this form of government can be rescued from the opprobrium under which it has so long labored, and be recommended to the esteem and adoption of mankind.

By what means is this object attainable? Evidently by one of two only. Either the existence of the same passion or interest in a majority at the same time, must be prevented; or the majority, having such co-existent passion or interest, must be rendered, by their number and local situation, unable to concert and carry into effect schemes of oppression. If the impulse and the opportunity be suffered to coincide, we well know that neither moral nor religious motives can be relied on as an adequate control. They are not found to be such on the injustice and violence of individuals, and lose their efficacy in proportion to the number combined together; that is, in proportion as their efficacy becomes needful.

From this view of the subject, it may be concluded, that a pure Democracy, by which I mean, a Society, consisting of a small number of citizens, who assemble and administer the Government in person, can admit of no cure for the mischiefs of faction. A common passion or interest will, in almost every case, be felt by a majority of the whole; a communication and concert results from the form of Government itself; and there is nothing to check the inducements to sacrifice the weaker party, or an obnoxious individual. Hence it is, that such Democracies have ever been spectacles of turbulence and contention; have ever been found incompatible with personal security, or the rights of property; and have in general been as short in their lives, as they have been violent in their deaths. Theoretic politicians, who have patronized this species of Government, have erroneously supposed, that by reducing mankind to a perfect equality in their political rights, they would, at the same time, be perfectly equalized and assimilated in their possessions, their opinions, and their passions.

A Republic, by which I mean a Government in which the scheme of representation takes place, opens a different prospect, and promises the cure for which we are seeking. Let us examine the points in which it varies from pure Democracy, and we shall comprehend both the nature of the cure, and the efficacy which it must derive from the Union.

The two great points of difference between a Democracy and a Republic are, first, the delegation of the Government, in the latter, to a small number of citizens elected by the rest: secondly, the greater number of citizens, and greater sphere of country, over which the latter may be extended.

The effect of the first difference is, on the one hand to refine and enlarge the public views, by passing them through the medium of a chosen body of citizens, whose wisdom may best discern the true interest of their country, and whose patriotism and love of justice, will be least likely to sacrifice it to temporary or partial considerations. Under such a regulation, it may well happen that the public voice pronounced by the representatives of the people, will be more consonant to the public good, than if pronounced by the people themselves convened for the purpose. On the other hand, the effect may be inverted. Men of factious tempers, of local prejudices, or of sinister designs, may be intrigue, by corruption or by other means, first obtain the suffrages, and then betray the interests of the people. The question resulting is, whether small or extensive Republics are most favorable to the election of proper guardians of the public weal; and it is clearly decided in favor of the latter by two obvious considerations.

In the first place it is to be remarked that however small the Republic may be, the Representatives must be raised to a certain number, in order to guard against the cabals of a few; and that however large it may be, they must be limited to a certain number, in order to guard against the confusion of a multitude. Hence the number of Representatives in the two cases, not being in proportion to that of the Constituents, and being proportionally greatest in the small Republic, it follows, that if the proportion of fit characters, be not less, in the large than in the small Republic, the former will present a greater option, and consequently a greater probability of a fit choice.

In the next place, as each Representative will be chosen by a greater number of citizens in the large than in the small Republic, it will be more difficult for unworthy candidates to practise with success the vicious arts, by which elections are too often carried; and the suffrages of the people being more free, will be more likely to centre on men who possess the most attractive merit, and the most diffusive and established characters.

It must be confessed, that in this, as in most other cases, there is a mean, on both sides of which inconveniencies will be found to lie. By enlarging too much the number of electors, you render the representative too little acquainted with all their local circumstances and lesser interests; as by reducing it too much, you render him unduly attached to these, and too little fit to comprehend and pursue great and national objects. The Federal Constitution forms a happy combination in this respect; the great and aggregate interests being referred to the national, the local and particular, to the state legislatures.

The other point of difference is, the greater number of citizens and extent of territory which may be brought within the compass of Republican, than of Democratic Government; and it is this circumstance principally which renders factious combinations less to be dreaded in the former, than in the latter. The smaller the society, the fewer probably will be the distinct parties and interests composing it; the fewer the distinct parties and interests, the more frequently will a majority be found of the same party; and the smaller the number of individuals composing a majority, and the smaller the compass within which they are placed, the more easily will they concert and execute their plans of oppression. Extend the sphere, and you take in a greater variety of parties and interests; you make it less probable that a majority of the whole will have a common motive to invade the rights of other citizens; or if such a common motive exists, it will be more difficult for all who feel it to discover their own strength, and to act in unison with each other. Besides other impediments, it may be remarked, that where there is a consciousness of unjust or dishonorable purposes, communication is always checked by distrust, in proportion to the number whose concurrence is necessary.

Hence it clearly appears, that the same advantage, which a Republic has over a Democracy, in controling the effects of faction, is enjoyed by a large over a small Republic—is enjoyed by the Union over the States composing it. . . .

The influence of factious leaders may kindle a flame within their particular States, but will be unable to spread a general conflagration through the other States: a religious sect, may degenerate into a political faction in a part of the Confederacy; but the variety of sects dispersed over the entire face of it, must secure the national Councils against any danger from that source: a rage for paper money, for an abolition of debts, for an equal division of property, or for any other improper or wicked project, will be less apt to pervade the whole body of the Union, than a particular member of it; in the same proportion as such a malady is more likely to taint a particular country or district, than an entire State.

In the extent and proper structure of the Union, therefore, we behold a Republican remedy for the diseases most incident to Republican Government. . . .

Source: Daily Advertiser (New York, November 22, 1787).

DOCUMENT 49: Letter IV (Agrippa [James Winthrop], December 4, 1787)

James Winthrop of Massachusetts, a scholar at Harvard University, tried to persuade the people of his state to reject the Constitution of 1787. He wrote sixteen letters for publication in a Boston newspaper in which he strongly disagreed with the Federalist's conception of republican government and federalism. Agrippa claimed it would be impossible to create a true republican government of the entire United States of America, because the size of the realm was too great. Madison's concept of an "extended federal republic" seemed unworkable to Agrippa, the pseudonym of John Winthrop.

What were Agrippa's criticisms of the 1787 Constitution? How does his view of republican government differ from the position of Publius in *Federalist* 10, 39, and 51? (See Documents 48, 50, and 51.)

To the PEOPLE.

Having considered some of the principal advantages of the happy form of government under which it is our peculiar good fortune to live, we find by experience, that it is the best calculated of any form hitherto invented, to secure to us the rights of our persons and of our property, and that the general circumstances of the people shew an advanced state of improvement never before known. We have found the shock given by the war in a great measure obliterated, and the publick debt contracted at that time to be considerably reduced in the nominal sum. The Congress lands are fully adequate to the redemption of the principal of their debt, and are selling and populating very fast. The lands of this state, at the west, are, at the moderate price of eighteen pence an acre, worth near half a million pounds in our money. They ought, therefore, to be sold as quick as possible. An application was made lately for a large tract at that price, and continual applications are made for other lands in the eastern part of the state. Our resources are daily augmenting.

We find, then, that after the experience of near two centuries our separate governments are in full vigour. They discover, for all the purposes of internal regulation, every symptom of strength, and none of decay. The new system is, therefore, for such purposes, useless and burdensome.

Let us now consider how far it is practicable consistent with the happiness of the people and their freedom. It is the opinion of the ablest writers on the subject, that no extensive empire can be governed upon republican principles, and that such a government will degenerate to a despotism, unless it be made up of a confederacy of smaller states, each having the full powers of internal regulation. This is precisely the principle which has hitherto preserved our freedom. No instance can be found of any free government of considerable extent which has been supported upon any other plan. Large and consolidated empires may indeed dazzle the eyes of a distant spectator with their splendour, but if examined more nearly are always found to be full of misery. The reason is obvious. In large states the same principles of legislation will not apply to all the parts. The inhabitants of warmer climates are more dissolute in their manners, and less industrious, than in colder countries. A degree of severity is, therefore, necessary with one which would cramp the spirit of the other. We accordingly find that the very great empires have always been despotick. They have indeed tried to remedy the inconveniences to which the people were exposed by local regulations; but these contrivances have never answered the end. The laws not being made by the people, who felt the inconveniences, did not suit their circumstances. It is under such tyranny that the Spanish provinces languish, and such would be our misfortune and degradation, if we should submit to have the concerns of the whole empire managed by one legislature. To promote the happiness of the people it is necessary that there should be local laws; and it is necessary that those laws should be made by the representatives of those who are immediately subject to the want of them. By endeavouring to suit both extremes, both are injured.

It is impossible for one code of laws to suit Georgia and Massachusetts. They must, therefore, legislate for themselves. Yet there is, I believe, not one point of legislation that is not surrendered in the proposed plan. Questions of every kind respecting property are determinable in a continental court, and so are all kinds of criminal causes. The continental legislature has, therefore, a right to make rules *in all cases* by which their judicial courts shall proceed and decide causes. No rights are reserved to the citizens. The laws of Congress are in all cases to be the supreme law of the land, and paramount to the constitutions of the individual states. The Congress may institute what modes of trial they please, and no plea drawn from the constitution of any state can avail. This new system is, therefore, a consolidation of all the states into one large mass, however diverse the parts may be of which it is to be composed. The idea of an uncompounded republick, on an average, one thousand miles in length, and eight hundred in breadth, and containing six millions of white inhabitants all reduced to the same standard of morals, or habits, and of laws, is in itself an absurdity, and contrary to the whole experience of mankind. The attempt made by Great-Britain to introduce such a system, struck us with horrour, and when it was proposed by some theorists that we should be represented in parliament, we uniformly declared that one legislature could not represent so many different interests for the purposes of legislation and taxation. This was the leading principle of the revolution, and makes an essential article in our creed. All that part, therefore, of the new system, which relates to the internal government of the states, ought at once to be rejected.

Source: Massachusetts Gazette (Boston, December 4, 1787).

DOCUMENT 50: *The Federalist* 39 (Publius [James Madison], January 16, 1788)

Publius gave new meaning to the term *federal republic,* a definition that has persisted. He argued that it was possible and desirable to combine federalism and republicanism in the government of a large territory, such as the federal government of the United States in the 1787 Constitution. Further, Publius claimed that his new conception of federalism held the middle ground between the extreme confederalism of the Anti-Federalists and the extreme nationalism of a unitary or consolidated government.

In *Federalist* 39, Publius connected his concepts of federalism and republicanism. The essential characteristics of a republic are that it is a representative government in which all branches are either directly or indirectly based on the people. His concept of federalism involved a compound of federal and national elements. For example, he claimed that the ratification of the Constitution would be a federal act because it would be done by state-based conventions. The operations of the new U.S. government would be national, because the government could act directly on citizens rather than exercising power only through the states. Further, the sources of power for the Congress would be partly national and partly federal. The members of the Senate would be elected by the state governments, an example of the federal principle. The members of the House of Representatives, by contrast, would be elected directly by the people of each state, an example of the national principle.

What other examples did Publius provide to show the mixture of federal and national elements in his concept of a compound federal republic? Which characteristics, the federal or the national, prevailed in Publius's model of a compound federal republic? Refer to Articles IV, V, and VI of the Constitution of 1787 (Document 43). Find at least five examples that show how government under this Constitution conformed to Publius's definition of a federal republic. Compare Publius's model of a federal republic to the model preferred by Brutus (Document 44). What are the essential differences? Do you agree with Brutus that Publius provided a consolidationist model rather than a federal system?

To the People of the State of New-York.
The last paper having concluded the observations which were meant

to introduce a candid survey of the plan of government reported by the Convention, we now proceed to the execution of that part of our undertaking. The first question that offers itself is, whether the general form and aspect of the government be strictly republican? It is evident that no other form would be reconcileable with the genius of the people of America; with the fundamental principles of the revolution; or with that honorable determination, which animates every votary of freedom, to rest all our political experiments on the capacity of mankind for self-government. If the plan of the Convention therefore be found to depart from the republican character, its advocates must abandon it as no longer defensible. . . .

If we resort for a criterion, to the different principles on which different forms of government are established, we may define a republic to be, or at least may bestow that name on, a government which derives all its powers directly or indirectly from the great body of the people; and is administered by persons holding their offices during pleasure, for a limited period, or during good behaviour. It is *essential* to such a government, that it be derived from the great body of the society, not from an inconsiderable proportion, or a favored class of it; otherwise a handful of tyrannical nobles, exercising their oppressions by a delegation of their powers, might aspire to the rank of republicans, and claim for their government the honorable title of republic. It is *sufficient* for such a government, that the persons administering it be appointed, either directly or indirectly, by the people; and that they hold their appointments by either of the tenures just specified; otherwise every government in the United States, as well as every other popular government that has been or can be well organized or well executed, would be degraded from the republican character. . . .

On comparing the Constitution planned by the Convention, with the standard here fixed, we perceive at once that it is in the most rigid sense conformable to it. . . .

But it was not sufficient, say the adversaries of the proposed Constitution, for the Convention to adhere to the republican form. They ought, with equal care, to have preserved the *federal* form, which regards the union as a *confederacy* of sovereign States; instead of which, they have framed a *national* government, which regards the union as a *consolidation* of the States. And it is asked by what authority this bold and radical innovation was undertaken. The handle which has been made of this objection requires, that it should be examined with some precision. . . .

First. In order to ascertain the real character of the government it may be considered in relation to the foundation on which it is to be established; to the sources from which its ordinary powers are to be drawn; to the operation of those powers; to the extent of them; and to the authority by which future changes in the government are to be introduced.

On examining the first relation, it appears on one hand that the Constitution is to be founded on the assent and ratification of the people of America, given by deputies elected for the special purpose; but on the other that this assent and ratification is to be given by the people, not as individuals composing one entire nation; but as composing the distinct and independent States to which they respectively belong. It is to be the assent and ratification of the several States, derived from the supreme authority in each State, the authority of the people themselves. The act therefore establishing the Constitution, will not be a *national* but a *federal* act. . . .

Each State in ratifying the Constitution, is considered as a sovereign body independent of all others, and only to be bound by its own voluntary act. In this relation then the new Constitution will, if established, be a *federal* and not a *national* Constitution.

The next relation is to the sources from which the ordinary powers of government are to be derived. The house of representatives will derive its powers from the people of America, and the people will be represented in the same proportion, and on the same principle, as they are in the Legislature of a particular State. So far the Government is *national* not *federal.* The Senate on the other hand will derive its powers from the States, as political and co-equal societies; and these will be represented on the principle of equality in the Senate, as they now are in the existing Congress. So far the government is *federal,* not *national.* . . .

The difference between a federal and national Government as it relates to the *operation of the Government* is supposed to consist in this, that in the former, the powers operate on the political bodies composing the confederacy, in their political capacities: In the latter, on the individual citizens, composing the nation, in their individual capacities. On trying the Constitution by this criterion, it falls under the *national,* not the *federal* character; . . .

But if the Government be national with regard to the *operation* of its powers, it changes its aspect again when we contemplate it in relation to the *extent* of its powers. The idea of a national Government involves in it, not only an authority over the individual citizens; but an indefinite supremacy over all persons and things, so far as they are objects of lawful Government. Among a people consolidated into one nation, this supremacy is completely vested in the national Legislature. Among communities united for particular purposes, it is vested partly in the general, and partly in the municipal Legislatures. In the former case, all local authorities are subordinate to the supreme; and may be controuled, directed or abolished by it at pleasure. In the latter the local or municipal authorities form distinct and independent portions of the supremacy, no more subject within their respective spheres to the general authority, than the general authority is subject to them, within its own sphere. In this relation then the proposed Government cannot be deemed a *national* one; since its jurisdiction extends to certain enumerated objects only, and leaves to the several States a residuary and inviolable sovereignty over all other objects. . . .

If we try the Constitution by its last relation, to the authority by which amendments are to be made, we find it neither wholly *national*, nor wholly *federal*. Were it wholly national, the supreme and ultimate authority would reside in the *majority* of the people of the Union; and this authority would be competent at all times, like that of a majority of every national society, to alter or abolish its established Government. Were it wholly federal on the other head, the concurrence of each State in the Union would be essential to every alteration that would be binding on all. The mode provided by the plan of the Convention is not founded on either of these principles. In requiring more than a majority, and particularly, in computing the proportion by *States*, not by *citizens*, it departs from the *national*, and advances towards the *federal* character: In rendering the concurrence of less than the whole number of States sufficient, it loses again the *federal*, and partakes of the *national* character.

The proposed Constitution therefore is in strictness neither a national nor a federal constitution; but a composition of both. In its foundation, it is federal, not national; in the sources from which the ordinary powers of the Government are drawn, it is partly federal, and partly national: in the operation of these powers, it is national, not federal: In the extent of them again, it is federal, not national: And finally, in the authoritative mode of introducing amendments, it is neither wholly federal, nor wholly national.

Source: Independent Journal (New York, January 16, 1788).

DOCUMENT 51: *The Federalist* 51 (Publius [James Madison], February 6, 1788)

In Publius's model of constitutional government, the separation of powers among three branches—legislative, executive, and judicial—was a primary means to limited government. This principle was built into the Constitution of 1787 to prevent any person or group in the government from acquiring too much power, which could be used for corrupt purposes. According to Publius, concentration of unlimited or insufficiently limited power leads inevitably to tyranny, because holders of such power cannot resist the temptation to abuse it.

In *Federalist* 51, Publius concluded his discussion of separation of powers and checks and balances as instruments for limited government. Publius wrote that the "great security" for maintenance of the Constitution's separation of powers is "giving those who administer each department, the necessary constitutional means, and personal motives, to resist the encroachment of others." What examples of constitutional means and personal motives are discussed by Publius? Refer to Articles I, II, and III of the Constitution of the United States (Document 43). What constitutional means are provided in Articles I, II, and III whereby one department can "resist the encroachment of others" (check them to balance the powers among the different branches of government)? Why does Publius argue for a bicameral legislature?

Publius discussed the relationship of human nature to government in several *Federalist* papers. In this paper, he wrote, "If men were angels, no government would be necessary. If angels were to govern men, neither external nor internal controuls on government would be necessary." What did this statement indicate about Publius's view of human nature and its relationship to government? What did this statement reveal about Publius's reasons for emphasizing separation of powers and checks and balances in the Constitution?

Publius discussed the problem of majority faction in republican government in the latter part of this paper, a topic he had also treated in *Federalist* 10 (see Document 48). What solution to this problem did he reject? What solution did he provide to prevent majoritarian tyranny and protect the rights of individuals in the minority?

In this paper, Publius tried to convince skeptics and critics of the Constitution that it would not violate a primary purpose of republican government, security for the natural rights of individuals. What is your evaluation of Publius's claim at the end of this paper that his conception of "the extended republic of the United States" provides the best protection for self-government and individual rights?

To the People of the State of New-York.

To what expedient then shall we finally resort for maintaining in practice the necessary partition of power among the several departments, as laid down in the constitution? The only answer that can be given is, that as all these exterior provisions are found to be inadequate, the defect must be supplied, by so contriving the interior structure of the government, as that its several constituent parts may, by their mutual relations, be the means of keeping each other in their proper places. Without presuming to undertake a full developement of this important idea, I will hazard a few general observations, which may perhaps place it in a clearer light, and enable us to form a more correct judgment of the principles and structure of the government planned by the convention.

In order to lay a due foundation for that separate and distinct exercise of the different powers of government, which to a certain extent, is admitted on all hands to be essential to the preservation of liberty, it is evident that each department should have a will of its own; and consequently should be so constituted, that the members of each should have as little agency as possible in the appointment of the members of the others. . . .

But the great security against a gradual concentration of the several powers in the same department, consists in giving to those who administer each department, the necessary constitutional means, and personal motives, to resist encroachments of the others. The provision for defence must in this, as in all other cases, be made commensurate to the danger of attack. Ambition must be made to counteract ambition. The interest of the man must be connected with the constitutional rights of the place. It may be a reflection on human nature, that such devices should be necessary to controul the abuses of government. But what is government itself but the greatest of all reflections on human nature? If men were angels, no government would be necessary. If angels were to govern men, neither external nor internal controuls on government would be necessary. In framing a government which is to be administered by men over men, the great difficulty lies in this: You must first enable the government to controul the governed; and in the next place, oblige it to controul itself. A dependence on the people is no doubt the primary controul on the government; but experience has taught mankind the necessity of auxiliary precautions.

This policy of supplying by opposite and rival interests, the defect of better motives, might be traced through the whole system of human affairs, private as well as public. We see it particularly displayed in all the subordinate distributions of power; where the constant aim is to divide and arrange the several offices in such a manner as that each may be a check on the other; that the private interest of every individual, may be a centinel over the public rights. These inventions of prudence cannot be less requisite in the distribution of the supreme powers of the state.

But it is not possible to give to each department an equal power of self defence. In republican government the legislative authority, necessarily, predominates. The remedy for this inconveniency is, to divide the legislature into different branches; and to render them by different modes of election, and different principles of action, as little connected with each other, as the nature of their common functions, and their common dependence on the society, will admit. It may even be necessary to guard against dangerous encroachments by still further precautions. . . .

First. In a single republic, all the power surrendered by the people, is submitted to the administration of a single government; and usurpations are guarded against by a division of the government into distinct and separate departments. In the compound republic of America, the power surrendered by the people, is first divided between two distinct governments, and then the portion allotted to each, subdivided among distinct and separate departments. Hence a double security arises to the rights of the people. The different governments will controul each other; at the same time that each will be controuled by itself.

Second. It is of great importance in a republic, not only to guard the society against the oppression of its rulers; but to guard one part of the society against the injustice of the other part. Different interests necessarily exist in different classes of citizens. If a majority be united by a common interest, the rights of the minority will be insecure. There are but two methods of providing against this evil: The one by creating a will in the community independent of the majority, that is, of the society itself; the other by comprehending in the society so many separate descriptions of citizens, as will render an unjust combination of a majority of the whole, very improbable, if not impracticable. The first method prevails in all governments possessing an hereditary or self appointed authority. This at best is but a precarious security; because a power independent of the society may as well espouse the unjust views of the major, as the rightful interests, of the minor party, and may possibly be turned against both parties. The second method will be exemplified in the federal republic of the United States. Whilst all authority in it will be derived from and dependent on the society, the society itself will be broken into so many parts, interests and classes of citizens, that the rights of individuals or of the minority, will be in little danger from interested combinations of the majority. In a free government, the security for civil rights must be the same as that for religious rights. It consists in the one case in the multiplicity of interests, and in the other, in the multiplicity of sects. The degree of security in both cases will depend on the number of interests and sects; and this may be presumed to depend on the extent of country and number of people comprehended under the same government. This view of the subject must particularly recommend a proper federal system to all the sincere and considerate friends of republican government: Since it shews that in exact proportion as the territory of the union may be formed into more circumscribed confederacies or states, oppressive combinations of a majority will be facilitated, the best security under the republican form, for the rights of every class of citizens, will be diminished; and consequently, the stability and independence of some member of the government, the only other security, must be proportionally increased. Justice is the end of government. It is the end of civil society. It ever has been, and ever will be pursued, untill it be obtained, or untill liberty be lost in the pursuit. In a society under the forms of which the stronger faction can readily unite and oppress the weaker, anarchy may as truly be said to reign, as in a state of nature where the weaker individual is not secured against the violence of the stronger: And as in the latter state even the stronger individuals are prompted by the uncertainty of their condition, to submit to a government which may protect the weak as well as themselves: So in the former state, will the more powerful factions or parties be gradually induced by a like motive, to wish for a government which will protect all parties, the weaker as well as the more powerful. It can be little doubted, that if the state of Rhode Island was separated from the confederacy, and left to itself, the insecurity of rights under the popular form of government within such narrow limits, would be displayed by such reiterated oppressions of factious majorities, that some power altogether independent of the people would soon be called for by the voice of the very factions whose misrule had proved the necessity of it. In the extended republic of the United States, and among the great variety of interests, parties and sects which it embraces, a coalition of a majority of the whole society could seldom take place on any other principles than those of justice and the general good; and there being thus less danger to a minor from the will of the major party, there must be less pretext also, to provide for the security of the former, by introducing into the government a will not dependent on the latter; or in other words, a will independent of the society itself. It is no less certain than it is important, notwithstanding the contrary opinions which have been entertained, that the larger the society, provided it lie within a practicable sphere, the more duly capable it will be of self government. And happily for the *republican cause*, the practicable sphere may be carried to a very great extent, by a judicious modification and mixture of the *federal principle*.

Source: Independent Journal (New York, February 6, 1788).

DOCUMENT 52: Essay XV (Brutus, March 20, 1788)

Brutus feared that the Supreme Court provided by the Constitution of 1787 would be an instrument for suppression of state government powers and oppression of individuals. He wrote, "I question whether the world ever saw, in any period of it, a court of justice invested with such immense power, and yet placed in a situation so little responsible." Later in this essay, Brutus claimed, "they are independent of the people, of the legislature, and of every power under heaven."

Brutus predicted that the proposed Supreme Court would exercise the power of judicial review, even though this power was not mentioned in the Constitution. Thus, the Court would, said Brutus, have supremacy over the legislature by its power to declare acts of Congress in violation of the Constitution. In summary, Brutus criticized the Supreme Court of the proposed Constitution as an undemocratic institution with no accountability to the people, upon whom the government was supposed to be based.

Why did Brutus draw these negative conclusions? How were Brutus's negative views of the federal judiciary related to his conceptions of true federalism and true republican government? (See Document 44, Essay I by Brutus, in addition to Essay XV.) What recommendations did Brutus provide about how the judicial department should be constituted and operated in a true republican government?

I said in my last number, that the supreme court under this constitution would be exalted above all other power in the government, and subject to no controul. The business of this paper will be to illustrate this, and to shew the danger that will result from it. I question whether the world ever saw, in any period of it, a court of justice invested with such immense powers, and yet placed in a situation so little responsible. . . .

The judges in England are under the controul of the legislature, for they are bound to determine according to the laws passed by them. But the judges under this constitution will controul the legislature, for the supreme court are authorised in the last resort, to determine what is the extent of the powers of the Congress; they are to give the constitution an explanation, and there is no power above them to sit aside their judgment. . . .

I do not object to the judges holding their commissions during good behaviour. I suppose it a proper provision provided they were made properly responsible. But I say, this system has followed the English government in this, while it has departed from almost every other principle of their juris-prudence, under the idea, of rendering the judges independent; which, in the British constitution, means no more than that they hold their places during good behaviour, and have fixed salaries, they have made the judges *independent*, in the fullest sense of the word. There is no power above them, to controul any of their decisions. There is no authority that can remove them, and they cannot be controuled by the laws of the legislature. In short, they are independent of the people, of the legislature, and of every power under heaven. Men placed in this situation will generally soon feel themselves independent of heaven itself. . . .

I have said that the judges under this system will be *independent* in the strict sense of the word: To prove this I will shew—That there is no power above them that can controul their decisions, or correct their errors. There is no authority that can remove them from office for any errors or want of capacity, or lower their salaries, and in many cases their power is superior to that of the legislature.

1st. There is no power above them that can correct their errors or controul their decisions—The adjudications of this court are final and irreversible, for there is no court above them to which appeals can lie, either in error or on the merits.—In this respect it differs from the courts in England, for there the house of lords is the highest court, to whom appeals, in error, are carried from the highest of the courts of law.

2d. They cannot be removed from office or suffer a dimunition of their salaries, for any error in judgement or want of capacity.

It is expressly declared by the constitution,—"That they shall at stated times receive a compensation for their services which shall not be diminished during their continuance in office."

The only clause in the constitution which provides for the removal of the judges from offices, is that which declares, that "the president, vice-president, and all civil officers of the United States, shall be removed from office, on impeachment for, and conviction of treason, bribery, or other high crimes and misdemeanors." By this paragraph, civil officers, in which the judges are included, are removable only for crimes. Treason and bribery are named, and the rest are included under the general terms of high crimes and misdemeanors.—Errors in judgement, or want of capacity to discharge the duties of the office, can never be supposed to be included in these words, *high crimes and misdemeanors*. A man may mistake a case in giving judgment, or manifest that he is incompetent to the discharge of the duties of a judge, and yet give no evidence of corruption or want of integrity. To support the charge, it will be necessary to give in evidence some facts that will shew, that the judges commited the error from wicked and corrupt motives.

3d. The power of this court is in many cases superior to that of the legislature. I have shewed, in a former paper, that this court will be authorised to decide upon the meaning of the constitution, and that, not only according to the natural and obvious meaning of the words, but also according to the spirit and intention of it. In the exercise of this power they will not be subordinate to, but above the legislature. For all the departments of this government will receive their powers, so far as they are expressed in the constitution, from the people immediately, who are the source of power. The legislature can only exercise such powers as are given them by the constitution, they cannot assume any of the rights annexed to the judicial, for this plain reason, that the same authority which vested the legislature with their powers, vested the judicial with theirs—both are derived from the same source, both therefore are equally valid, and the judicial hold their powers independently of the legislature, as the legislature do of the judicial.—The supreme court then have a right, independent of the legislature, to give a construction to the constitution and every part of it, and there is no power provided in this system to correct their construction or do it away. If, therefore, the legislature pass any laws, inconsistent with the sense the judges put upon the constitution, they will declare it void; and therefore in this respect their power is superior to that of the legislature. In England the judges are not only subject to have their decisions set aside by the house of lords, for error, but in cases where they give an explanation to the laws or constitution of the country, contrary to the sense of the parliament, though the parliament will not set aside the judgement of the court, yet, they have authority, by a new law, to explain a former one, and by this means to prevent a reception of such decisions. But no such power is in the legislature. The judges are supreme—and no law, explanatory of the constitution, will be binding on them.

From the preceding remarks, which have been made on the judicial powers proposed in this system, the policy of it may be fully developed.

I have, in the course of my observation on this constitution, affirmed and endeavored to shew, that it was calculated to abolish entirely the state governments, and to melt down the states into one entire government, for every purpose as well internal and local, as external and national. In this opinion the opposers of the system have generally agreed—and this has been uniformly denied by its advocates in public. Some individuals, indeed, among them, will confess, that it has this tendency, and scruple not to say, it is what they wish; and I will venture to predict, without the spirit of prophecy, that if it is adopted without amendments, or some such precautions as will ensure amendments immediately after its adoption, that the same gentlemen who have employed their talents and abilities with such success to influence the public mind to adopt this plan, will employ the same to persuade the people, that it will be for their good to abolish the state governments as useless and burdensome.

Perhaps nothing could have been better conceived to facilitate the abolition of the state governments than the constitution of the judicial. They will be able to extend the limits of the general government gradually, and by insensible degrees, and to accomodate themselves to the temper of the people. Their decisions on the meaning of the constitution will commonly take place in cases which arise between individuals, with which the public will not be generally acquainted; one adjudication will form a precedent to the next, and this to a following one. These cases will immediately affect individuals only; so that a series of determinations will probably take place before even the people will be informed of them. In the mean time all the art and address of those who wish for the change will be employed to make converts to their opinion. The people will be told, that their state officers, and state legislatures are a burden and expence without affording any solid advantage, for that all the laws passed by them, might be equally well made by the general legislature. If to those who will be interested in the change, be added, those who will be under their influence, and such who will submit to almost any change of government, which they can be persuaded to believe will ease them of taxes, it is easy to see, the party who will favor the abolition of the state governments would be far from being inconsiderable.—In this situation, the general legislature, might pass one law after another, extending the general and abridging the state jurisdictions, and to sanction their proceedings would have a course of decisions of the judicial to whom the constitution has committed the power of explaining the constitution.—If the states remonstrated, the constitutional mode of deciding upon the validity of the law, is with the supreme court, and neither people, nor state legislatures, nor the general legislature can remove them or reverse their decrees.

Had the construction of the constitution been left with the legislature, they would have explained it at their peril; if they exceed their powers, or sought to find, in the spirit of the constitution, more than was expressed in the letter, the people from whom they derived their power could remove them, and do themselves right; and indeed I can see no other remedy that the people can have against their rulers for encroachments of this nature. . . .

Source: New York Journal (New York, March 20, 1788).

DOCUMENT 53: *The Federalist* 78 (Publius [Alexander Hamilton], May 28, 1788)

Alexander Hamilton was very concerned about Brutus's criticism of the judiciary in the 1787 Constitution. He feared a positive public response to Brutus's Essay XV (see Document 52) and decided to rebut his Anti-Federalist critic. He argued that an independent judicial branch of government, with the power of judicial review, was necessary to achieve limited government and security for individual rights under the supreme law of the Constitution. Lifetime tenure of office would be a key to judicial independence from partisan influences and public pressures to violate the rights of unpopular individuals. Further, the power of judicial review would be a key to prevent actions of the legislature that violated the Constitution and threatened the people's freedoms.

Publius responded brilliantly to Brutus's charge that the Supreme Court of the proposed Constitution contradicted the idea of republican government because it was not directly accountable to the people. He argued that this Constitution could not become the law of the land unless it was ratified in state conventions by elected representatives of the people. If so, everything in this document, including the judiciary, would have been confirmed by an act of popular sovereignty or consent by the governed.

What is your evaluation of Hamilton's response to Brutus's critique of the judicial branch in the 1787 Constitution? How did he use the ideas of judicial independence, judicial review, and popular sovereignty? Did he succeed in his attempt to refute Brutus's criticisms?

We proceed now to an examination of the judiciary department of the proposed government. . . .

According to the plan of the convention, all the judges who may be appointed by the United States are to hold their offices *during good behaviour*, which is conformable to the most approved of the state constitutions; and among the rest, to that of this state. Its propriety having been drawn into question by the adversaries of that plan, is no light symptom of the rage for objection which disorders their imaginations and judgments. The standard of good behaviour for the continuance in office of the judicial magistracy is certainly one of the most valuable of the modern improvements in the practice of government. In a monarchy it is an excellent barrier to the despotism of the prince: In a republic it is a no less excellent barrier to the encroachments and oppressions of the representative body. And it is the best expedient which can be devised in any government, to secure a steady, upright and impartial administration of the laws.

Whoever attentively considers the different departments of power must perceive, that in a government in which they are separated from each other, the judiciary, from the nature of its functions, will always be the least dangerous to the political rights of the constitution; because it will be least in a capacity to annoy or injure them. The executive not only dispenses the honors, but holds the sword of the community. The legislature not only commands the purse, but prescribes the rules by which the duties and rights of every citizen are to be regulated. The judiciary on the contrary has no influence over either the sword or the purse, no direction either of the strength or of the wealth of the society, and can take no active resolution whatever. It may truly be said to have neither Force nor Will, but merely judgment; and must ultimately depend upon the aid of the executive arm even for the efficacy of its judgments.

This simple view of the matter suggests several important consequences. It proves incontestibly that the judiciary is beyond comparison the weakest of the three departments. . . .

The complete independence of the courts of justice is peculiarly essential in a limited constitution. By a limited constitution I understand one which contains certain specified exceptions to the legislative authority; such for instance as that it shall pass no bills of attainder, no *ex post facto* laws, and the like. Limitations of this kind can be preserved in practice no other way than through the medium of the courts of justice; whose duty it must be to declare all acts contrary to the manifest tenor of the constitution void. Without this, all the reservations of particular rights or privileges would amount to nothing.

Some perplexity respecting the right of the courts to pronounce legislative acts void, because contrary to the constitution, has arisen from an imagination that the doctrine would imply a superiority of the judiciary to the legislative power. It is urged that the authority which can declare the acts of another void, must necessarily be superior to the one whose acts may be declared void. As this doctrine is of great importance in all the American constitutions, a brief discussion of the grounds on which it rests cannot be unacceptable.

There is no position which depends on clearer principles, than that every act of a delegated authority, contrary to the tenor of the commission under which it is exercised, is void. No legislative act therefore contrary to the constitution can be valid. To deny this would be to affirm that the deputy is greater than his principal; that the servant is above his master; that the representatives of the people are superior to the people themselves; that men acting by virtue of powers may do not only what their powers do not authorise, but what they forbid.

If it be said that the legislative body are themselves the constitutional judges of their own powers, and that the construction they put upon them is conclusive upon the other departments, it may be answered, that this cannot be the natural presumption, where it is not to be collected from any particular provisions in the constitution. It is not otherwise to be supposed that the constitution could intend to enable the representatives of the people to substitute their *will* to that of their constituents. It is far more rational to suppose that the courts were designed to be an intermediate body between the people and the legislature, in order, among other things, to keep the latter within the limits assigned to their authority. The interpretation of the laws is the proper and peculiar province of the courts. A constitution is in fact, and must be, regarded by the judges as a fundamental law. It therefore belongs to them to ascertain its meaning as well as the meaning of any particular act proceeding from the legislative body. If there should happen to be an irreconcileable variance between the two, that which has the superior obligation and validity ought of course to be preferred; or in other words, the constitution ought to be preferred to the statute, the intention of the people to the intention of their agents.

Nor does this conclusion by any means suppose a superiority of the judicial to the legislative power. It only supposes that the power of the people is superior to both; and that where the will of the legislature declared in its statutes, stands in opposition to that of the people declared in the constitution, the judges ought to be governed by the latter, rather than the former. They ought to regulate their decisions by the fundamental laws, rather than by those which are not fundamental.

This exercise of judicial discretion in determining between two contradictory laws, is exemplified in a familiar instance. It not uncommonly happens, that there are two statutes existing at one time, clashing in whole or in part with each other, and neither of them containing any repealing clause or expression. In such a case, it is the province of the courts to liquidate and fix their meaning and operation: So far as they can by any fair construction be reconciled to each other; reason and law conspire to dictate that this should be done. Where this is impracticable, it becomes a matter of necessity to give effect to one, in exclusion of the other. The rule which has obtained in the courts for determining their relative validity is that the last in order of time shall be preferred to the first. But this is mere rule of construction, not derived from any positive law, but from the nature and reason of the thing. It is a rule not enjoined upon the courts by legislative provision, but adopted by themselves, as consonant to truth and propriety, for the direction of their conduct as interpreters of the law. They thought it reasonable, that between the interfering acts of an *equal* authority, that which was the last indication of its will, should have the preference.

But in regard to the interfering acts of a superior and subordinate authority, of an original and derivative power, the nature and reason of the thing indicate the converse of that rule as proper to be followed. They teach us that the prior act of a superior ought to be preferred to the subsequent act of an inferior and subordinate authority; and that, accordingly, whenever a particular statute contravenes the constitution, it will be the duty of the judicial tribunals to adhere to the latter, and disregard the former. . . .

If then the courts of justice are to be considered as the bulwarks of a limited constitution against legislative encroachments, this consideration will afford a strong argument for the permanent tenure of judicial offices, since nothing will contribute so much as this to that independent spirit in the judges, which must be essential to the faithful performance of so arduous a duty.

This independence of the judges is equally requisite to guard the constitution and the rights of individuals from the effects of those ill humours which the arts of designing men, or the influence of particular conjunctures, sometimes disseminate among the people themselves, and which, though they speedily give place to better information and more deliberate reflection, have a tendency in the mean time to occasion dangerous innovations in the government, and serious oppressions of the minor party in the community. . . .

That inflexible and uniform adherence to the rights of the constitution and of individuals, which we perceive to be indispensable in the courts of justice, can certainly not be expected from judges who hold their offices by a temporary commission. Periodical appointments, however regulated, or by whomsoever made, would in some way or other be fatal to their necessary independence. If the power of making them was committed either to the executive or legislature, there would be danger of an improper complaisance to the branch which possessed it; if to both, there would be an unwillingness to hazard the displeasure of either; if to the people, or to persons chosen by them for the special purpose, there would be too great a disposition to consult popularity, to justify a reliance that nothing would be consulted but the constitution and the laws. . . .

Upon the whole there can be no room to doubt that the convention acted wisely in copying from the models of those constitutions which have established *good behaviour* as the tenure of their judicial offices in point of duration; and that so far from being blameable on this account, their plan would have been inexcuseably defective if it had wanted this important feature of good government. The experience of Great Britain affords an illustrious comment on the excellence of the institution.

Source: New York Packet (New York, June 20, 1788).

FURTHER READING

Carey, George. *The Federalist: Design for a Constitutional Republic.* Urbana: University of Illinois Press, 1989.

Cooke, Jacob E. *Alexander Hamilton: A Biography.* New York: Charles Scribner's Sons, 1982.

De Pauw, Linda Grant. *The Eleventh Pillar: New York State and the Federal Convention.* Ithaca, N.Y.: Cornell University Press, 1966.

Gillespie, Michael, and Michael Liensch, eds., *Ratifying the Constitution.* Lawrence: University of Kansas Press, 1989.

Kessler, Charles R., ed. *Saving the Revolution: The Federalist Papers and the American Founding.* New York: The Free Press, 1987.

Ketcham, Ralph. *James Madison: A Biography.* Charlottesville: University Press of Virginia, 1990.

Morris, Richard B. *Witnesses at the Creation: Hamilton, Madison, Jay, and the Constitution.* New York: Henry Holt and Company, 1985.

Pacheco, Josephine F. *Antifederalism.* Fairfax, Va.: George Mason University Press, 1992.

Schechter, Stephen L., ed. *The Reluctant Pillar: New York and the Adoption of the Federal Constitution.* Albany: New York State Commission on the Bicentennial of the United States Constitution, 1987.

Storing, Herbert J. *What the Anti-Federalists Were For.* Chicago: University of Chicago Press, 1981.

Part VII

The First Federal Congress and the Bill of Rights, 1788–1792

During the autumn and winter of 1788–1789, a new federal government was born. The first elections were held, and Congress convened in New York City, the temporary federal capital. The work of governance began in April after a quorum was achieved in the House of Representatives and Senate. The new president and vice-president, George Washington and John Adams, were inaugurated (April 30).

The first federal Congress, in collaboration with the first president, had to create and initiate operations of government under the Constitution. The first federal taxes were levied and collected, and the first federal regulations of interstate commerce were enacted and enforced. Further, institutions of the three branches of government were established.

Amid this flurry of governmental activity, James Madison, representative to Congress from Virginia, reminded his colleagues of a promise made to the American people at several ratifying conventions. In order to win support for the controversial Constitution of 1787, Federalists had pledged to introduce constitutional amendments at the first federal Congress that would guarantee the rights and liberties of the people against the strong powers of the federal government. James Madison had won his seat in Congress, in close contest with James Monroe (1,308 votes to 972), only by convincing constituents that he would propose constitutional amendments—a bill of rights—to the first federal Congress.

At first, Madison had opposed a federal bill of rights. He had joined others at the Federal Convention to vote down George Mason's proposal, near the end of the proceedings, to include a "declaration of rights" in the Constitution. However, neither Madison nor the other delegates were opponents of civil liberties and rights for the people of the United States. Madison, for example, had been a champion of religious liberty and other freedoms for the people of his state, Virginia. He believed ardently that the ultimate purpose of a good government, as stated in the American Declaration of Independence, was "to secure these rights." Thus, he had endeavored to achieve a "well-constructed Union" and Constitution that would protect the people's rights through such practical principles of government as separation of powers, checks and balances, limited grants of power, and regular election of legislators responsible to the people.

Madison and other Federalists had advanced arguments in defense of a U.S. Constitution without a bill of rights. First, there would be protection for rights in the bills of rights of the state constitutions. Second, the federal Constitution could not negate rights guaranteed in state constitutions. Third, it would be unnecessary to declare in the Constitution that certain rights of the people may not be denied by the federal government, because there was no power granted to deny them; the federal government, for example, was not granted power to deny freedom of the press, so it could not do it. Fourth, if certain rights were listed in a formal bill of rights, other rights that the people should possess could be denied them on the grounds that what was not listed was not protected. Fifth, the entire Constitution could be viewed as a bill of rights because it was designed, as the Preamble says, to "secure the Blessings of Liberty to ourselves and our Posterity." And, finally, without effective institutions of government, designed to provide ordered liberty, the people's rights could never be secure, no matter how eloquently they might be stated in a written declaration.

George Mason, a colleague of Madison in the Virginia delegation to the Federal Convention, disagreed adamantly with the arguments and decision against a bill of rights in the Constitution. His influential essay against the Constitution of 1787 (Document 47), distributed throughout the United States, began with this ringing objection, "There is no declaration of rights." An alarmed James Madison wrote to Thomas Jefferson (October 24, 1787), "Colonel Mason left Philadelphia in an exceeding ill humor. . . . He returned to Virginia with a fixed disposition to prevent the adoption of the plan [Constitution] if possible. He considers the want of a Bill of Rights a fatal objection."[1]

Jefferson wrote back to Madison from Paris, France, agreeing with Mason's primary objection to the Constitution, although he generally approved the document (see Document 54). He advised Madison that "a bill of rights is what the people are entitled to against every government on earth, general or particular, and what no just government should refuse, or rest on inference."

Many Americans, perhaps a majority, agreed with Jefferson and Mason about the need for amendments to the Constitution to guarantee the people's rights against the federal government's powers. The Anti-Federalists used this public sentiment to oppose ratification of the Constitution, unless public pledges were made by the Federalists to amend the Constitution to correct certain deficiencies. However, the Anti-Federalists' call for amendments was two sided. One side, in concert with Jefferson and Mason, proposed amendments to protect certain natural rights, such as freedom of the press, free exercise of religion, due process in legal proceedings, and so forth. The second side, in concert with Anti-Federalist conceptions of republican government and confederation, was a call for amendments to change the structure of the federal government to greatly restrict its powers in favor of greater powers for the state governments.

This second side of the call for amendments was revealed clearly in statements issued by the ratifying conventions of several states, beginning with Massachusetts (February 6, 1788). These state ratifying conventions listed proposed amendments to the Constitution, which should be addressed by the first federal Congress. The nine amendments proposed by Massachusetts, for example (Document 55), mostly pertained to stronger limits on federal government power to enhance the state governments' powers. Only two of the nine proposed amendments (numbers six and eight) pertained to the natural rights of individuals.

This same kind of emphasis on amendments to change the structure of government and the balance of power between the federal and state governments is revealed by the proposals from other state ratifying conventions. The New York Convention, for example, combined its plea for amendments to protect natural rights with amendments to protect state powers (see Document 56). The New York Convention put forth several striking alterations in the 1787 Constitution to protect the states' rights and powers. Consider this example: "That the senators and representatives, and all executive and judicial offices of the United States, shall be bound by oath or affirmation not to infringe or violate the constitutions or rights of the respective states." If this proposal, and others like it, had become constitutional amendments, the locus of power in the federal system would have reverted decisively to the states, as it was under the Articles of Confederation.

Several state ratifying conventions had proposed nearly 200 separate amendments, which were compiled in a pamphlet. James Madison sent it to Thomas Jefferson with his letter of October 17, 1788 (Document 57). In this remarkable letter, Madison informed Jefferson that he would support the addition of a bill of rights to the Constitution, "because it is anxiously desired by others." But he also decided to oppose any amendments that would alter the federal government's structure or the balance of power between the federal and state governments. Above all, Madison wanted to prevent any significant reduction in the power of the federal government vis-à-vis the several state governments.

Madison continued to believe that a bill of rights, if added to the Constitution, would not be an effective safeguard for the people's liberties unless it were embedded in a well-constructed government that could enforce it. Otherwise, a bill of rights would be a mere "parchment barrier" to tyranny, not an enforceable instrument for protection of natural rights.

On June 8, 1789, James Madison addressed the House of Representatives to propose addition of a bill of rights to the Constitution (see Document 58). He included only provisions to protect the natural rights of individuals, such as freedom of speech, press, and religion and other protections of persons against the power of government. Madison, however, ignored recommendations from state ratifying conventions to protect or expand the powers of state governments relative to the federal government, which greatly disappointed Anti-Federalists in Congress. They tried, at least, to insert the words "expressly delegated" in the proposal that became the Tenth Amendment, so that it would be stated as follows: "The powers not *expressly* delegated to the United States by the Constitution, nor prohibited by it to the States, are reserved to the States respectively, or to the people." By including the words "expressly delegated" instead of merely "delegated," the Anti-Federalists wanted to strictly limit the powers granted to the federal government in the Constitution. They especially intended to neuter the "necessary and proper" clause of Article I, Section 8, by which the powers of Congress could be stretched through a loose interpretation of the Constitution.

James Madison organized opposition in Congress to insertion of the word "expressly" before "delegated" in this amendment, and Madison's side won. By omitting the strictly limiting word "expressly," Madison and his supporters defeated the final Anti-Federalist attempt to alter the balance of power in the federal system away from the U.S. government and toward the states. Further, they opened the way to the doctrine of implied powers and a loose construction of the Constitution, by which the powers of the federal government might be stretched by the majority in Congress in response to future issues and needs.

On August 24, after deliberation and discussion, the House of Representatives adopted, with minor changes, Madison's proposals of June 8 in the form of seventeen articles to be added to the Constitution. On September 9, the Senate adopted its own version of the proposed amendments. Differences between the two houses were settled by September 25, when the Congress officially proposed twelve articles as amendments to the Constitution (see Document 59).

The proposed amendments were sent to the states, in accord with the Constitution's Article V, for their approval or rejection. Article V requires that three-fourths of the states must approve a proposed amendment before it is ratified and added to the Constitution.

James Madison was generally satisfied with the amendments proposed by Congress. They proclaimed civil liberties and rights of the people against the powers of government, and they did not alter the structure or the enumerated powers of the federal government. So, this proposed Bill of Rights did not violate Madison's conception of what the federal system should be. However, he was greatly disappointed by defeat in the Senate of his specific proposal to restrict the state governments from abridging the rights of individuals to freedom of the press and religion and to trial by jury in criminal cases. (See the fifth provision in Madison's June 8 speech to Congress, Document 58.) Madison warned, "I think there is more danger of those powers [against the people's rights] being abused by the State Governments than by the Government of the United States." Madison's warning was not heeded until passage of the Fourteenth Amendment in 1868, which restricts the power of state governments in order to protect certain rights of individuals.

Anti-Federalist stalwarts were very disappointed in the proposed amendments. For example, the two Senators from Virginia, William Grayson and Richard Henry Lee, were sharply critical in a letter to the Virginia House of Delegates. They did not disagree with guarantees of individual rights in the Amendment. Rather, they were fearful that, without additional Amendments to alter the structure of the federal system, the states would be subordinated to the federal government, and the people's liberties ultimately would be lost. William Grayson wrote to Patrick Henry (September 29, 1789) that the amendments "are good for nothing."[2] Another Anti-Federalist, Thomas Tudor Tucker of South Carolina, wrote, "You will find our Amendments to the Constitution calculated merely to amuse, or rather to deceive."[3]

The few Anti-Federalist dissidents, however, were not able to obstruct the ratification of the proposed amendments. Most Americans were reassured by them, including the majority of Anti-Federalists who had responded to George Mason's objection to the 1787 Constitution—"There is no declaration of rights." So, the ratification of the federal Bill of Rights proceeded slowly but surely during the next two years. Not until December 15, 1791, however, did a sufficient number of states ratify ten of the twelve proposed Amendments.

The first and second of the original list of twelve amendments were rejected. The defeated amendments were not directly related to civil liberties or rights. The first unratified proposal would have modified apportionment of delegates to the House of Representatives. The second provided that, "No law, varying the compensation for services of the Senators and Representatives, shall take effect, until an election of Representatives shall have intervened." Only six states had approved this amendment by the end of 1791, not enough to ratify it. But in 1978 public interest in this proposed amendment was revived, and by May 7, 1992, a sufficient number had ratified it to meet the three-fourths requirement of Article V. So, the rejected Second Amendment of the original list of twelve became the Twenty-Seventh Amendment to the Constitution, more than 200 years after it was initially proposed by Congress.

On March 1, 1792, the secretary of state, Thomas Jefferson, sent to the governor of each state official notice of ratification of ten amendments to the Constitution (see Document 60). Most Americans seemed satisfied that their natural rights would be protected against the power of the new federal government.

The federal Bill of Rights (Document 60), proposed initially by Anti-Federalists, became a special project of James Madison and his Federalist supporters. But certain Anti-Federalist proposals for protecting the powers and rights of the states were not included in Amendments I–X. Documents 54–60 reveal the similarities and differences in the ideas of Federalists and Anti-Federalists about a Bill of Rights and other amendments to the Constitution.

From the founding era until the present, Americans treated unjustly have appealed to the Bill of Rights to achieve redress of their grievances. And people around the world have seen this appendage to the 1787 Constitution as a universal symbol of liberty.

NOTES

1. Michael Kammen, ed., *The Origins of the American Constitution: A Documentary History* (New York: Viking Penguin, 1986), p. 74.

2. Helen E. Veit, Kenneth R. Bowling, and Charlene Bangs Bickford, eds., *Creating the Bill of Rights: The Documentary Record from the First Federal Congress* (Baltimore: The Johns Hopkins University Press, 1991), p. 300.

3. Ibid.

DOCUMENT 54: Letter to James Madison (Thomas Jefferson, December 20, 1787)

Thomas Jefferson was in Paris, serving as the Minister to France from the United States, when he received a copy of the 1787 Constitution with a letter from his friend, James Madison. Jefferson generally approved the new frame of government and reported to Madison the many features of it that he approved. He liked the separation of powers among three branches of government and lauded the bicameral legislature, which included a House of Representatives elected by the people and a Senate elected by the state governments. What else did Jefferson especially like about the new Constitution?

Jefferson was disappointed that the 1787 Constitution did not include a bill of rights. Why? What were his reasons? What other criticisms did Jefferson make against the 1787 Constitution?

The season admitting only of operations in the Cabinet, and these being in a great measure secret, I have little to fill a letter. I will therefore make up the deficiency by adding a few words on the Constitution proposed by our Convention. I like much the general idea of framing a government which should go on of itself peaceably, without needing continual recurrence to the state legislatures. I like the organization of the government into Legislative, Judiciary and Executive. I like the power given the Legislature to levy taxes; and for that reason solely approve of the greater house being chosen by the people directly. For tho' I think a house chosen by them will be very illy qualified to legislate for the Union, for foreign nations &c. yet this evil does not weigh against the good of preserving inviolate the fundamental principle that the people are not to be taxed but by representatives chosen immediately by themselves. I am captivated by the compromise of the opposite claims of the great and little states, of the latter to equal, and the former to proportional influence. I am much pleased too with the substitution of the method of voting by persons, instead of that of voting by states: and I like the negative given to the Executive with a third of either house, though I should have liked it better had the Judiciary been associated for the purpose, or invested with a similar and separate power. There are other good things of less moment. I will now add what I do not like. First the omission of a bill of rights providing clearly and without the aid of sophisms for freedom of religion, freedom of the press, protection against standing armies, restriction against monopolies, the eternal and unremitting force of the habeas corpus laws, and trials by jury in all matters of fact triable by the laws of the land and not by the law of Nations. To say, as Mr. Wilson does that a bill of rights was not necessary because all is reserved in the case of the general government which is not given, while in the particular ones all is given which is not reserved might do for the Audience to whom it was addressed, but is surely gratis dictum, opposed by strong inferences from the body of the instrument, as well as from the omission of the clause of our present confederation which had declared that in express terms. It was a hard conclusion to say because there has been no uniformity among the states as to the cases triable by jury, because some have been so incautious as to abandon this mode of trial, therefore the more prudent states shall be reduced to the same level of calamity. It would have been much more just and wise to have concluded the other way that as most of the states had judiciously preserved this palladium, those who had wandered should be brought back to it, and to have established general right instead of general wrong. Let me add that a bill of rights is what the people are entitled to against every government on earth, general or particular, and what no just government should refuse, or rest on inference. The second feature I dislike, and greatly dislike, is the abandonment in every instance of the necessity of rotation in office, and most particularly in the case of the President. Experience concurs with reason in concluding that the first magistrate will always be reelected if the constitution permits it. He is then an officer for life. . . . An incapacity to be elected a second time would have been the only effectual preventative. The power of removing him every fourth year by the vote of the people is a power which will not be exercised. . . .

Source: H. A. Washington, ed., *The Writings of Thomas Jefferson,* Vol. I (Washington, D.C.: Taylor and Maury, 1853), pp. 322–23.

DOCUMENT 55: Amendments to the U.S. Constitution Proposed by the Massachusetts Ratifying Convention (February 6, 1788)

Anti-Federalists were unrelenting in their demands for constitutional amendments to protect the rights of the people and the states. The Federalists prevailed at the Massachusetts ratifying convention and in several other states only by promising to support amendments to the Constitution proposed by the Anti-Federalists. In exchange for this pledge, many Anti-Federalist delegates voted for ratification. Notice that only two of the nine proposed amendments (items VI and VIII) pertain directly to rights of individuals. The others pertain primarily either to the rights of powers of state governments or to the operations of the federal government.

What guarantees for individual rights were proposed as amendments to the Constitution? What were the proposals to protect or expand the powers and rights of the states?

. . . And as it is the opinion of this Convention, that certain amendments and alterations in the said Constitution would remove the fears, and quiet the apprehensions, of many of the good people of this commonwealth, and more effectually guard against an undue administration of the federal government,—the Convention do therefore recommend that the following alterations and provisions be introduced into the said Constitution:—

I. That it be explicitly declared that all powers not expressly delegated by the aforesaid Constitution are reserved to the several states, to be by them exercised.

II. That there shall be one representative to every thirty thousand persons, according to the census mentioned in the Constitution, until the whole number of the representatives amounts to two hundred.

III. That Congress do not exercise the powers vested in them by the 4th section of the 1st article, but in cases where a state shall neglect or refuse to make the regulations therein mentioned, or shall make regulations subversive of the rights of the people to a free and equal representation in Congress, agreeably to the Constitution.

IV. That Congress do not lay direct taxes but when the moneys arising from the impost and excise are insufficient for the public exigencies, nor then until Congress shall have first made a requisition upon the states to assess, levy, and pay, their respective proportions of such requisition, agreeably to the census fixed in the said Constitution, in such way and manner as the legislatures of the states shall think best; and in such case, if any state shall neglect or refuse to pay its proportion, pursuant to such requisition, then Congress may assess and levy such state's proportion, together with interest thereon at the rate of six per cent-per annum, from the time of payment prescribed in such requisition.

V. That Congress erect no company of merchants with exclusive advantages of commerce.

VI. That no person shall be tried for any crime by which he may incur an infamous punishment, or loss of life, until he be first indicted by a grand jury, except in such cases as may arise in the government and regulation of the land and naval forces.

VII. The Supreme Judicial Federal Court shall have no jurisdiction of causes between citizens of different states, unless the matter in dispute, whether it concerns the realty or personalty, be of the value of three thousand dollars at the least; nor shall the federal judicial powers extend to any actions between citizens of different states, where the matter in dispute, whether it concerns the realty or personalty, is not of the value of fifteen hundred dollars at least.

VIII. In civil actions between citizens of different states, every issue of fact, arising in actions at common law, shall be tried by a jury, if the parties, or either of them, request it.

IX. Congress shall at no time consent that any person, holding an office of trust or profit under the United States, shall accept of a title of nobility, or any other title or office, from any king, prince, or foreign state.

Source: Jonathan Elliot, ed., *The Debates in the Several State Conventions on the Adoption of the Federal Constitution,* Vol. 2 (Philadelphia: J. B. Lippincott, 1881), pp. 322–23.

DOCUMENT 56: Amendments to the U.S. Constitution Proposed by the New York Ratifying Convention (July 26, 1788)

The New York State Ratifying Convention approved the 1787 Constitution by a narrow vote of thirty to twenty-seven. But to mollify the dissenters, the Convention also proposed amendments to the Constitution that reflected Anti-Federalist viewpoints. Several proposed amendments guaranteed traditional individual rights against federal government power. Most of the proposed amendments, however, pertained to structural changes in the federal system.

Anti-Federalists in New York criticized the proposed Constitution because it shifted power away from the states toward a powerful central government. They demanded amendments to bring significant powers back to the states. Several examples of these proposals to enhance state government powers under the Constitution are presented in this document issued by the New York Convention.

What changes in the structure of the federal government or the nature of the federal system were proposed? If these amendments had been approved, how would the constitutional government of the United States have changed? What might have been the political consequences of these changes?

. . . And the Convention do, in the name and behalf of the people of the state of New York, enjoin it upon their representatives in Congress to exert all their influence, and use all reasonable means, to obtain a ratification of the following amendments to the said Constitution, in the manner prescribed therein; and in all laws to be passed by the Congress, in the mean time, to conform to the spirit of the said amendments, as far as the Constitution will admit. . . .

That the compensation for the senators and representatives be ascertained by standing laws; and that no alteration of the existing rate of compensation shall operate for the benefit of the representatives until after a subsequent election shall have been had. . . .

That no capitation tax shall ever be laid by Congress.

That no person be eligible as a senator for more than six years in any term of twelve years; and that the legislatures of the respective states may recall their senators, or either of them, and elect others in their stead, to serve the remainder of the time for which the senators so recalled were appointed.

That no person shall be eligible to the office of President of the United States a third time.

That the executive shall not grant pardons for treason, unless with the consent of the Congress; but may, at his discretion, grant reprieves to persons convicted of treason, until their cases can be laid before the Congress.

That the President, or person exercising his powers for the time being, shall not command an army in the field in person, without the previous desire of the Congress. . . .

That the militia of any state shall not be compelled to serve without the limits of the state, for a longer term than six weeks, without the consent of the legislature thereof. . . .

That the senators and representatives, and all executive and judicial officers of the United States, shall be bound by oath or affirmation not to infringe or violate the constitutions or rights of the respective states. . . .

Source: Jonathan Elliot, ed., *The Debates in the Several State Conventions on the Adoption of the Federal Constitution,* Vol. 2 (Philadelphia: J. B. Lippincott, 1881), pp. 327–31.

DOCUMENT 57: Letter to Thomas Jefferson (James Madison, October 17, 1788)

James Madison communicated with Thomas Jefferson, who was in France, about proposals to amend the 1787 Constitution put forward by Anti-Federalists at several state ratifying conventions. He explained to Jefferson why he at first opposed a bill of rights in the Constitution. His main reason was a firm belief that a formal declaration of rights was not necessary, because the Constitution was designed to secure the rights of individuals. What were his other reasons?

Then, he told Jefferson why he changed his mind. Madison decided to support a bill of rights in the Constitution because the people strongly desired it. What benefits, according to Madison, could a bill of rights provide in a popular government?

Madison was very concerned about securing the rights of individuals against a peculiar source of oppression in a republican government: tyranny of majority rule by the elected representatives of the people. What were Madison's reasons for fearing majoritarian tyranny? How could the Constitution be used to prevent this threat to individual rights?

DEAR SIR,—The little pamphlet herewith inclosed will give you a collective view of the alterations which have been proposed [by the State Ratifying Conventions] for the new Constitution. . . . Various and numerous as they appear, they certainly omit many of the true grounds of opposition. The articles relating to Treaties, to paper money, and to contracts, created more enemies than all the errors in the system, positive and negative, put together.

It is true, nevertheless, that not a few, particularly in Virginia, have contended for the proposed alterations from the most honorable and patriotic motives; and that among the advocates for the Constitution there are some who wish for further guards to public liberty and individual rights. As far as these may consist of a constitutional declaration of the most essential rights, it is probable they will be added; though there are many who think such addition unnecessary, and not a few who think it misplaced in such a Constitution. There is scarce any point on which the party in opposition is so much divided as to its importance and its propriety. My own opinion has always been in favor of a bill of rights, provided it be so framed as not to imply powers not meant to be included in the enumeration. At the same time, I have never thought the omission a material defect, nor been anxious to supply it even by *subsequent* amendment, for any other reason than that it is anxiously desired by others. I have favored it because I supposed it might be of use, and, if properly executed, could not be of disservice.

I have not viewed it in an important light—1. Because I conceive that in a certain degree, though not in the extent argued by Mr. Wilson, the rights in question are reserved by the manner in which the federal powers are granted. 2. Because there is great reason to fear that a positive declaration of some of the most essential rights could not be obtained in the requisite latitude. I am sure that the rights of conscience in particular, if submitted to public definition, would be narrowed much more than they are likely ever to be by an assumed power. One of the objections in New England was, that the Constitution, by prohibiting religious tests, opened a door for Jews, Turks, and infidels. 3. Because the limited powers of the federal Government, and the jealousy of the subordinate Governments, afford a security which has not existed in the case of the State Governments, and exists in no other. 4. Because experience proves the inefficacy of a bill of rights on those occasions when its controul is most needed. Repeated violations of these parchment barriers have been committed by overbearing majorities in every State.

In Virginia, I have seen the bill of rights violated in every instance where it has been opposed to a popular current. Notwithstanding the explicit provision contained in that instrument for the rights of conscience, it is well known that a religious establishment would have taken place in that State, if the Legislative majority had found, as they expected, a majority of the people in favor of the measure; and I am persuaded that if a majority of the people were now of one sect, the measure would still take place, and on narrower ground than was then proposed, notwithstanding the additional obstacle which the law has since created.

Wherever the real power in a Government lies, there is the danger of oppression. In our Governments the real power lies in the majority of the community, and the invasion of private rights is *chiefly* to be apprehended, not from acts of Government contrary to the sense of its constituents, but from acts in which the Government is the mere instrument of the major number of the Constituents. This is a truth of great importance, but not yet sufficiently attended to; and is probably more strongly impressed on my mind by facts and reflections suggested by them than on yours, which has contemplated abuses of power issuing from a very different quarter. Wherever there is an interest and power to do wrong, wrong will generally be done, and not less readily by a powerful and interested party than by a powerful and interested prince. The difference, so far as it relates to the superiority of republics over monarchies, lies in the less degree of probability that interest may prompt abuses of power in the former than in the latter; and in the security in the former against an oppression of more than the smaller part of the Society, whereas, in the latter, it may be extended in a manner to the whole.

The difference, so far as it relates to the point in question—the efficacy of a bill of rights in controuling abuses of power—lies in this: that in a monarchy the latent force of the nation is superior to that of the Sovereign, and a solemn charter of popular rights must have a great effect as a standard for trying the validity of public acts, and a signal for rousing and uniting the superior force of the community; whereas, in a popular Government, the political and physical power may be considered as vested in the same hands, that is, in a majority of the people, and, consequently, the tyrannical will of the Sovereign is not to be controuled by the dread of an appeal to any other force within the community.

What use, then, it may be asked, can a bill of rights serve in popular Governments? I answer, the two following, which, though less essential than in other Governments, sufficiently recommend the precaution: 1. The political truths declared in that solemn manner acquire by degrees the character of fundamental maxims of free Government, and as they become incorporated with the National sentiment, counteract the impulses of interest and passion. 2. Although it be generally true, as above stated, that the danger of oppression lies in the interested majorities of the people rather than in usurped acts of the Government, yet there may be occasions on which the evil may spring from the latter source; and on such, a bill of rights will be a good ground for an appeal to the sense of the community. Perhaps, too, there may be a certain degree of danger that a succession of artful and ambitious rulers may, by gradual and well-timed advances, finally erect an independent Government on the subversion of liberty. Should this danger exist at all, it is prudent to guard against it, especially when the precaution can do no injury. . . .

Source: Gaillard Hunt, ed., *The Writings of James Madison,* Vol. 5 (New York: G. P. Putnam's Sons, 1900), pp. 271–75.

DOCUMENT 58: Speech in the U.S. House of Representatives (James Madison, June 8, 1789)

In a carefully prepared speech in the House of Representatives, James Madison of Virginia introduced proposals for a bill of rights in the U.S. Constitution. These proposals were influenced by the 1776 Virginia Declaration of Rights. He recommended that these amendments be inserted into sections of the Constitution rather than appended to it. Roger Sherman of Connecticut, however, rallied opposition to this recommendation about placement of the amendments, and the House of Representatives decided that they should be appended to the Constitution as a separate Bill of Rights.

Madison emphasized item five in his list of proposals. If practiced, it would have guaranteed certain individual rights against the power of state governments. Madison believed a primary threat to rights would come from the small republics of the Union, the states.

Madison predicted that the federal courts would become "the guardians of these rights" in the Bill of Rights. He said in this speech that the federal judges "will be naturally led to resist every encroachment upon rights expressly stipulated for in the Constitution by the declaration of rights."

What specific guarantees of rights of individuals did Madison propose to include in the constitution? What were his reasons for proposing these amendments? What were the similarities of Madison's proposals to the Virginia Declaration of Rights?

. . . I will state my reasons why I think it proper to propose amendments, and state the amendments themselves. . . .

It cannot be a secret to the gentlemen in this House, that, notwithstanding the ratification of this system of Government by eleven of the thirteen United States, in some cases unanimously, in others by large majorities; yet still there is a great number of our constituents who are dissatisfied with it, among whom are many respectable for their talents and patriotism, and respectable for the jealousy they have for their liberty, which, though mistaken in its object is laudable in its motive. There is a great body of the people falling under this description, who at present feel much inclined to join their support to the cause of Federalism, if they were satisfied on this one point. We ought not to disregard their inclination, but, on principles of amity and moderation, conform to their wishes, and expressly declare the great rights of mankind secured under this Constitution. . . .

The amendments which have occurred to me, proper to be recommended by Congress to the State Legislatures, are these:

First. That there be prefixed to the Constitution a declaration, that all power is originally vested in, and consequently derived from, the people.

That Government is instituted and ought to be exercised for the benefit of the people; which consists in the enjoyment of life and liberty, with the right of acquiring and using property, and generally of pursuing and obtaining happiness and safety.

That the people have an indubitable, unalienable, and indefeasible right to reform or change their Government, whenever it be found adverse or inadequate to the purposes of its institution.

Secondly. That in article 1st, section 2, clause 3, these words be struck out, to wit: "The number of Representatives shall not exceed one for every thirty thousand, but each State shall have at least one Representative, and until such enumeration shall be made;" and that in place thereof be inserted these words, to wit: "After the first actual enumeration, there shall be one Representative for every thirty thousand, until the number amounts to———, after which the proportion shall be so regulated by Congress, that the number shall never be less than—, nor more than—, but each State shall, after the first enumeration, have at least two Representatives; and prior thereto."

Thirdly. That in article 1st, section 6, clause 1, there be added to the end of the first sentence, these words, to wit: "But no law varying the compensation last ascertained shall operate before the next ensuing election of Representatives."

Fourthly. That in article 1st, section 9, between clauses 3 and 4, be inserted these clauses, to wit: The civil rights of none shall be abridged on account of religious belief or worship, nor shall any national religion be established, nor shall the full and equal rights of conscience be in any manner, or on any pretext, infringed.

The people shall not be deprived or abridged of their right to speak, to write, or to publish their sentiments; and the freedom of the press, as one of the great bulwarks of liberty, shall be inviolable.

The people shall not be restrained from peaceably assembling and consulting for their common good; nor from applying to the Legislature by petitions, or remonstrances, for redress of their grievances.

The right of the people to keep and bear arms shall not be infringed; a well armed and well regulated militia being the best security of a free country: but no person religiously scrupulous of bearing arms shall be compelled to render military service in person.

No soldiers shall in time of peace be quartered in any house without the consent of the owner; nor at any time, but in a manner warranted by law.

No person shall be subject, except in cases of impeachment, to more than one punishment or one trial for the same offence; nor shall be compelled to be a witness against himself; nor be deprived of life, liberty, or property, without due process of law; nor be obliged to relinquish his property, where it may be necessary for public use, without a just compensation.

Excessive bail shall not be required, nor excessive fines imposed, nor cruel and unusual punishments inflicted.

The rights of the people to be secured in their persons, their houses, their papers, and their other property, from all unreasonable searches and seizures, shall not be violated by warrants issued without probable cause, supported by oath or affirmation, or not particularly describing the places to be searched, or the persons or things to be seized.

In all criminal prosecutions, the accused shall enjoy the right to a speedy and public trial, to be informed of the cause and nature of the accusation, to be confronted with his accusers, and the witnesses against him; to have a compulsory process for obtaining witnesses in his favor; and to have the assistance of counsel for his defence.

The exceptions here or elsewhere in the Constitution, made in favor of particular rights, shall not be so construed as to diminish the just importance of other rights retained by the people, or as to enlarge the powers delegated by the Constitution; but either as actual limitations of such powers, or as inserted merely for greater caution.

Fifthly. That in article 1st, section 10, between clauses 1 and 2, be inserted this clause, to wit:

No State shall violate the equal rights of conscience, or the freedom of the press, or the trial by jury in criminal cases.

Sixthly. That, in article 3d, section 2, be annexed to the end of clause 2d, these words, to wit:

But no appeal to such court shall be allowed where the value in controversy shall not amount to ——— dollars: nor shall any fact triable by jury, according to the course of common law, be otherwise re-examinable than may consist with the principles of common law.

Seventhly. That in article 3d, section 2, the third clause be struck out, and in its place be inserted the clauses following, to wit:

The trial of all crimes (except in cases of impeachments, and cases arising in the land or naval forces, or the militia when on actual service, in time of war or public danger) shall be by an impartial jury of freeholders of the vicinage, with the requisite of unanimity for conviction, of the right of challenge, and other accustomed requisites; and in all crimes punishable with loss of life or member, presentment or indictment by a grand jury shall be an essential preliminary, provided that in cases of crimes committed within any county which may be in possession of an enemy, or in which a general insurrection may prevail, the trial may by law be authorized in some other county of the same State, as near as may be to the seat of the offence.

In cases of crimes committed not within any county, the trial may by law be in such county as the laws shall have prescribed. In suits at common law, between man and man, the trial by jury, as one of the best securities to the rights of the people, ought to remain inviolate.

Eighthly. That immediately after article 6th, be inserted, as article 7th, the clauses following, to wit:

The powers delegated by this Constitution are appropriated to the departments to which they are respectively distributed: so that the Legislative Department shall never exercise the powers vested in the Executive or Judicial, nor the Executive exercise the powers vested in the Legislative or Judicial, nor the Judicial exercise the powers vested in the Legislative or Executive Departments.

The powers not delegated by this Constitution, nor prohibited by it to the States, are reserved to the States respectively.

Ninthly. That article 7th be numbered as article 8th.

The first of these amendments relates to what may be called a bill of rights. I will own that I never considered this provision so essential to the Federal Constitution as to make it improper to ratify it, until such an amendment was added; at the same time, I always conceived, that in a certain form, and to a certain extent, such a provision was neither improper nor altogether useless. . . .

Having done what I conceived was my duty, in bringing before this House the subject of amendments, and also stated such as I wish for and approve, and offered the reasons which occurred to me in their support, I shall content myself, for the present, with moving "that a committee be appointed to consider of and report such amendments as ought to be proposed by Congress to the Legislatures of the States, to become, if ratified by three-fourths thereof, part of the Constitution of the United States." By agreeing to this motion, the subject may be going on in the committee, while other important business is proceeding to a conclusion in the House. I should advocate greater despatch in the business of amendments, if I were not convinced of the absolute necessity there is of pursuing the organization of the Government; because I think we should obtain the confidence of our fellow-citizens, in proportion as we fortify the rights of the people against the encroachments of the Government.

Source: Gaillard Hunt, ed., *The Writings of James Madison,* Vol. 5 (New York: G. P. Putnam's Sons, 1900), pp. 370–89.

DOCUMENT 59: Amendments Passed by the U.S. Congress (September 25, 1789)

After more than two months of deliberation and discussion, the House of Representatives agreed to seventeen amendments on rights. They were sent to the Senate for review and possible revision. Both branches of Congress had to approve any proposed amendments, by a two-thirds vote, before they could be sent to the states for ratification.

The Senate received and reflected upon the proposals for amendments sent to it by the House of Representatives. The Senators significantly revised the House's work and passed their own version of proposed amendments on rights.

Members of the House of Representatives and Senate met in a conference committee to discuss the differences in their proposals on amendments. They compromised to create a Bill of Rights that both houses of Congress could accept. The report of the Conference Committee was passed by the House of Representatives on September 24, 1789 and by the Senate on September 25, which is the official date of enactment by Congress of the Bill of Rights. These twelve proposed Amendments were transmitted to the states for ratification according to Article V of the Constitution. To what extent were Madison's proposals of June 8 (Document 58) included in the Bill of Rights passed by Congress?

Article the first. After the first enumeration required by the first Article of the Constitution, there shall be one Representative for every thirty thousand, until the number shall amount to one hundred, after which, the proportion shall be so regulated by Congress, that there shall be not less than one hundred Representatives, nor less than one Representative for every forty thousand persons, until the number of Representatives shall amount to two hundred, after which the proportion shall be so regulated by Congress, that there shall not be less than two hundred Representatives, nor more than one Representative for every fifty thousand persons.

Article the second. No law, varying the compensation for the services of the Senators and Representatives, shall take effect, until an election of Representatives shall have intervened.

Article the third. Congress shall make no law respecting an establishment of religion, or prohibiting the free exercise thereof; or abridging the freedom of speech, or of the press, or the right of the people peaceably to assemble, and to petition the Government for a redress of grievances.

Article the fourth. A well regulated Militia, being necessary to the security of a free State, the right of the people to keep and bear Arms, shall not be infringed.

Article the fifth. No Soldier shall, in time of peace be quartered in any house, without the consent of the Owner, nor in time of war, but in a manner to be prescribed by law.

Article the sixth. The right of the people to be secure in their persons, houses, papers, and effects, against unreasonable searches and seizures, shall not be violated, and no Warrants shall issue, but upon probable cause, supported by Oath or affirmation, and particularly describing the place to be searched, and the persons or things to be seized.

Article the seventh. No person shall be held to answer for a capital, or otherwise infamous crime, unless on a presentment or indictment of a Grand Jury, except in cases arising in the land or naval forces, or in the Militia, when in actual service in time of War or public danger; nor shall any person be subject for the same offence to be twice put in jeopardy of life or limb, nor shall be compelled in any criminal case to be a witness against himself, nor be deprived of life, liberty, or property, without due process of law; nor shall private property be taken for public use without just compensation.

Article the eighth. In all criminal prosecutions, the accused shall enjoy the right to a speedy and public trial, by an impartial jury of the State and district wherein the crime shall have been committed, which district shall have been previously ascertained by law, and to be informed of the nature and cause of the accusation; to be confronted with the witnesses against him; to have compulsory process for obtaining witnesses in his favor, and to have the Assistance of Counsel for his defence.

Article the ninth. In suits at common law, where the value in controversy shall exceed twenty dollars, the right of trial by jury shall be preserved, and no fact tried by a jury shall be otherwise re-examined in any Court of the United States, than according to the rules of the common law.

Article the tenth. Excessive bail shall not be required, nor excessive fines imposed, nor cruel and unusual punishments inflicted.

Article the eleventh. The enumeration in the Constitution, of certain rights, shall not be construed to deny or disparage others retained by the people.

Article the twelfth. The powers not delegated to the United States by the Constitution, nor prohibited by it to the States, are reserved to the States respectively, or to the people.

Source: National Archives and Records Administration, *The Bill of Rights: Milestone Documents in the National Archives* (Washington, D.C.: National Archives Trust Fund Board, 1986), pp. 22–23.

DOCUMENT 60: The Bill of Rights, Amendments I–X to the U.S. Constitution (Ratified December 15, 1791 and Certified by Thomas Jefferson, Secretary of State, in a Letter to the State Governors, March 1, 1792)

On December 15, 1791, Virginia became the eleventh of the fourteen American states to ratify Articles 3 through 12 of the proposed Bill of Rights. Thus, three-fourths of the states had approved these ten amendments, which then became part of the U.S. Constitution. The U.S. secretary of state, Thomas Jefferson, notified the governors of the fourteen states in a circular letter about ratification of the ten amendments.

How did the numbering of the amendments change as a result of the ratifying process? Compare the ten amendments of the federal Bill of Rights with state declarations of rights in Part II (see Documents 10, 12, and 15). How is the federal Bill of Rights similar to and different from the Declarations of Rights of Virginia, Pennsylvania, and Massachusetts?

Sir,   Mar. 1, 1792

I have the honor to send you herein enclosed, two copies duly authenticated, of an Act concerning certain fisheries of the United States, and for the regulation and government of the fishermen employed therein; also of an Act to establish the post office and post roads within the United States; also the ratifications by three fourths of the Legislatures of the Several States, of certain articles in addition and amendment of the Constitution of the United States, proposed by Congress to the said Legislatures, and of being with sentiments of the most perfect respect, your Excellency's &.

Th. Jefferson

[Amendment I]

Congress shall make no law respecting an establishment of religion, or prohibiting the free exercise thereof, or abridging the freedom of speech, or of the press; or the right of the people peaceably to assemble, and to petition the Government for a redress of grievances.

[Amendment II]

A well regulated Militia, being necessary to the security of a free State, the right of the people to keep and bear Arms, shall not be infringed.

[Amendment III]

No Soldier shall, in time of peace be quartered in any house, without the consent of the Owner, nor in time of war, but in a manner to be prescribed by law.

[Amendment IV]

The right of the people to be secure in their persons, houses, papers, and effects, against unreasonable searches and seizures, shall not be violated, and no Warrants shall issue, but upon probable cause, supported by Oath or affirmation, and particularly describing the place to be searched, and the persons or things to be seized.

[Amendment V]

No person shall be held to answer for a capital, or otherwise infamous crime, unless on a presentment or indictment of a Grand Jury, except in cases arising in the land or naval forces, or in the Militia, when in actual service in time of War or public danger, nor shall any person be subject for the same offence to be twice put in jeopardy of life or limb, nor shall be compelled in any criminal case to be a witness against himself, nor be deprived of life, liberty, or property, without due process of law; nor shall private property be taken for public use, without just compensation.

[Amendment VI]

In all criminal prosecutions, the accused shall enjoy the right to a speedy and public trial, by an impartial jury of the State and district wherein the crime shall have been committed, which district shall have been previously ascertained by law, and to be informed of the nature and cause of the accusation; to be confronted with the witnesses against him, to have compulsory process for obtaining Witnesses in his favor, and to have the Assistance of Counsel for his defence.

[Amendment VII]

In Suits at common law, where the value in controversy shall exceed twenty dollars, the right of trial by jury shall be preserved, and no fact tried by a jury, shall be otherwise re-examined in any Court of the United States, than according to the rules of the common law.

[Amendment VIII]

Excessive bail shall not be required, nor excessive fines imposed, nor cruel and unusual punishments inflicted.

[Amendment IX]

The enumeration in the Constitution, of certain rights, shall not be construed to deny or disparage others retained by the people.

[Amendment X]

The powers not delegated to the United States by the Constitution, nor prohibited by it to the States, are reserved to the States respectively, or to the people.

Source: National Archives and Records Administration, *The Bill of Rights: Milestone Documents in the National Archives* (Washington, D.C.: National Archives Trust Fund Board, 1986), pp. 5–6, 25.

FURTHER READING

Banning, Lance. *Jefferson and Madison: Three Conversations from the Founding.* Madison, Wis.: Madison House, 1994.

Barnett, Randy E., ed. *The Rights Retained by the People.* Fairfax, Va.: George Mason University Press, 1989.

Bickford, Charlene Bangs, and Kenneth R. Bowling. *Birth of the Nation: The First Federal Congress, 1789–1791.* Madison, Wis.: Madison House, 1992.

Christman, Margaret C. S. *The First Federal Congress, 1789–1791.* Washington, D.C.: Smithsonian Institution, 1989.

Conley, Patrick T., and John P. Kaminski, eds. *The Bill of Rights and the States.* Madison, Wis.: Madison House, 1992.

Lacy, Michael J., and Knud Kaakonssen, eds. *A Culture of Rights: The Bill of Rights in Philosophy, Politics and Law, 1795–1991.* Cambridge: Cambridge University Press, 1991.

Rutland, Robert Allen. *The Birth of the Bill of Rights, 1776–1791.* Chapel Hill: University of North Carolina Press, 1955.

Schechter, Stephen L., and Richard B. Bernstein, eds. *Contexts of the Bill of Rights.*

Albany: New York State Commission on the Bicentennial of the United States Constitution, 1990.

Schwartz, Bernard. *The Great Rights of Mankind: A History of the American Bill of Rights.* Madison, Wis.: Madison House, 1992.

Index

Abolition of slavery, 74–75

Adams, Abigail, 75–76, 79–80

Adams, John, 1; and the Declaration of Independence, 3, 24–27; and state constitutions, 35–39, 45–46, 61, 67; Vice-President of the United States, 243; women's rights, 75–76, 79, 80–81

Adams, Samuel, 1, 67, 112, 127

African American, 73–74, 85–88, 102

Agrippa (pseudonym of James Winthrop), 222

American Revolution, 1, 35, 85, 97, 147. *See also* Revolutionary War

Annapolis Convention, 112–13, 133–35, 147

Anti-Federalist, 197–202, 203, 237, 245–48, 251, 253, 255. *See also* Agrippa; Brutus

Articles of Confederation, 109–14, 115–24, 147–48

Banneker, Benjamin, 75, 102, 105–7

Bicameral legislature, 36, 43–44, 148, 167, 173, 229, 249

Bill of Rights, 152, 243–50, 255–58, 262–64

Bowdoin, James, 67

Brutus (pseudonym of an unknown Anti-Federalist), 198–99, 203, 210, 233, 237

Burke, Thomas, 109–10

Carrington, Edward, 113, 136, 138

Checks and balances, 36, 45, 61, 184, 229, 244. *See also* Separation of powers

Church-state separation, 76–78. *See also* Religious freedom; Virginia Statute for Religious Freedom

Common Sense (Paine), 2, 14–19, 36, 41, 45, 58

Commonwealth v. Nathaniel Jennison (1783), 74–75, 87–88. *See also* Walker, Quock

Confederation, 199, 203–4. *See also* Articles of Confederation

Constitutional amendments, 243–48, 251–55, 262, 265–267

Constitutional government, 35–41, 45, 52, 56, 115, 147, 153, 155, 170, 200, 229, 253

Constitutionalism, 37–39, 147, 198

Constitution of the United States, 39, 77, 112, 149, 151–53, 173, 184–96, 197–202, 225, 229, 244, 247–49, 251, 253, 255, 258, 262, 265

Continental Congress, 1–3, 7, 24–25,

29, 35, 45, 75–76, 79, 109–13, 147–
48, 153, 159, 184, 197, 201
Cushing, C. J., 87–88

Dana, James, 75, 99
Declaration of the Causes and Necessity of Taking Up Arms, 2, 7–12
Declaration of Independence, 2–4, 24–
27, 29–33, 37, 52, 56, 65, 73, 85, 102,
109, 185, 244
Democracy, 36, 149, 216–17, 219–21
Dickinson, John, 1–3, 7, 25, 28, 109–
10, 133, 149, 163, 165–66, 177, 179

Ellicott, Andrew, 102
Ellsworth, Oliver, 151, 177, 179
Equality, 29, 37, 52, 69, 73, 75, 79–88,
102, 185
The Essex Result (Parsons), 37, 61–64

Federal Convention, 147–53, 155, 181,
184, 243–44
Federalism, 147, 149, 184, 198–201,
203, 222, 225
The Federalist (Publius), 149, 197–98,
200–201, 207, 216, 225, 229, 237. See
also Federalist Papers; Federalists
Federalist Papers (Publius), 149, 197.
See also Federalists; The Federalist
Federalists, 197–202, 243, 248. See also
The Federalist
Federal republic, 149, 225. See also
Federalism; Republican govern-
ment; Republicanism
First Federal Congress, 243
Franklin, Benjamin, 3, 27, 152, 181–82
Freedom: of the press, 247, 129; of re-
ligion, 73, 76–78, 89, 244, 247, 249;
of speech, 58. See also Liberty
Free government, 4, 99, 198, 204, 223,
257

George III, King, 2, 7, 12
Gerry, Elbridge, 149, 152–53, 177, 179,
181–82, 210
Grayson, William, 247
Great Compromise, 150–51

Hamilton, Alexander, 112–13, 133,
147, 197–98, 200, 207, 237
Hancock, John, 3
Henry, Patrick, 77, 247
Human nature, 29, 37, 52, 73, 94, 99,
229–30

Indians. See Native Americans
Individual rights, 37–38, 52, 56, 58, 67,
73, 89, 99, 111, 129, 140, 143–45,
147, 149, 185, 198–201, 203, 229–30,
237, 251, 253, 258. See also Bill of
Rights; Massachusetts Declaration
of Rights; Virginia Declaration of
Rights
Inglis, Charles, 19

Jay, John, 112, 129, 131, 136, 138, 197–98
Jefferson, Thomas, 2; Banneker, correspondence with, 75, 102, 106–7;
the Bill of Rights, 248–49, 255, 265;
Declaration of Independence, 3–4,
7, 25–33, 52; Federal Convention
and Constitution of 1787, correspondence on, 153, 244–45; Ordinances of 1784 and 1785, 111, 113;
religious liberty, 94–96
Judicial independence, 39, 46, 234,
237, 240
Judicial review, 39, 233, 237

Lansing, John, 173–74
Lee, Richard Henry, 3, 24, 26, 45, 77,
109, 112, 127, 131, 247
Legislative supremacy, 36, 39, 52, 149
Liberty, 4, 29–30, 37, 41, 52, 58, 67, 73,
76–79, 85–89, 94, 102, 147–49, 185,
199–201, 208–9, 213, 243–44, 248. See
also Freedom
Limited government. See Constitution-
al government; Constitutionalism
Lincoln, Levi, 74
Livingstone, Robert, 3, 25, 27
Locke, John, 38
Loyalists, 2, 19

Madison, James: and Annapolis Convention, 112–13, 133; and the Bill of

Rights, 243–47, 255–61; and the
Federal Convention, 147–51, 155–59,
163–64; and *The Federalist*, 197–98,
200, 207, 216–21, 225–31
Majoritarian tyranny. *See* Majority
faction; Tyranny of the majority
Majority faction, 163–65, 216, 221, 229,
231–32. *See also* Tyranny of the ma-
jority
Martin, Luther, 177–78
Mason, George, 52, 58, 149, 151–53,
177–79, 181–82, 213, 243–45, 247
Massachusetts Constitution, 37–39, 61,
65, 67, 76
Massachusetts Declaration of Rights,
38, 67–72, 75–76, 87–88, 184
Memorial and Remonstrance Against
Religious Assessments (Madison),
77, 89–93
Morris, Gouverneur, 151–52

Native Americans, 76–77, 97–98
Natural rights, 4, 29–30, 37–38, 52, 56,
58, 61, 67, 73–76, 85–89, 94–96, 99–
102, 111, 140, 185, 198–201, 245–46,
248
New Jersey Plan, 150–51, 170–73
New York Constitution, 37, 39, 52
Northwest Ordinance, 11–12, 114,
140–45

Olive Branch Petition, 2, 12
Ordered liberty, 147–48, 200
Ordinance of 1784, 111
Ordinance of 1785, 111, 114

Paine, Thomas, 2, 14, 19, 36–38, 45, 58
Parliament, 7, 12, 29
Parsons, Theophilus, 37–38, 61, 64
Paterson, William, 150, 170, 173–74
Pennsylvania Constitution, 38–39, 41,
52, 56, 58, 65, 67
Pennsylvania Declaration of Rights,
38, 56, 58–60
Pinckney, Charles Cotesworth (Gen-
eral), 149, 163, 177–78, 179
Popular sovereignty, 37–38, 56, 61,
147, 184, 237

Property rights, 73
Publius (pseudonym for authors of
The Federalist), 197, 200–202, 207,
216, 225, 229, 237. *See also The Federalist*; Federalists

Randolph, Edmund, 148, 153, 159,
170, 173, 175–76, 181–82
Ratifying Conventions, 197, 201, 237,
243, 245, 251–52, 253–54
Religious freedom, 73, 76–78, 89, 244,
247, 249. *See also* Memorial and Re-
monstrance Against Religious As-
sessments; Virginia Statute for
Religious Freedom
Representative government, 37, 148–
50, 216, 225
Republican government, 37–38, 81,
147, 149–50, 153, 184, 198–201, 203,
216, 219–22, 225–26, 233, 255–56
Republicanism, 149–50, 184, 199, 225
Resolution for Independence, 24
Revolutionary War, 1–2, 35. *See also*
American Revolution
Rodney, Caesar, 3
Rule of law, 45, 52, 56, 61, 67. *See also*
Constitutional government; Consti-
tutionalism
Rutledge, John, 177–79

Separation of powers, 36, 45, 61, 67,
89, 148, 167, 184, 200–201, 229–31,
244, 249. *See also* Checks and bal-
ances
Shays's Rebellion, 113, 136, 138
Sherman, Roger, 3, 27, 149, 163–64,
177–78, 258
Sidney, Algernon, 38
Slavery, 73–75, 85–88, 99–102; debates
in Federal Convention, 151–52, 177–
79
Slave trade, 25, 27–28, 74, 99–100,
151–52
Social compact, 65
The Spirit of the Laws (Montesquieu),
199
State constitutions. *See* Massachusetts
Constitution; New York Constitu-

tion; Pennsylvania Constitution; Virginia Constitution

State government powers, 35, 41, 233, 245, 251, 253. *See also* Federalism

Suffrage, 36. *See also* Voting rights

Sullivan, James, 76, 81

Supreme Court, 233, 237

Thoughts on Government (Adams), 36–37, 39, 45–51, 61, 67, 184

Three-Fifths Compromise, 151–52

Treaty of Paris (1783), 76, 97, 97, 110–11, 114

Tyranny of the majority, 149, 200–201, 216–17, 229, 255–56. *See also* Majority faction

Unicameral legislature, 36, 41, 115, 148, 150, 170, 173

Virginia Act of Cession, 110

Virginia Constitution, 37–38, 52, 76

Virginia Declaration of Rights, 38, 52–54, 56, 58, 65, 67, 76, 94, 152, 258

Virginia Plan, 148–50, 155, 159–162, 167–70, 173

Virginia Statute for Religious Freedom (Jefferson), 87, 94–96. *See also* Religious freedom

Voting rights, 36, 73

Walker, Quock, 74–75, 87–88

Washington, George, 7, 77, 79, 97, 112, 125, 129, 131, 136, 138, 148, 155, 197, 243

Weightman, Roger D., 4

Williamson, Hugh, 177, 179

Wilson, James, 25, 149, 163, 173–75, 181, 250, 256

Winthrop, James, 222

Women's rights, 75–77, 79–81

Yates, Robert, 203

About the Editor

JOHN J. PATRICK is Director of the Social Studies Development Center and Professor of Education at Indiana University. A specialist in the history of the Founding Period, he is the author of more than 25 books on civic history education and a member of the Governing Body of the National Council for History Standards that prepared the National History Standards Project in 1994. In addition, Patrick served as chief consultant to the Agency for Instructional Technology in developing the prize-winning video program series on the U.S. Constitution for use in history classrooms and public television.

Recent Titles in the New Series Primary Documents in American History and Contemporary Issues

The Abortion Controversy: A Documentary History
Eva R. Rubin, editor

Women Rights in the United States: A Documentary History
Winston E. Langley and Vivian C. Fox, editors